Preventive
Defense

Preventive Defense

A New Security Strategy for America

Ashton B. Carter
and
William J. Perry

BROOKINGS INSTITUTION PRESS
Washington, D.C.

ABOUT BROOKINGS

The Brookings Institution is a private nonprofit organization devoted to research, education, and publication on important issues of domestic and foreign policy. Its principal purpose is to bring knowledge to bear on current and emerging policy problems. The Institution maintains a position of neutrality on issues of public policy. Interpretations or conclusions in Brookings publications should be understood to be solely those of the authors.

Library of Congress Cataloging-in-Publication data
Carter, Ashton B.
Preventive defense : a new security strategy for America / Ashton B. Carter and William J. Perry.
p. cm.
Includes bibliographical references and index.
ISBN 0-8157-1308-8 (cloth : acid-free paper)
ISBN 0-8157-1307-X (pbk. : acid-free paper)
1. National security—United States. 2. United States—Military policy. 3. World politics—1989– 4. Twenty-first century—Forecasts. I. Perry, William James, 1927– II. Title.
UA23 .C275 1998
355'.03373—dc21   98-51245
                                                                        CIP

(First paperback printing, September 2000)
9 8 7 6 5 4 3

The paper used in this publication meets minimum requirements of the American National Standard for Information Sciences—Permanence of Paper for Printed Library Materials: ANSI Z39.48-1984.

Typeset in Sabon

Composition by R. Lynn Rivenbark
Macon, Georgia

Printed by R. R. Donnelley and Sons
Harrisonburg, Virginia

Preface

The thoughts we express in this book are informed by our service in the Pentagon during the first term of the Clinton administration and with the reflection of a year of distance from the fray. This book includes both our recollections of some of the efforts we have made to initiate a Preventive Defense strategy and our analyses and recommendations for U.S. defense policy in the future. This design, while perhaps unorthodox, seemed most appropriate to us because Preventive Defense is an unfinished mission, one on which we continue to work.

We arrived in the Pentagon in January 1993, a few days after President Bill Clinton took office; Bill Perry became, first, deputy secretary of defense and, a year later, secretary of defense, while Ash Carter became assistant secretary of defense. The ideas and commitments reflected here began, however, with work we did well before we began this period of government service. The national security problems we describe in these pages are far from resolved, and we continue to think about them and to seek solutions. Bill Perry, as the nation's nineteenth secretary of defense and earlier the Pentagon's technology chief at the height of the cold war, might have chosen to write a straightforward memoir. Instead, in this book we attempt to be analytical and forward looking, using the past to suggest and illuminate approaches to national security that might be effective in the future. It omits many subjects that were in the headlines in the first Clinton term and dwells at length on some subjects that were not in the headlines at all. The emphasis is on vital dangers to national security and on strategies of lasting value, not on the *crise du jour* that makes the headlines. Making the distinction between larger and lesser dangers to national security is in fact one of the bases of the Preventive Defense approach.

Bill Perry served as deputy secretary of defense from March 1993 until February 1994, when he succeeded Les Aspin as secretary, and he continued as secretary of defense until January 1997. More than a decade earlier, during the Carter administration, he had been undersecretary for research and engineering, in charge of technology development and weapons acquisition. In between tours in Washington, he returned to California and eventually to Stanford, where he became deputy director of the Center for International Security and Arms Control (CISAC, now called the Center for International Security and Cooperation). Ash Carter was then director of Harvard's Center for Science and International Affairs, and the two of us began a collaboration on many of the ideas we relate in this book. In 1993 Carter became assistant secretary of defense for international security policy, with responsibility for policy regarding weapons of mass destruction and proliferation, nuclear strategy and arms control, the former Soviet Union and NATO matters covered in this book. After our term in office, we both returned to academic life, Carter to Harvard in September 1996 and Perry to Stanford in February 1997, and we resumed our collaboration, launching a joint university program called the Preventive Defense Project. Our work together thus spans over a decade, and this book is a product both of that collaboration and of Perry's previous work in the Carter administration.

We owe a great debt of gratitude to our colleagues in the Pentagon from 1993 to 1997—the group that came to call itself the "Perry A Team"—and we are also indebted to President Clinton for inviting us to serve.

The thinking and drafting that lie behind this book were made possible by the generosity and trust of the Carnegie Corporation of New York, especially David Hamburg and David Speedie, and of the John D. and Catherine T. MacArthur Foundation, especially Adele Simmons and Vic Rabinovitch. Private supporters of our work have included Daniel Case, Bill Edwards, Tom Ford, Franklin Johnson, Jeong Kim, and Elliott Levinthal. Corporate sponsors included The Boeing Company, Lockheed Martin Corporation, and United Technologies Corporation.

The sponsorship of these foundations and of private and corporate supporters makes possible the Preventive Defense Project, a research collaboration of Stanford University and Harvard University, our respective academic homes. Through the Preventive Defense Project, we were able to conduct research into the various facets of the Preventive Defense strategy, and this book is one fruit of that research. We are grateful to John Shalikashvili and Liz Sherwood-Randall, our project colleagues during this first year, for their friendship and advice.

Others who contributed to the thoughts contained here, but who remain blameless for any errors, are Commander Mike Abrashoff, Chip Blacker, Robert D. Blackwill, Melba Boling, Kurt Campbell, Carol Chaffin, Warren Christopher, Ambassador James Collins, John Deutch, Donna Ditoto, Robert Hermann, Laura S. H. Holgate, Lieutenant General Randy House, Paul Kaminski, Lieutenant General Paul Kern, Mike Lampton, Franklin C. Miller, Steven E. Miller, Katherine Mooney, Joe Nye, Brent Scowcroft, Mitch Wallerstein, John P. White, Philip Zelikow, and many others who are still in government service.

Deborah Gordon and Hilary Driscoll are the anchors of the Preventive Defense Project at, respectively, Stanford's Center for International Security and Cooperation (CISAC) and Harvard's Belfer Center for Science and International Affairs (BCSIA). Without them, nothing would get done—surely not this book. Celeste Johnson at BCSIA contributed her superb research, editorial, and strategic gifts to every chapter. Our editor, Teresa J. Lawson, made structural and substantive contributions that went well beyond her nominal role. Gretchen Bartlett at Harvard and Lainie Dillon at Stanford kept our drafts and our schedules straight.

It is in the nature of the Preventive Defense approach that it requires U.S. defense policymakers to forge strong relationships with security leaders in other countries. We thank our many colleagues in foreign defense establishments who continue to contribute to Preventive Defense from their end; some of them are mentioned by name in these pages.

Dedicated to

A. Clayton Spencer
and
Lee Green Perry

*whose love, support,
and intellect inspired
this book, and much
else that we have done.*

—ABC and WJP

Contents

ix

Preventive
Defense

Four Trips to Pervomaysk: Preventive Defense at Work

In March 1994 melting snowdrifts still marked the rolling farmland around Pervomaysk. The Ukrainian Air Force helicopter in which we were riding settled through the wintry wind and onto the mud atop an isolated knoll. Our host was General Vitaly Radetsky, minister of defense of the two-year-old nation of Ukraine, one of fifteen republics of the former Soviet Union. Here in the "breadbasket of the USSR," there was little to distinguish this hill from others, apart from its barbed wire and two armored doors mounted almost flush with the hillside. Radetsky led us through one of the armored doors into a concrete bunker, where a small elevator about the size of a phone booth took us deep underground to a dimly lit passageway. At the end of the passageway was a modest-sized room: a nuclear missile control center.

We were the first Americans to visit this facility, which, as Radetsky explained, controlled 700 nuclear warheads. Across one wall of the command center stretched a map of the United States. Another map showed Europe. Small lights dotted across the maps indicated the targets of the nuclear warheads controlled from this center. A few of the lights had been turned off, but most were still lit.

Two young duty officers in the uniform of the newly established Ukrainian armed forces stood at attention at their launch consoles. We could see, from the bunks and the samovar, that they were prepared to live down there for a long period. Clearly nervous, they had apparently been told that we were very important visitors, and they proceeded with their "show and tell." They began with their communication equipment, and then they went through every step of a practice launch sequence, stopping just short of the actual launch command. We watched the countdown and stared at the targets highlighted on the maps—cities in Germany and England, in Kansas and Oregon. We had known from U.S. intelligence, collected laboriously over decades of cold war, that facilities like this one would control the launch of Soviet nuclear-armed ICBMs aimed at the United States. We had both done analyses and papers on how to maintain the uneasy balance that constituted nuclear deterrence. But never had the "balance of terror" seemed as real and as terrible to either of us as it was at that moment.

General Radetsky led us across the knoll to another heavily armored door. This one was open: it was the lid of one of the missile silos that had been built to hold the SS-24 nuclear-tipped intercontinental ballistic missiles controlled by the command center we had just left. We peered inside. We had seen photos of Soviet ICBMs rolling through Moscow's Red Square in the May Day parades, and even satellite photos of these Pervomaysk missile silos. But now we were looking down at the very missile that had been the subject of so much of our professional work, so many defense studies, so much concern, for so many years. This was the business end of the cold war's nuclear "balance of terror."

As we could see, the ten warheads that would normally be atop this SS-24 missile had been removed. Under the Trilateral Agreement recently reached between Ukraine, Russia, and the United States to eliminate Ukraine's nuclear weapons, the missiles had been loaded on a train and sent back to the factory in Russia that had made them, where they would be dismantled and eliminated.

That explained why some of the lights on the target map in the control center were unlit: some American cities were no longer targets of these missiles. The nuclear weapons aimed at them had been put away: Ukraine's denuclearization had begun.

Ukraine: A State Born Nuclear

When the USSR disintegrated, no fewer than 176 SS-19 and SS-24 intercontinental ballistic missiles were on what was no longer Soviet soil but Ukrainian soil. All carried multiple warheads, the "MIRVs" of cold war fame. Ukraine found itself in possession of some of the Soviet Union's most modern bombers, too, and a stock of the long-range nuclear cruise missiles they carried. Altogether, Ukraine was born as a state in possession of nearly 2,000 nuclear weapons. Had Ukraine retained them, the new state, of which many Americans had never even heard, would have been the third most powerful nuclear nation on earth after Russia and the United States, with many more nuclear warheads than China, France, or the United Kingdom. This would have been the biggest setback in the history of nonproliferation.

The Clinton administration had therefore set a high priority on removing this lethal legacy from Ukraine. Russia's participation was key, since the warheads would need to be returned to Russia for elimination. The way in which the first trilateral talks came about was especially memorable for us. We had accompanied Vice President Al Gore to Moscow in December 1993 for his semiannual meeting with Russian Prime Minister Viktor Chernomyrdin as part of the Gore-Chernomyrdin Commission. The first night we were in Moscow, the startling news came that our boss, Defense Secretary Les Aspin, had abruptly resigned. We spent much of the night pondering our futures and talking to friends and family back home.

After a restless night, we rejoined Vice President Gore and Strobe Talbott, President Clinton's point man on the former Soviet Union (later deputy secretary of state), who suggested that we simply continue our mission as originally planned. Since after leaving

Moscow we planned to travel to Macedonia to visit U.S. troops on peacekeeping duty there, we suggested stopping first in Kiev, taking a Russian team with us to hold trilateral talks with Ukraine on what to do with its nuclear weapons. Gore discussed the plan with Chernomyrdin, who readily agreed, and Gore dispatched Talbott to go with us, while Chernomyrdin sent a solitary Russian, Georgiy Mamedov. Mamedov had been the Soviet Union's and was now Russia's chief "American-handler," and was respected by all of us. Mamedov and Talbott boarded the U.S. Department of Defense plane with us, and we arrived in Kiev late that evening.

Trilateral talks made for an awkward diplomatic seating problem that was finally resolved by having the Americans sit along one side of the meeting table, the Ukrainians along the other, and Mamedov perched alone at one end. Once the right three parties were around the table, however, progress was quick, and soon the main lines of the agreement had been decided. Perry then departed, leaving Carter behind with the others to work out the details. By this time it was the middle of the night, and the previous night's uncertainty and sleeplessness began to catch up with Carter. Shortly after Perry left, he fell fast asleep there in the meeting room, a fact of which he would be mercilessly reminded many times in coming years by Ukrainians, Russians, and above all Talbott.

In January 1994 the Trilateral Agreement was signed in Moscow by President Clinton, President Boris Yeltsin, and President Leonid Kravchuk, but the agreement to denuclearize Ukraine was fragile. It was controversial in Ukraine, where some felt the new state needed nuclear weapons for its security. Eliminating the nuclear weapons was also a mammoth and expensive task: under the Ukrainian timetable, the process would take seven years, a very long time in turbulent post-Soviet Ukraine and Russia. Would the Trilateral Agreement ever be fully implemented? We believed the answer was critical for American and international security and that it required the fullest effort of the Department of Defense.

Thus we made our first trip to Pervomaysk a few months after the Trilateral Agreement was signed to begin the task of working with the Ukrainian military. Our descent into the missile command center made it chillingly clear that we could not afford to miss this opportunity for Preventive Defense. Over the next two years, therefore, we would make a total of four trips to Pervomaysk together, and Carter would make many additional trips as part of an immense U.S. Department of Defense effort to ensure that the nuclear weapons of Ukraine were eliminated.

A Second Visit to Pervomaysk: Defense by Other Means

We returned to Pervomaysk a second time a year later, in April 1995, to monitor the progress of the effort begun a year earlier. This time, we watched a crane lift an SS-19 missile, its warheads already removed, straight up out of the silo in what looked for all the world like a slow-motion launch. Soon the huge object, several stories high, towered over our heads, a gratifying symbol of the results of the Pentagon's efforts to help the Ukrainians get the job done. After it was removed from the silo, the toxic fuel would be drained into tanks provided by the Department of Defense under programs we had struggled to push through the bureaucracy and Congress. The missile would be transported by rail to a special facility elsewhere in Ukraine that had been built by the DOD, and there it would be chopped up into scrap metal.

We went into the nearby town to inspect newly constructed houses. Ukrainian law required that retiring military be provided with housing, and without such housing for its officers, the missile base could not be closed. But the new government of Ukraine could not afford to build housing by itself, so we had arranged for DOD funds to convert a nearby naval weapons factory to the production of prefabricated housing based on the design of an American company. The housing had gone up here for officers who would no longer be needed to guard and launch the Pervomaysk nuclear missiles. This program simultaneously had the effect of making possible the closing of the missile base, ending production of new weapons in this former Soviet factory, and providing a new economic opportunity for the workers at the factory. When we arrived, an Orthodox priest sprinkled holy water on the site and on us in blessing, and a retired officer and his wife proudly showed us their new home, modest but comfortable.

Without DOD assistance, the job could never have been done, and nuclear weapons would remain still on the rolling hills of Ukraine. The Defense Department's program in Ukraine was truly "defense by other means." The cost to the U.S. defense budget of this innovative program was tiny compared with the cost of defending against the missiles we were now dismantling. Dollar for dollar, the country got at least as much security from this program as from any other expenditure in the defense budget.

Another Return: Missile Silos Turned to Dust

Our third joint visit to Pervomaysk took place almost a year later, in the dead of winter. In the Ukrainian Air Force plane with us that January 1996 were Russia's defense minister, Pavel Grachev, and Radetsky's successor as Ukraine's defense minister, Valeriy Shmarov; U.S. Ambassador to Ukraine William Miller; Igor Sergeyev, the chief of Russia's nuclear rocket forces, who would later be Russian defense minister; the Ukrainian president's national security adviser, Volodymyr Horbulin; and President Clinton's senior National Security Council aide for the former Soviet Union, Coit D. ("Chip") Blacker.

At Uman airfield outside Pervomaysk, the pilot made a hair-raising blind descent through thick snow and fog, approaching the runway dangerously askew. A wingtip caught a snowbank—in any other season the wing would have caught the ground and flipped the plane over, but this time, mercifully, it skidded over the soft snow. The jolt nevertheless flung Perry under the aircraft's conference table and Grachev into the galley. Carter, looking across at General Sergeyev, thought grimly for a few moments that this face might be the last he ever saw on earth. In spite of this inauspicious arrival, however, our third trip to Pervomaysk was a triumph.

There, in the blowing snow and freezing rain, the three defense ministers—Perry, Shmarov, and Grachev—simultaneously turned the keys that, two years earlier, would have launched nuclear missiles toward the United States. This time, the turn of the keys ignited high explosives that blew up the empty concrete SS-19 silo. When we recall that day, we think not of the near-disaster of our arrival, but of the sight of the SS-19 silo disintegrating in a cloud of smoke. With U.S. assistance and skillful diplomacy, we were eliminating the nuclear threat, silo by silo.

A Fourth Visit to Pervomaysk: From Silos to Sunflowers

We returned to Pervomaysk for the fourth and last time on a beautiful summer day in June 1996. We were going to observe the final shipment of Ukraine's nuclear warheads to dismantlement facilities in Russia, but right up to the last minute, Ukrainian officials were arguing about whether to keep the weapons instead. Thus we chose not to go to Pervomaysk directly. Instead, we went first to a base where the Ukrainian Army was conducting a training exercise with soldiers from the United States, Russia, Poland, and six other European countries under NATO's Partnership for Peace program. Our detour was meant to send a message—a reminder that Ukraine's security would be assured by joining the family of European nations, not by hanging on to the illusory protection of nuclear weapons. Our message was heard: late in the night, just before we arrived at Pervomaysk, the last nuclear warheads left Ukraine and crossed the border into Russia, heading for a dismantlement facility.

At Pervomaysk, we met again with Defense Minister Grachev and Defense Minister Shmarov. On the little knoll in the middle of the rolling farmland, the barbed wire and steel doors were gone. The warheads and missiles had been taken away, the concrete silo blown to rubble and covered with soil. Around us, the fields had been plowed and planted. In place of nuclear missile silos and weapons control bunkers and barbed wire, a beautiful and lucrative crop of sunflowers now bloomed. We walked to the spot where the lid of the missile silo had been, and there the three defense ministers planted sunflowers, sowing more seeds of peace.

Preventive Defense

Now that an immediate peril is not plainly visible, there is a natural tendency to relax and to return to business as usual. . . . But I feel that we are seriously failing in our attitude toward the international problems whose solution will largely determine our future.

George C. Marshall,
Washington's Birthday Remarks at Princeton University, February 22, 1947

Our tale of four visits to Pervomaysk illustrates the paradox brought about by the end of the cold war. On the one hand, the familiar threat of imminent global nuclear war ended when the Soviet Union ended. But the result was not a world guaranteed free of risk for U.S. security. At Pervomaysk, a new and unfamiliar danger—an unprecedented surge of nuclear proliferation in the heart of Europe—took the place of the familiar military threat. As the term is usually understood, "threat" is imminent and well defined. The situation at Pervomaysk in 1993, in contrast, might better be termed a "danger." It was not imminent: it might have taken some years and several turns of the wheel of history and social revolution in the former Soviet Union for these missiles and nuclear warheads to fall into the hands of those who might once again use them to threaten American lives and interests. But if the danger had been ignored and allowed to fester and grow, the resulting threat would be as fearsome as the cold war's balance of terror. The post–cold war world has other Pervomaysks: other dangers that might become cold war–scale threats. A new strategy, with new tactics like those of the Nunn-

Lugar Cooperative Threat Reduction program that provided U.S. Department of Defense aid to Ukrainian denuclearization, is needed to identify these dangers and apply U.S. influence to avert them. We call this strategy "Preventive Defense." Like preventive medicine, Preventive Defense seeks to forestall dangerous developments before they require drastic remedies. Preventive Defense is about both grave dangers to U.S. security and great opportunities to safeguard it.[1]

From Deterrence to Prevention

Through more than four decades of the cold war, American national security strategy, although difficult to implement, was easy to understand. America was set on a clear course to contain Soviet expansionism anywhere in the world, all the while building a formidable arsenal of nuclear weapons to deter the Soviet Union from using military force against the United States or its allies. Then the underlying rationale for that strategy—the threat from the Soviet Union—disappeared. For a time, American policy focused on the immediate task of peaceful adjustment to the collapse of communism in Europe and Russia. But the transition period has ended, and a new strategy is urgently needed. What should the American security strategy be as the twenty-first century opens?

Much depends on arriving at the correct answer to this question. The world survived three global wars this century. The first two resulted in tens of millions of deaths, but the third—the cold war—would have been even more horrible had deterrence failed. American strategy after these wars contains some clues to the strategy we need now.

At the end of World War I, the victorious European allies sought revenge and reparations, but what they got was a massive depression and another world war. The United States sought "normalcy" and isolation, but what it got was total war and the job of winning it. Because it failed both to prevent the rise of a dangerous adversary, and then to deter that adversary's aggression, America was forced to mobilize a second time to defeat Germany.

At the end of World War II, America initially took an approach to strategy centered on prevention. Vowing not to repeat the mistakes made after World War I, the Truman administration created the Marshall Plan to assist the devastated nations of Europe, friends and foes alike, to rebuild. This strategy, aimed at preventing the conditions that would lead to a future world war, was an outstanding success in Western Europe and in Japan as well. The economic chaos, political instability, isolation, and paranoia that might have followed in the wake of defeat and destruction in Germany and Japan were averted. These two countries, and the regions around them that war had ravaged, were brought into normal alignment with the rest of the world, and Germany and Japan reclaimed leading international roles in a peaceful fashion.

The Soviet Union, however, turned down the Marshall Plan, and instead persisted in a program of expansion, trying to take advantage of the weakened condition of most of the European countries. The resulting security problem was famously articulated by George Kennan, who predicted that U.S. wartime cooperation with the Soviet Union would be replaced by a struggle for the heart of Europe, and that the United States should prepare for a protracted period of confrontation. Based on Kennan's analysis, the Truman administration formulated a strategy that would get the United States through the cold war: we would seek to deter another global war, while containing the Soviet Union's expansionist ambitions. Containment and deterrence supplanted prevention as the top U.S. priority: there was no other choice.

Deterrence was a new departure for American military strategy. The United States had twice risen to defeat aggression after it occurred, but it had not maintained the peacetime military establishment or diplomatic engagement necessary to deter World War I or World War II. The national security team around Truman, led by Dean Acheson, created the peacetime posture and new security institutions required.[2] The United States avoided war with the Soviet Union, which in time disintegrated as a result of the contradictions in its political and economic systems. Containment and deterrence had worked to keep the peace.

Strategy in the Absence of a Major Threat

Throughout the cold war, the Soviet Union posed a threat to the very survival of the United States. But with the cold war over, it is necessary to rethink the risks to U.S. security. Conceptually, they can be arrayed in a hierarchy from most dangerous to least dangerous. At the top of the hierarchy would be an "A list" of threats to U.S. survival of the kind and scale that the Soviet Union presented during the cold war. But this list is empty today: there are no imminent military threats to the very survival of the United States. The two "major regional contingencies" in the Persian Gulf and on the Korean peninsula that undergird Pentagon planning and budgeting form a "B list" of imminent threats to U.S. interests, but not to the survival or way of life of Americans. The third place in this hierarchy is occupied by the Kosovos, Bosnias, Somalias, Rwandas, and Haitis that compose a "C list" of important contingencies that indirectly affect U.S. security but do not directly threaten U.S. interests.

The emptiness of the A list is disorienting for Americans, who made the huge transition from defeating aggression to deterring aggression after World War II, but who now, in consequence, tend to conceive national security strategy exclusively in terms of threats to be deterred or defeated. Thus the focus tends to be on B-list and C-list threats. We believe, however, that long-range strategic thinking about how to prevent the rise of new A-list threats is sorely needed, and it is for that reason we have written this book.

Political and economic transformations now under way in Eastern Europe and the former Soviet Union are unprecedented in their scale and scope. This vast redistribution of political and economic power extends throughout Eurasia, and includes the gradual emergence of China as a true world power. Meanwhile, the nuclear, chemical, and biological weapons that made deterrence both dangerous and necessary have not been fully dismantled, let alone disinvented, and they now threaten to fall into the hands of unstable nations, groups, and terrorists. Thus while threats of the traditional sort might be hard to find, danger to the security of Americans is not.

However, in the years since the cold war ended, the evening news has given the impression that the primary security challenges of the new era are those that arise in remote places such as Kosovo, Bosnia, Rwanda, Haiti, and Somalia. For many, these conflicts seem to define the national security dangers of the post–cold war world. But in fact, these are third-order or C-list threats; they are places and problems that do not threaten America's survival as World War II and the cold war did. This is not to say that they are unimportant; we must meet challenges such as Bosnia not only for humanitarian reasons, but to stop the killing and atrocities before they undermine the foundations of regional and international stability. However, a price is paid for such actions: resources are diverted to military operations, and they demand the time and attention of our national leaders. Because such C-list issues do not threaten America's vital security interests, dealing with them individually or as classes—peacekeeping, peacemaking, humanitarian operations, operations other than war, and the like—cannot make up the core national security strategy of the United States.

Nor can U.S. strategy be wholly determined by what we call B-list threats: those that may threaten vital U.S. interests, but not America's survival. These are the major regional contingencies—specifically, the threat of Iraqi aggression in the Persian Gulf and the threat of North Korean invasion of South Korea—around which the Pentagon must organize much of its military planning and force structure. While a look at the newspapers suggests that the United States places a high priority on peacekeeping and humanitarian operations, a look at the defense budget shows the higher priority the United States places on these regional wars. They constitute familiar cold war–like strategic territory for Americans: clear and imminent threats, which must be deterred by ready military forces.

If deterrence fails, the U.S. military is capable of inflicting a decisive defeat on today's two potential regional aggressors. Saddam Hussein's Iraq is militarily weaker today than it was in 1990, while U.S. forces are better positioned to repel Iraqi aggression. North Korea still has the capability to launch a horribly destructive war on the Korean peninsula, but the capability of its collapsing economy and starving population to sustain the campaign is far less than during the 1994 crisis over North Korea's nuclear program. And, as in the Gulf, the posture of the United States and the U.S.-Korean Combined Forces Command has been substantially improved.

The reason for the preoccupation of American strategy with these B-list and C-list issues in the early post–cold war period has been the current unusual and happy circumstance in which there is no A-list threat to the United States. The Soviet Union is gone. Russia does not pose a conventional military threat to Europe and shows little inclination to pose a nuclear threat to the United States. Some Americans conjure up China as the enemy of the future, but China's future role in the world will be influenced by contingencies over which U.S. policy can exert some positive influence.

Thus, the United States is enjoying a period of peace and influence like it has never had before. But while this should be savored by the public, foreign policy and defense leaders cannot afford to be so complacent. A period of absence of A-list threats must stretch us strategically; it calls for vision and foresight to act strategically when events and imminent threats do not compel us to do so. That should be the primary business of statecraft in the post–cold war era.

The way to sharpen focus on the strategic requirements of our time is to ask the questions, "How might the post–cold war era end?" "How can the United States prolong this period of peace and influence?" "How can we ensure that if it must end, it ends gracefully, without cataclysm?" and "What is the character of the era that will follow it?" The answers to these questions define the fundamental long-term strategic challenges of the post–cold war era.

Because the security strategy created to deal with the threats of the cold war is not suitable for dealing with the dangers to our security in the twenty-first century, we believe that the United States should now follow the example of Truman, Marshall, and Acheson at America's last great strategic transition: it should formulate a new security strategy appropriate for this new world and should create the policies and programs capable of carrying out that strategy. In essence, America has another chance to realize Marshall's initial vision at the end of World War II: a world not of threats to be deterred, but a world "united in peace, freedom, and prosperity." To realize this vision, America should return to a prevention strategy like that embodied so successfully in the Marshall Plan: a strategy of Preventive Defense.

Preventive Defense is a defense strategy for the United States in the twenty-first century that concentrates national security strategy on the dangers that, if mismanaged, have the potential to grow into true A-list-scale threats to U.S. survival in the next century, bringing the current era to an abrupt and painful end. These dangers are not yet threats to be defeated or deterred; they are dangers that can be prevented.

We argue that developing and implementing a strategy of Preventive Defense is the most important mission of today's national security leaders and defense establishment. They must dedicate themselves to Preventive Defense at the same time they deter lesser but existing threats—in Iraq and North Korea—and conduct selected peacekeeping and humanitarian missions—in Bosnia, Haiti, Rwanda, and so on—where conflict threatens long-term interests.

Heading off the Dangers of the Twenty-First Century

In the first five chapters of this book, we focus on the five dangers that we believe have the potential to become A-list threats to U.S. and international security in the twenty-first century. These are the targets of Preventive Defense; its goals are to keep these dangers from becoming major threats. We define these dangers as follows:

— that Russia might descend into chaos, isolation, and aggression as Germany did after World War I;

— that Russia and the other Soviet successor states might lose control of the nuclear legacy of the former Soviet Union;

— that China could grow hostile rather than becoming cooperatively engaged in the international system;

— that weapons of mass destruction will proliferate and present a direct military threat to the United States;

— that "catastrophic terrorism" of unprecedented scope and intensity might occur on U.S. territory.

We devote a chapter to each of these dangers, beginning each with an illustrative tale drawn from our time in office and then offering an analysis of the issues and a set of Preventive Defense prescriptions for U.S. policy.[3]

However, Preventive Defense could fail and any of these dangers become A-list threats. Therefore the United States will continue to need a strong military on into the twenty-first century, and so chapter 6 addresses the management issues of keeping it so.

"Weimar Russia"

Harking back to the disastrous failures of the international community in dealing with Germany after World War I, we focus attention on the risk of parallel developments in post-Soviet Russia. A primary goal of Preventive Defense is to help Russia establish a self-respecting place for itself in the post–cold war world and to establish a stable security order on the territory of the former Warsaw Treaty Organization states. In chapter 1 we tell the story of how we sought to forward these ends by "defense diplomacy," engaging Russia in mutually beneficial cooperative efforts and particularly in the NATO-led international peacekeeping force sent to Bosnia to enforce the Dayton Accords. Such defense diplomacy grows even more important as the "honeymoon" phase of the post–cold war "partnership" with Russia ends, the Yeltsin era draws to a close, and a more difficult era begins.

"Loose Nukes"

Failure to reduce and secure the deadly legacy of the cold war—nuclear, chemical, and biological weapons in Russia and the rest of the former Soviet Union—could quickly resurrect a top-priority A-list threat if these weapons were to fall into the hands of disaffected custodial personnel, rebellious factions, rogue regimes, or terrorists. In chapter 2, we relate the history and successes of the Nunn-Lugar Cooperative Threat Reduction program and other efforts to control the lethal legacy of the cold war. But our success so far is only small comfort in view of the sheer size of that legacy and its longevity: plutonium, for example, has a half-life of twenty-four thousand years, an eternity in Russian politics. As Russia enters the second post–cold war era, arms control has been at an impasse, and threat reduction programs such as Nunn-Lugar need reinvention and reinvigoration.

Tension with a Rising China

Chapter 3 argues that the United States must act to help shape the course of China's rise to Asian superpower status so that it emerges in future decades as a partner rather than an adversary. Failure here would lead to the Pacific's greatest danger. We give a glimpse of that danger by describing the 1996 crisis over China's missile firings into the waters around Taiwan. The Clinton administration has called for a strategy of "engagement" in the U.S.-China relationship that reflects the principles of Preventive Defense, but engagement needs specific content if it is to be more than just a diplomatic slogan. Chapter 3, therefore, outlines content for U.S. engagement with China based on Preventive Defense principles.

Proliferation of Weapons of Mass Destruction

The spread of weapons of mass destruction (WMD) has always been regarded as a cardinal danger to international peace and security, but the nature of proliferation is now sharpening from diplomatic problem to direct military threat to the United States and its interests. Potential opponents in regional conflicts are amassing weapons of mass destruction in an attempt to sidestep U.S. conventional military forces, which they cannot hope to defeat in head-to-head "symmetric" warfare. The U.S. military therefore needs to develop counters to "asymmetrical" threats like weapons of mass destruction. In chapter 4, we describe the way the proliferation danger nearly became a direct threat on the Korean peninsula in 1994 and our efforts to promote military countermeasures in the so-called Counterproliferation Initiative. But this effort to equip the U.S. military for asymmetrical warfare is only beginning; chapter 4 charts the next steps.

Catastrophic Terrorism

The widening availability of destructive technology and the growing complexity and consequent vulnerability of twenty-first century societies suggest that terrorism might make a quantum leap in the decades ahead, from airline hijacking, ordinary explosives, and hostage taking to attack with nuclear, chemical, biological, and cyber weapons of enormous destructiveness. Terrorism with such weapons could cross borders as easily as people, goods, and capital do, bringing the threat directly to the U.S. homeland for the first time. To many, the end of the cold war implied that threats to U.S. personnel and interests would be remote, taking place in Europe, the Persian Gulf, or the Korean Peninsula. However, this threat has the potential to change Americans' perception of their security within their own homeland and thus to change our society itself; we therefore term this specter "catastrophic terrorism." It is a military-scale threat divorced from the traditional context of foreign military conflict, and this is entirely new in American experience. Catastrophic terrorism challenges the U.S. government to invent a new security structure from the bottom up. Chapter 5 reports the results of an effort, with our colleagues John M. Deutch and Philip Zelikow, to lay the first bricks in that structure.

Fallback: Maintaining a Strong U.S. Military

We have argued that the end of the cold war has induced a false sense of comfort that the dangers to American security are confined to the B-list and C-list threats that have dominated the

headlines in the last decade of the twentieth century. There is growing evidence that the absence of imminent A-list threat might also
lull the United States into sloppy and wasteful mismanagement of
its defense establishment. We call the danger of such mismanagement "the threat within." Chapter 6 describes this threat and the
actions already taken to overcome some of its consequences.
However, we argue, a new effort is needed. The United States must
have a strong military to cope with continuing B-list and C-list
contingencies, and a strong military will be even more essential if
Preventive Defense strategies are not able to keep future threats
from emerging.

Preventive Defense as a Defense Strategy

As a guide to national security strategy, Preventive Defense is
fundamentally different from deterrence: it is a broad politico-
military strategy, and therefore it draws on all the instruments of
foreign policy: political, economic, and military. But the role of
the U.S. Department of Defense is central: the department's contacts with its counterpart militaries in Russia, China, and
Europe will influence their views of themselves and thus their
propensity to threaten U.S. interests. The Defense Department's
resources and technology are critical to countering loose nukes,
proliferation, and terrorism. And the DOD has an enormous
stake in the success of Preventive Defense, since the price of failure is nothing less than the emergence of new A-list military
threats against which it would have to respond.

During our time at the Pentagon, we established a number of
programs and initiatives that made a strong start at incorporating
the strategy of Preventive Defense into the activities of the Defense
Department; these are described in the chapters that follow. After
we left the Pentagon in 1996, the department reinforced its commitment to these programs by adding "shaping the international
environment" to the DOD missions identified in the Quadrennial
Defense Review, a full-scale review of department programs com-

pleted in 1997. The second mission identified by the Quadrennial Review is "responding"—to aggression in Korea and the Persian Gulf and to peacekeeping and humanitarian emergencies such as Bosnia and Rwanda, our B-list and C-list threats. The third mission identified is "preparing" to use new technology to defeat major new threats if they emerge in the future (the subject of chapter 6). In our view, most of the department's efforts go to "responding"; a still insufficient but growing effort goes to "preparing"; and as yet far too little effort goes to "shaping," that is, to Preventive Defense. We hope that this book begins to redress the balance.

The Challenge Ahead

Today we are at a unique point in the history of American security. The United States faces no direct threats to its national survival, and it is the dominant military force in the world. To some, these conditions are contradictory. They argue that because we have no threat to our survival, America does not need to maintain its military dominance. Others argue, at least implicitly, that because of America's military dominance, our nation does not need to take measures to keep threats from reemerging. But we believe that a primary goal of our nation's security strategy should be to ensure that both of these conditions are perpetuated.

Preventive Defense programs, sustained and expanded, hold great promise for preventing conflict and should be a key component of American security strategy. But Preventive Defense is a strategy for influencing the rest of the world, not compelling it: Preventive Defense will not always work, and the United States will have to deal with a continuing parade of challenges that, while they threaten neither a global war nor our national survival, do threaten the survival of an ally, economic strangulation, or the use of weapons of mass destruction. We have no reason to expect these regional threats to disappear; rather, they are likely to get more severe. So, in addition to Preventive Defense, American defense strategy must maintain the military forces that are able to deter regional aggressors and that, if deterrence fails, can win quickly, decisively, and with minimal casualties.

Much work lies ahead to sustain the existing Preventive Defense programs and to build on them. The purpose of this book is to describe the new policies and programs needed to take maximum advantage of the current unprecedented opportunity to base American and international security in the twenty-first century on our ability to keep trouble from starting.

CHAPTER 1

Pursuing Marshall's Vision with Russia and NATO

During the tense days of the cold war, the windowless Boeing 747 was called the Doomsday plane. Painted bright white and sealed to protect its electronic communication gear from the huge electromagnetic pulse generated by a nuclear detonation, it was meant to be the sole surviving command post from which the president or the president's successor would order retaliation to a Soviet nuclear attack. Assured retaliation against any attack by Moscow was the essence of deterrence—the reason why the Soviets would not attack in the first place. The aircraft was designed to fly continuously during a nuclear war, refueled every few hours by U.S. Air Force tankers while thousands of Soviet nuclear weapons rained down on the United States.

Now the Soviet Union was gone and with it the priority given the "Doomsday" mission. The four Doomsday planes had been given an additional post–cold war role as operations centers for disaster relief officials responding to floods and hurricanes. In the Pentagon's "acronymania," the plane's official name, the National Emergency Airborne Command Post—NEACP, pronounced "kneecap"—had been changed to NAOC, National Airborne Operations Center.

Even with these new duties, however, at least one plane in the NAOC fleet was almost always unused, and so the secretary of defense had begun using the extra plane for overseas travel.[1] Now the Doomsday plane of the cold war had become the primary means of transportation for the secretary of defense and his team as we traveled to the many new nations that had emerged from the Soviet Union and Warsaw Pact. We formed close working relationships with their defense ministers, foreign ministers, heads of state, and chiefs of staff, all the while staying in touch with the 200,000 U.S. troops based overseas. One might call this new breed of Pentagon work "Preventive Defense" diplomacy, since its purpose was to bring together the militaries of Europe to find solutions to common problems rather than working in isolation against one another. This had been George Marshall's vision for Europe after World War II. He had been successful in Western Europe, but not Eastern Europe.

In the post–cold war world, adjustments were taking place everywhere, and everywhere, as with NEACP, old missions for the cold war's military tools were replaced with new ones. NATO, the North Atlantic Treaty Organization, had been founded in the 1950s to throw back a Soviet European invasion that never came. Now NATO was preparing to carry out its first-ever military operation, but with a very different mission: enforcing the peace in Bosnia that everyone hoped would result from the talks scheduled to open in Dayton, Ohio, on November 1, 1995.

Reaching and keeping the peace in Bosnia would be the greatest test yet of the security system in Europe that replaced the bloc structure of the cold war. When the iron grip of communism relaxed its hold on the states of the former Warsaw Pact, ethnic conflict had welled up and had done so with a vengeance in the former Yugoslavia. The security system for Europe thus put to the test was the "Europe whole and free" proclaimed by President George Bush and the "undivided continent" called for by his successor, President Bill Clinton, whom we had served in the Pentagon since early 1993.

The Dayton talks were expected to call for an international peacekeeping force to separate Serb, Croat, and Muslim factions, confiscate heavy weapons, and prevent violence while economic and political reconstruction took place. The United States, under the leadership of Richard Holbrooke, was brokering the peace process, and it was expected to take a lead role in organizing the peacekeeping force.

We believed it was essential that Russia also participate in the peacekeeping force. To exclude Russia from the operation in which Europe coped with its first post–cold war security emergency would create a division of the continent in deed, whatever we might say in diplomatic words. Yet bringing together the former cold war enemies in a joint peacekeeping force was no easy matter. The story of our travels aboard NAOC to negotiate with Russia over how its troops would work with NATO to keep the peace in Bosnia is a tale both cautionary and exemplary.

The Partnership for Peace and the Pragmatic Partnership

Military-to-military links are the key to preventing new divisions and new wars in Europe. We came into office believing that reaching out to these new militaries should be one of the principal tasks of the U.S. military in the post–cold war era. We were determined to forge new links with our former enemies; we wanted to draw them into the community of western nations and into the vision of a Europe whole and free. We wanted them to plan, train, and exercise together with the U.S. military to solve common problems. If they did so, they would be more likely to trust one another and avoid the intrigue that had been the bane of Europe ever since it became a system of nation states.

The rigid war machine of the Warsaw Pact had been replaced by a host of independent militaries. From Kazakhstan on the Chinese border to Poland on the German border, and from Estonia on the Baltic to Albania on the Adriatic, the United States and NATO had drawn these new nations into working together with NATO nations in a "Partnership for Peace." When it was established in January

1994, membership in the Partnership for Peace (PFP) was offered to all the states of the former Warsaw Pact and Soviet Union. The dream for this partnership was that the partners would see ethnic wars like the one in Bosnia as a common security problem and would cooperate as partners in solving it, rather than designating proxies and taking sides as in the cold war.[2]

We strongly believed that Russia should take part in peace-keeping in Bosnia. This would be a defining event for the new Russia, just as the international community's response to Dayton would be a defining event for the new Europe. The role of Russia's military was key because it was the institution that would endure, whatever might happen to Boris Yeltsin's democrats or their successors.

The Department of Defense had dubbed the U.S.-Russian security relationship, including the military-to-military program, the Pragmatic Partnership.[3] Our new links to the Russian military were crucial to realizing an undivided Europe. Russia's empire and war machine were much reduced, but it still had the world's largest nuclear arsenal and a power and position in Eurasia that made its participation in the emerging European security system essential. Our objective was to promote common action between our militaries where Russian and American interests converged, building a foundation of cooperation that would survive the inevitable differences.

Starting in 1993, we had established a system of regular meetings between senior DOD and Russian Ministry of Defense officials. Russians, long jaded by the phoniness of their official relationships under the Soviet system, valued such personal contacts. Every few months, Carter would take a delegation of senior Pentagon officials and military officers to Moscow to meet with the Russian Defense Ministry and General Staff officers in what was called the Bilateral Working Group (the Russian Ministry of Defense was all military, with no civilians as in the U.S. Defense Department).

On one such visit, Carter had brought the commander of the U.S. missile defense program, a three-star general, to brief the Russians on the new technologies the United States was developing for the theater missile defense system intended to replace the Patriot missile. Carter had asked all briefers who came to Moscow to have translated into Russian the ubiquitous colored charts without which no proper Pentagon briefing could be given. When the Air Force general called for his first chart, it came up on the projection screen in Russian—totally unreadable to the American briefer! The briefing came to an abrupt halt until an English-language version of the charts could be found to give the general his cues.

Perry and Carter had even briefed Russia's Defense Minister Pavel Grachev and the Russian General Staff on the results of the Nuclear Posture Review, an in-depth look at the role of the U.S. nuclear arsenal after the cold war that had been completed in September 1994. At this briefing in New York, we used the same charts with which we had briefed President Clinton, minus the classified details.

We regularly joined the meetings of the Gore-Chernomyrdin Commission to report on the progress of our Pragmatic Partnership with the Russian military. These twice-yearly meetings, begun in 1993 under the auspices of U.S. Vice President Al Gore and Russia's Prime Minister Viktor Chernomyrdin, were remarkable affairs. Virtually the entire U.S. cabinet would sit along one side of a giant meeting table and their Moscow counterparts would sit along the other: the U.S. secretary of health and human services across from Russia's health minister, the head of NASA across from the head of the Russian space program, the secretary of energy across from the minister of atomic energy, the director of the Environmental Protection Agency across from the environment minister, and so on. Each pair would report on their progress in crafting joint projects that pooled the technology of each country for the good of both. At first, this dialogue was difficult for these officials whose two nations had developed their technology independently of one another for half a century. But a large number of worthy joint projects were begun through this mechanism.

At the Gore-Chernomyrdin meetings, defense cooperation was just one topic among many: there was no longer any reason for security to monopolize the U.S.-Russian relationship as it had done in Soviet times. The breadth of these meetings is a tribute to the vision of Gore and Chernomyrdin, who recognized that a durable post–cold war peace would need to be broad-based and to engage the everyday interests of the Russian and American people.

However, the U.S. stakes in Russia's evolution remained concentrated in the security sphere. Here the relationships between the defense ministers and their ministries were key. Perry had worked hard to forge a bond with Pavel Grachev. They could not have been more different from one another. Grachev was twenty years younger than Perry, a barrel-chested soldier's soldier with a scar across his lower jaw from his years with the airborne forces. He was one of the young *Afghansi* officers, veterans of the Soviet Union's disastrous decade-long war in Afghanistan. Another prominent *Afghansi*, Alexander Rutskoi, had led the October 1993 parliamentary putsch against Yeltsin. At that time, Grachev had stood by Yeltsin and had even ordered his forces to attack the rebels in the parliamentary headquarters; his tanks had fired into the "White House" from a bridge over the Moscow River. For this and other reasons, Grachev was unpopular with some of the Russian military, but he clearly had Yeltsin's ear and support.

Russia's foreign minister, Andrei Kozyrev, did not. Kozyrev, a brilliant political scientist who was admired in the West, was regarded by Russian nationalists as having sold out Moscow's superpower status. Yeltsin, always willing to deflect criticism from himself onto subordinates, had been hinting for some time that Kozyrev was on the way out. The Foreign Ministry had accordingly lost clout in policymaking, and the Defense Ministry had taken it up. The Perry-Grachev relationship seemed, for the time being, to be the best channel for getting serious business done with the Russians.

We had worked hard to establish good working relationships with Grachev and his staff. When we met with them we took small mementos: a framed picture of our last meeting for Grachev, a copy of the popular American children's book *Curious George* for his young interpreter's family. We had a special direct phone circuit—a "hotline"—installed between Grachev's desk and Perry's. The line was encrypted to protect the ministers' conversation from eavesdropping by foreign powers (or by Grachev's colleagues in Russia's intelligence services). It was a source of constant frustration: we would come into the Pentagon early in the morning to speak to Grachev late in his day in Moscow. After five or ten minutes of conversation, the line would begin to whistle, hum, and crackle; it would finally disconnect. We pleaded with our communications specialists to fix the problem, and they traced it to the Russian end: Russian security officials, afraid that the phone was bugged, had tampered with it. Nonetheless, the hotline was a sign of the two defense ministers' personal commitment to work together to solve problems.

Briefings and frequent meetings were important to instill a spirit of openness in the U.S.-Russian relationship. In the initial post–cold war period it was enough simply to meet and talk as "Joe" and "Ivan." But these military-to-military contacts shortly wore thin. What really matters to military professionals is joint professional activity: training and exercises, with the prospect of actually operating in combat on the same side someday.

Not since World War II had Russian and American soldiers fought together. We could not consider operating with the Russians in Bosnia without practicing with them first. Russia's homegrown "peacekeeping" operation in the breakaway republic of Chechnya, launched in December 1994, had been a disaster. (A Russian briefing Carter's Bilateral Working Group had treated the astonished Americans to a presentation on "artillery tactics in urban areas.") We needed to make sure that the Russian units that went to Bosnia were trained in NATO tactics, which included the use of nonlethal means for containing the feuding Bosnian armies and dealing with angry civilian populations, and even extended to guidance on handling the ever-present international press.

We therefore proposed to the Russians a program of joint military exercises. The first joint war games, which we planned for Totskoye, in Russia, for September 1994, and Fort Riley, Kansas, in November 1995, would simulate a combined peacekeeping mission, just like Bosnia. It had been difficult to persuade the suspicious Russian military to agree to the exercises. When the first exercise was scheduled for Totskoye, some rabble-rousers in the overheated Russian political arena accused the Russian military of

submitting to an American "invasion."[4] Money was also a problem. The dwindling Russian military budget was stretched with
just feeding and housing the troops in their swollen ranks; there
was little money left to train them to be effective soldiers.

NATO Expansion and the Souring of U.S.-Russian Relations

The Pragmatic Partnership had gotten off to a good start in 1994,
but by late 1995 these relations had soured; it had not been a ban-
ner year. The first dent had come in September 1994. The Russians
had not opposed the U.S. operation to restore Jean-Bertrand
Aristide to his legitimate post in Haiti, and indeed had voted for
the UN resolution approving the U.S. operation. But military planning for the Haiti operation reached a critical phase in early
September, just at the time that the first joint peacekeeping exercise
between American and Russian forces was to be held at Totskoye.
As a result, it was impossible for Perry to leave Washington to
attend the exercise as we had planned. Pavel Grachev had stuck his
neck out to host this exercise on Russian soil against Russian
opposition, and when we canceled our visit to Totskoye, he was
bitter. Although the Totskoye exercises were successful, Grachev
deferred his agreement to send Russian troops to the follow-on
exercise at Fort Riley, Kansas, scheduled for November 1995, and
indicated that he would not come to the United States to attend the
exercise even if it did take place.

But the deeper source of trouble in the relationship was
NATO, and in particular NATO expansion. Grachev, like almost
all Russians, regarded NATO as a throwback to the cold war, a
sign that Europe would never welcome Russia as a security partner.
NATO was the enemy against which he and all other Russian officers had trained for their entire careers. Now that the cold war
was over, most Russians thought NATO should vanish as the
Warsaw Pact had done. Its continued existence, they complained,
meant that the western countries saw themselves as victors and
were not ready to put the past behind them. They charged that the
United States was using NATO to press its advantage as the sole

remaining superpower. They saw NATO expansion as directed squarely at them. Under the Partnership for Peace, which we were trying to nurture, all former Warsaw Pact countries could forge the same links to NATO, even Russia; none would be singled out. But Russia saw NATO expansion as a repudiation of the Partnership for Peace.

There was no question in our mind that NATO should continue to exist, and that it could usefully take on new missions in the post–cold war world. We also believed that NATO should not take the position that its membership was forever limited to its sixteen cold war members. Since the Berlin Wall fell, states liberated from the Warsaw Pact had been clamoring for membership in western European institutions. They wanted validation that their new governments were going concerns, and they wanted to associate themselves with the prosperity and security of the West. They wanted membership in western economic institutions and above all the European Union. But the EU did not want new members: that would incur real economic costs. Some cynical Europeans thought that offering NATO membership instead would satisfy their brethren to the east without the economic dislocation that would result from mixing the former Warsaw Pact nations' uncertain economic fortunes with those of western European nations.

While NATO could not declare itself closed to new members, we believed it was preferable to defer admission of new members from the former Warsaw Pact until Russia and other eastern European nations had more opportunity to work with NATO. By working on real operations with NATO, they would come to see NATO not as an enemy, but as a partner. This would be accomplished in time by the workings of the Partnership for Peace, enhanced by ad hoc joint operations such as in Bosnia. Indeed, Partnership for Peace activities would both help change NATO's image and also provide the major benefits of NATO enlargement: giving the militaries of the east the link to the West they sought, as well as the experience sought by NATO of planning together rather than against one another.

Through late 1994 and into early 1995 there had been debate within the Clinton administration over the timing of NATO enlargement. The question was not whether NATO should expand, but when. We thought the question should be deferred until later in the decade. By then the Partnership for Peace (PFP) would be fully developed, extending the benefits of affiliation with NATO to all the new militaries to the east. We thought that premature speculation about who would become members of NATO would derail the PFP and spawn invidious distinctions among its members. There was also the question of whether NATO was itself ready to absorb new members. NATO was undergoing an identity crisis, seeking a new role for its unrivaled joint military capabilities. Above all, strains over how to handle Bosnia were eroding goodwill within NATO to an unprecedented degree. We were concerned that prematurely adding untried militaries and fledgling democracies from the former Warsaw Pact to this mix would make NATO's transformation more difficult. Undercutting the Pragmatic Partnership with Russia was therefore just one of several factors counseling a go-slow approach to NATO expansion.

On the other side of the balance was the fervent desire of the eastern European nations, which had essentially been occupied for the previous half century, to become part of the West at last by joining at least NATO, if not the European Union. Their tragic history argued that they should not be kept waiting long. And proponents of immediate expansion argued that delaying the accession of new members would not really help the problems with which we were most concerned.

Debate within the Clinton administration over NATO expansion came to a head in late 1994. Early in December, NATO held its usual twice-yearly meetings of foreign and defense ministers at NATO headquarters in Brussels. These were usually routine affairs at which most of the real business was done in the hallways and side meeting rooms, and as usual, before this one, the staffs of NATO's sixteen member nations and its permanent officials began to negotiate a communiqué that would "emerge" from the meeting with fictional spontaneity. This time, the bureaucratic process resulted in a December 1994 communiqué that included the declaration that NATO would expand.

The storm in Moscow was immediate. In Budapest a few days after the release of the NATO communiqué, Carter, accompanying President Clinton, witnessed a performance by Boris Yeltsin reminiscent of Khrushchev's cold war UN shoe-banging. Yeltsin warned that Europe "runs the risk of plunging into a cold peace." He viewed expansion as a sign of the West's doubt that Russia's democratic experiment would succeed. "It's too early to bury democracy in Russia!" he declared. Yeltsin ended his peroration with an argument that could have been taken from George Marshall after World War II: "The year 1995 is the year of the 50th anniversary of the end of World War II. Today, half a century on, we come to realize the true meaning of the great victory—the need for historic reconciliation in Europe. There should no longer be enemies, winners or losers in it. For the first time in history, our continent has a real opportunity to achieve unity. To miss it means to forget the lessons of the past and to jeopardize our future."

A few days later, as we accompanied Vice President Gore at a Moscow meeting of the Gore-Chernomyrdin Commission, we had another first-hand taste of Russia's condemnation of NATO expansion. As we met with defense and Duma leaders, the press, and scholars, it was clear to us that the NATO communiqué on expansion had created an issue on which the usually fractious Moscow foreign policy elite could agree unanimously. Speaking with the vice president and with Strobe Talbott, President Clinton's point man on Russia, Perry argued that the NATO communiqué was making policy—and unnecessary waves—when the president had not yet made a final decision on NATO expansion. Perry asked for a meeting with the president when they returned to Washington.

Thus on December 21, 1994, Perry joined Gore and Talbott, as well as Secretary of State Warren Christopher, National Security Advisor Anthony Lake, Deputy National Security Advisor Sandy Berger, and President Clinton in the president's personal study in the White House. Perry argued that the communiqué implied that NATO would be expanding soon, but that early expansion was a mistake. Provoking distrust and dismay in Russia was just one reason to defer expansion until later in the decade.

Their trips to Budapest and Moscow had made the president and vice president sensitive to the Russian angle, and they listened intently to Perry's other concerns about NATO's readiness to expand and the importance of not undermining the Partnership for Peace. But they felt that right was on the side of the eastern European countries that wanted to enter NATO soon, that deferring expansion until later in the decade was not feasible, and that the Russians could be convinced that expansion was not directed against them.

On his return to the Pentagon, therefore, Perry summoned Carter as well as Carter's deputy for Russia, the energetic and able Elizabeth Sherwood. Expansion would go forward on a brisk schedule, he explained, and so we would have to make an extra effort to create positive momentum elsewhere in the Pragmatic Partnership, including more Bilateral Working Group meetings with the Russian General Staff, more Perry-Grachev meetings, more consultation over the hotline between Perry's and Grachev's offices, and above all an effort to get the Russian military and NATO working together, especially in Bosnia. It would be an uphill struggle.

Not only was NATO expanding; it was also taking on a larger and larger role in Bosnia. By late summer 1995, NATO was conducting air strikes in Bosnia, over Russian objections. We made it a point to phone Grachev after each strike to explain the justification, but we did not think it was appropriate to inform the Russians before the strike. That would have risked a leak, possibly jeopardizing the lives of NATO aircrews. Grachev, however, objected that these phone calls were only informing him, not consulting him.

Thus by the time peace seemed within reach in Bosnia in October 1995, U.S.-Russian relations and our Pragmatic Partnership with the Russian military were at an all-time low. In early October, when we asked Grachev for a meeting to discuss a role for Russia in the Bosnian peace force, we offered him a choice of three locations. He chose Geneva, a "neutral" site where some of the toughest negotiations of the cold war had been held. The tone of Grachev's choice was unmistakably chilly.

Bringing Russia In

Russia's military forces were not essential to the peacekeeping operation in Bosnia: the United States and its NATO allies could handle the job. Moreover, the warring parties in the former Yugoslavia were themselves indifferent about Russian participation. Even the Serbs, Russia's "Slavic brethren," as the Russian nationalists called them, did not press for Russia to be part of the peacekeeping force. The Muslims and Croats did not seem to fear that if they spurned Russia, these "Slavic brethren" of the Serbs might begin to interfere rather than support the peace process, by arming the Serbs or by encouraging hard-liners among the Bosnian Serb forces to resist the Dayton agreement. With atrocities running nightly on the television news, most of the American and European officials were preoccupied with seeking peace in Bosnia and desperate to end the years of frustration and humiliation. As a consequence, they could no longer see any larger meaning in how the peace was accomplished, such as the need to give Russia a role.

We disagreed. We believed that the reason to include Russia in the Bosnian peace force was bigger than the Bosnian operation and had to do with Russia itself. Exclusion would be taken by Russians as a sign that the extended hand of post–cold war "partnership" was a false gesture, that our military-to-military relationship was for show but not for real. The Yeltsin government was already under attack by domestic critics of reform and democracy who argued that Yeltsin's policies had demolished Russia's international standing. The reward for allowing the Warsaw Pact to disintegrate peacefully, they charged, had not been respectful inclusion in the club of leading nations, but instead the back of the hand. Yeltsin was polling in the single digits, and communists, nationalists, agrarians, and a host of other factions were contending with him for the electorate in upcoming parliamentary and presidential elections.

Earlier in this century, European statesmen had spurned a former enemy, the Weimar Republic of Germany, and allowed it to fall prey to its worst tendencies. The result was the rise of Adolf Hitler and World War II. The parallels to Boris Yeltsin's Russia were alarming. A crisis for democratic Russia akin to the demise of Weimar Germany could loom in the near future.

Aboard NAOC for Geneva

Thus the stakes were very high as we boarded NAOC at Andrews Air Force Base on Saturday, October 7, 1995, heading for Geneva and our meeting with Grachev. NAOC has a conference room and an amphitheater with projection screen and podium for formal briefings: no Pentagon meeting, even in the air, is complete without a colonel wielding a pointer and colored charts. Behind the amphitheater is a "battle room" where rows of high captain's chairs face consoles lined with buttons, switches, screens, and phones; they were designed for military officers directing the flow of satellite intelligence and launch messages during a nuclear war. On diplomatic trips, however, the battle room serves as office space for senior officials, who perch on the high chairs like Captain Kirk of the Starship Enterprise, ignoring the high-tech gear as they draft their talking points on laptop computers.

Behind the battle room is the communications suite where a team of enlisted personnel staffs an array of radios, satellite links, phones, and faxes. NAOC's communications were originally not very useful to us: they were designed to transmit one-way launch codes to nuclear forces: go or no-go. But post–cold war upgrades had made available normal office communications by phone or fax, either "in the clear" or encrypted. Perry would use the forward cabin, originally designed for the president or his successor during a nuclear war, to read up on the negotiations and work with his staff. Perhaps NAOC's most appreciated feature is its dozen or so bunks where the secretary's exhausted delegation can catnap between stops. They are stacked three high, small but horizontal: no better than a sailor's bunk on a submarine, but they are blessedly horizontal. Preventive Defense diplomacy is tough on the body.

Our October 1995 NAOC trip to meet Grachev in Geneva followed a familiar rhythm. Most of us had already put in a long day and night of preparation at the Pentagon. The first few hours of the flight would be spent reading briefing books, discussing the main issues to be addressed at the upcoming meetings, and receiving and transmitting cables. Then final changes would be made in the "talking points" that would guide our discussions with foreign leaders, the agreements to be negotiated, and the speeches to be given. Finally the traveling press would be brought forward from their compartment in the back of the plane and briefed on the main objectives of the trip. By then the destination would be only a few hours away. After a brief and fitful sleep, it would be time to awaken, shave, put on our suits, and step onto the tarmac to review the inevitable honor guard while the inevitable military band played.

Shortly after takeoff that Saturday, we met up forward in the conference room. Its long meeting table had headphones at each seat, so that we could hear one another above the engine and slip-stream noises of the giant 747. On the wall of the conference room was a chart that listed the line of succession to the presidency specified in the U.S. Constitution and the Presidential Succession Act, prepared for use when NAOC was performing its original duty rather than Preventive Defense diplomacy. If, in a nuclear war, the president did not survive to board the aircraft, the crew would refer to the chart and look for the next living successor, who would become president and begin giving the necessary orders. The line of succession ran from Vice President Al Gore to Speaker of the House Newt Gingrich, to Senator Strom Thurmond of South Carolina, president pro tempore of the Senate, and then to the Cabinet members: Secretary of State Warren Christopher, Treasury Secretary Robert Rubin, Defense Secretary Bill Perry, Attorney General Janet Reno, and so on down the Cabinet line. The chart seemed incongruous on a mission such as ours, which was trying to work cooperatively with the Russian military; it was a reminder of how far we had come since the cold war and the importance of not slipping backward.

Joining the two of us at the conference room table were Strobe Talbott; Walt Slocombe, the Pentagon's policy chief and point man on Bosnia; Lieutenant General Wes Clark, the "J-5" or director of policy and plans for the Joint Chiefs of Staff, who later became supreme commander of allied forces in Europe; and other senior National Security Council and State Department officials responsible for Europe and the former Soviet Union.

The mood at the conference table was pessimistic. Our position—Russians in Bosnia under NATO command—and the Russian position—Russians in Bosnia but not under NATO—seemed irreconcilable. We believed that the stakes were very high, but the prospects for success seemed dim. The problem was very simple.

Any military operation requires what the military calls "unity of command," meaning that each level of command responds to one and only one superior, with no possibility of conflicting orders at a dangerous moment. In Somalia two years earlier, the compromise of this principle had contributed to the disastrous outcome; the bodies of dead U.S. soldiers had been dragged through the streets of Mogadishu by exultant mobs, the grisly spectacle captured on television cameras for all the world to see. Putting U.S. soldiers in harm's way in the Balkans, one of history's cruelest regions to any great power trying to tame it, would be a grave matter.

The only international military organization we could trust to provide unity of command was NATO. The U.S. position, therefore, was that Russia's forces should serve in the Bosnian peace force under NATO command and control. This military necessity for the United States, however, ran headlong into a political necessity of the Yeltsin government. To Moscow, the idea of Russia's forces subordinated to NATO was unacceptable. Thus, beginning in Geneva the next day, we would seek to square this circle with Russian Defense Minister Pavel Grachev.

Adding to the pessimistic mood around NAOC's conference table was the fact that since the Bosnian conflict was such a thorn in the side of the United States, few others in the U.S. government had much patience for seeking an honorable role for the Russians. To most U.S. and NATO officials caught up in the Bosnia drama, Russia seemed like an unnecessary complication. We believed that they were not seeing the forest for the trees; they failed to recognize that Russia was an indispensable part of the larger European security order of which the Bosnian peace was supposed to be a part.

However, just days earlier the ministers of defense of the NATO nations, meeting in Williamsburg, Virginia, had urged Perry, their American counterpart, to find a solution to the Bosnian peacekeeping force that included Russia, although not at the price of displacing the NATO chain of command. With this encouragement, we resolved in the NAOC conference room to try to find some way of persuading Russia's Grachev to join a NATO-commanded peacekeeping operation in Bosnia. It would be a hard sell and a sharp test of the new relationship we had been striving to forge with the Russian military since taking office in 1993.

Averting Disaster at Geneva

We landed in Geneva in late afternoon and went to the hotel. There, following standard procedures on such trips, the military staff had taken over an entire floor. One room had been designated the "control room" and specially secured. The control room was a tangle of encrypted phones and faxes that would be set up and torn down on every trip by a dedicated set of technicians. They covered the walls with brown wrapping paper and pitched a tent in the middle of the floor to hide the equipment and documents from any cameras that might have been installed in the hotel's walls or ceiling by a foreign intelligence service. They installed secure phones in sound-proof phone booths lugged along for the purpose, sometimes asking the official who used the phone to put his or her face into a sealed rubber "oxygen mask" designed to muffle voices. While we unpacked our bags, the control room staff gathered cables, message traffic, intelligence bulletins, and press clips from around the world, as well as phone messages from Washington, where the Pentagon would be having its own typical day of feverish "inside-the-beltway" activity, seemingly oblivious to the fact that its chief officials were half a world away.

After we responded to what the control room staff calls "real-world" emergencies—to distinguish them from Washington's perceived crises—and dutifully returned calls to Washington, it was time for a casual dinner with the ambassador and his country team. We were grateful this time to be spared the lavish formal banquet, with its multiple toasts, often endured on such trips. At such affairs, one has to be gracious while staying alert to the tendency of wily foreign hosts, operating in their own time zone on plenty of sleep, to use such moments to press for a concession or exploit a drowsy lapse of discretion. This time, we could relax and turn in early. The next day we would arise at what the military calls "Oh-Dark-Thirty" to check our preparations, see what was happening in the rest of the world, and motorcade to the U.S. mission, where the morning meeting with Grachev would be held.

At the mission, the mood at the long table was surly from the outset. Those of us from the Pentagon and the Russian General Staff who knew each other well greeted one another with uncharacteristic grimness. The Bosnia experts on both sides were glowering.

Each minister got right to the point. The Bosnian peace force, said Perry, must be a NATO force, for military reasons. Grachev shot back that it could not be a NATO force, that Russia would not accept this. He gripped his throat with both hands: this is what would happen in Moscow, he said, to any Russian who agreed to such a humiliation. "And therefore you, Dr. Perry, have me by the throat."

Perry asked whether Russia would accept a noncombat role—maybe airlift, logistics, other supporting functions but not combat? The United States could accept a looser command and control system for Russian forces if they were limited to such functions. No, said Grachev; Russia had to be a full combatant participant.

Then he delivered more bad news as he raised other key issues in U.S.-Russian relations. One concerned the Conventional Forces in Europe (CFE) Treaty signed by the United States and the Soviet Union during the cold war. For years the Russian military had objected to the "flanks" provision of the treaty, which limited Russia's ability to move its tanks, armored personnel carriers, artillery pieces, assault helicopters, and strike aircraft to new locations on Russian territory. The provision had been meant to limit the ability of the Soviet Union to concentrate its armies for a westward strike against NATO.

The U.S. Defense Department was sympathetic to the Russian claim that the flanks provision was no longer militarily necessary, and we were working with the Europeans to amend the CFE Treaty. But now, at our meeting in Geneva, Grachev threatened that Russia could wait no longer. He told us that, as we spoke, a paper spelling out two options was being prepared for Boris Yeltsin. In one option, Russia would simply ignore the odious flanks provision; in the other, it would scrap the CFE Treaty entirely.

Deepening our gloom, Grachev went on to announce that he would not cooperate with the new Nunn-Lugar program proposed by the Pentagon to help safeguard Russian nuclear weapons against terrorism or theft. Fear of "loose nukes" in a fractious, revolutionary Russia was a chief U.S. security concern, and we were prepared to underwrite strengthened safeguards over the Russian arsenal with Defense Department funds, but now Grachev seemed to be slamming the door. Thus, the issue of Bosnian peacekeeping was threatening to undermine a vital security interest of the United States: nuclear safety.

Even so, we could not agree to a Russian combat force outside of NATO. Unclear command and control invited another Somalia-like debacle for our soldiers. Diplomatic disaster loomed. President Clinton would understand the source of the stalemate, but he would not welcome failure. In just two weeks he was scheduled to meet with Boris Yeltsin for a summit at Franklin D. Roosevelt's family home in Hyde Park, New York. It would not be serving the president well to hand him a mess of this magnitude on the eve of the summit. Presumably Grachev felt the same pressure from Yeltsin. Both presidents were facing tough reelection challenges in 1996, and both counted their ability to shepherd their two countries' post–cold war relationship as a deserved plus in their popularity. Neither the Russians nor the Americans were happy when we recessed for lunch.

As the U.S. delegation huddled over sandwiches in the U.S. Mission, the scene of innumerable tense cold war conclaves, we discussed how to proceed. Although we were disappointed with Grachev's position, we were not surprised. Back on NAOC, we had foreseen as much, and there we had devised a fallback plan. Experience had taught us that when diplomatic disaster looms, two things are crucial. First, no matter how wide the disagreement, we should try to find something, however small, that the two sides can agree to and announce to the anxiously watching world. Second, do not break off contact; try to get agreement to meet again. That keeps the process going and keeps hope alive. Over lunch, Carter reviewed the two-part "disaster plan" he had prepared aboard NAOC.

We reconvened after lunch, this time in the former Soviet mission that Russia now shared, somewhat awkwardly, with Ukraine and other former Soviet republics. There, Grachev reiterated his position on Russian participation in a NATO-led peacekeeping effort in Bosnia: "Nyet!" All afternoon, the discussion went back and forth. As the appointed time for adjournment approached, it was time to execute the disaster plan.

First, we proposed that Grachev send a military planning team to meet with NATO's supreme allied commander, Europe (SACEUR) at NATO headquarters in Mons, Belgium, where detailed planning for the Bosnia operation was taking place. There the Russians could see NATO at work and view the role they could play if they did relent and join the NATO operation. Maybe Russia's generals and NATO's military leaders, led by General George Joulwan, the straight-talking SACEUR, would find a practical way to meet both our military requirements and Russia's political requirements.

Would Grachev agree, Perry asked, to send a senior officer to Mons to participate in Joulwan's planning effort? Grachev was intrigued by the idea of a Russian officer actually working within NATO's precincts. His answer—to our relief—was "da."

Second, we asked Grachev to reverse his decision not to attend the upcoming U.S.-Russian exercise at Fort Riley, the follow-on to the Totskoye exercise that was scheduled to begin immediately after the Hyde Park summit. The two defense ministers could then try again to find a solution. On this question, Grachev demurred:

"I must ask Boris Nikolayevich," he said, but it was clear to us that his recommendation to Yeltsin would be positive.

That was enough to save the situation and the Hyde Park summit. The presidents would be able to say that the explosive issue of Russia's participation in Bosnian peacekeeping was under active discussion by their defense ministers; that although agreement was far from assured, the effort would continue; and that, as a sign of optimism, military planners were meeting at Mons.

The Hyde Park Summit

Before the summit, Coit D. ("Chip") Blacker, President Clinton's assistant for Russia and Eastern Europe, who had been working closely with us, advised the president to take the initiative and raise the issue of Russian participation in Bosnia immediately at Hyde Park. Carter, representing Perry, advised President Clinton to propose that the two presidents agree to remand the matter to their defense ministers and avoid getting into the details of how to square the circle of NATO command.

When the Hyde Park summit opened on October 23, 1995, Clinton followed this advice. Yeltsin, taken by surprise at Clinton's emphasis on this issue, was intrigued by his suggestion. He gave a strong "da," to the obvious discomfort of his staff. President Clinton then said that he believed that Perry and Grachev could solve this problem, but that time was of the essence. He asked whether Yeltsin would allow Grachev to come to the Fort Riley exercise with Perry so they could continue their discussions in an expedited way. "I will order him to," said Yeltsin. It seemed that the Russians wanted to find a solution, too.

The mood in Hyde Park was much better than at Geneva. The presidents were giving their defense leaders the chance to solve the security problems. Yeltsin directed his deputy foreign minister, Georgiy Mamedov, to hand Carter a map of the CFE flanks showing the disposition of Russian forces and proposing a change in the treaty. It was an extreme proposal, but it was not the total repudiation of the treaty that Grachev had threatened at Geneva.

As for Bosnia, Yeltsin wanted in. "The minimum," he said, was that Russia should perform noncombat missions outside of the NATO command system, as Perry had indicated in Geneva was acceptable to the United States. Yeltsin asked that these functions be called "special operations" so they would not sound merely custodial. Yeltsin then said that Perry and Grachev should explore "the maximum." Clinton agreed.[5]

Second Try with Grachev

We planned meticulously for Grachev's return visit, so that events would be conducive to agreement. On October 27, 1995, the two of us accompanied him to Fort Riley, where U.S. and Russian troops were practicing peacekeeping together: how to secure a town, how to guard a checkpoint, even how to deal with inquisitive reporters. It was clear that the troops on the ground could work together, if only their leaders could agree on how to command them. Grachev got the point, and mixing with the troops, as always, put him in good spirits.

The next day we went to Whiteman Air Force Base, where Grachev and Perry pushed the plunger to set off a high-explosive charge under a Minuteman intercontinental missile silo, destroying it in accordance with the START I arms control agreement. This was a reminder to both delegations of the stakes involved in the U.S.-Russian relationship and the price of undermining that relationship. No single issue, not even Bosnian peacekeeping, should be permitted to throw us back into confrontation. Photos of Grachev and Perry at the plunger, a huge cloud of dust rising into the sky behind them, appeared on front pages across the United States and Russia. It was important for Grachev to get good press on this trip; as he had told us in Geneva, Moscow politicians were looking to "get him by the throat" over Bosnia. We also invited Grachev into the cockpit of a B-2 "stealth" bomber; he was the first Russian ever allowed to approach the once-secret plane.

To top off his visit, we presented a proposal on the CFE flank issue that responded to key Russian concerns. NATO had worked with U.S. negotiators on the proposal; the implicit message for

Grachev was, "you can work with NATO." Perry also invited Grachev to come to NATO headquarters in Brussels for the semi-annual meeting of NATO defense ministers to be held later in November. Grachev could see NATO for himself and decide whether it was still an enemy of Russia.

Between events at Fort Riley and Whiteman, and on the airplane as we flew about, the two delegations worked together on the Bosnia problem. Exploring various command and control arrangements for the Russian contingent, we drew boxes indicating the various levels of command and lines connecting them on napkins and scraps of paper. We agreed that the officer whom Grachev would send to work with General Joulwan could assume the title of "deputy commander for Russian forces" if Russia joined the operation. A special command chain, outside of NATO channels, would be set up for the Russians, but the "unity of command" principle meant that the Russian contingent could not have a combat role. Instead, it would perform engineering, transport, and construction tasks, which we would term "special operations," as President Yeltsin had asked. U.S. engineers would work alongside the Russians in a joint division. The special operations division would come into Bosnia a month after the combat force.

Thus we had achieved "the minimum" Yeltsin had asked for: the Russians were in. Beyond that, no agreement was reached, but neither side was ready to stop at restricting the Russians to "special operations." Perry and Grachev agreed to ask General Joulwan and the Russian general sent by Grachev to try to devise a command scheme for the Russians to play a full combat role. Perry and Grachev would review their commanders' proposals when Grachev came to Brussels for the NATO ministerial meeting.

The Generals Square the Circle

The general whom Grachev sent to NATO headquarters was Colonel General Leontiy Shevtsov (three stars in the Russian system). Both he and General Joulwan were practical, inventive commanders. Working intently together during the first week of November, as the peace talks opened in Dayton, they swept aside abstractions and focused on the military tasks. The result was a brilliant scheme to bring about Russian participation in Bosnia.[6]

Their scheme hinged upon the distinction between what the military calls "operational control," or OPCON, and "tactical control," or TACON. OPCON refers to the selection of tasks a given unit is assigned (such as, "separate Serb and Muslim forces in Sector A") and the rules of engagement (such as, "you may fire your weapons only in the following circumstances"). TACON refers to minute-by-minute orders to go somewhere and do something called for by the OPCON tasks.

Joulwan and Shevtsov agreed that Joulwan, as overall commander, would exercise OPCON over the Russian contingent through Shevtsov as deputy commander for Russian forces rather than through ordinary NATO channels, as Perry and Grachev had agreed for the noncombat special operations. But TACON would be exercised over the Russian forces through NATO channels, specifically through American Major General Bill Nash, who would command a multinational division consisting of Russian, American, and other NATO forces. With such unity of command for TACON, the Russians could be given a combat role.

The Russians cared about OPCON. We cared about TACON. Under the Joulwan-Shevtsov scheme, we got what we wanted: unity of command, under Joulwan, for all combat forces, including Russian forces. And the Russians got what they wanted: a role "with, but not under" NATO.

By the time the NATO meeting convened in Brussels on November 8, the seed planted in Geneva had sprouted. Joulwan and Shevtsov began their briefing to Perry and Grachev with a simple chart. It had the NATO insignia and the Russian flag, side by side. Underneath were the words: "Intended Outcome: NATO + Russia = Success."

Keeping the Spirit of Bosnia Peacekeeping Alive

So Russia did go into Bosnia, shoulder to shoulder with American troops and other NATO troops. Over the next year it was not uncommon to read such headlines as "Fighting in Bosnia as Exiles

Go Home," with the subtitle almost matter-of-fact: "U.S. and Russian Troops Quell Battle in Serb-Held Village."[7] Soon the world seemed almost to take for granted that American and Russian troops should be fighting together side by side against disorder and violence in an undivided Europe.

But if the circle had not been squared with OPCON and TACON, Russia would have been excluded from Europe's most significant security event of the decade and its only large-scale military operation in decades. In a year of presidential elections in Moscow and Washington, a year of heart attacks for Boris Yeltsin, a year of NATO expansion, Bosnia would have become a political football in Moscow. Russia might not have been co-peacemaker but spoiler of the Dayton accords. The result would have been a disaster for U.S.-Russian relations, for NATO-Russia relations, and for the Bosnian peace.

Instead, major political disaster was averted through practical defense-to-defense cooperation. Such cooperation between militaries is the key to Preventive Defense for the undivided Europe so yearned for and so needed after the cold war. Defense cooperation generates practical, down-to-earth solutions to thorny diplomatic problems. It wins support for such solutions within a critical constituency: the militaries themselves. It changes attitudes by creating new historical experience, new "facts on the ground," to supplant old suspicions and hostilities and to dispel the memory of cold war. And it builds on itself, as Perry and Grachev were able to build on Totskoye, Fort Riley, and the Joulwan-Shevtsov relationship.

Postscript: Building on Success

So successful were the defense ministers and generals at solving the problem of military control for Bosnia that a few weeks later President Clinton and President Yeltsin sent Perry and Joulwan, Grachev and Shevtsov back to Brussels for another meeting. The objective of this meeting on November 28, 1996—it was the defense leaders' fourth in a month, their seventh in a year—was to solve the problem of "political control" as distinct from military control: what role would Russia play with NATO in the overall peace process in Bosnia? And so we boarded NAOC once again.

This time the mood at our meeting was jocular. Grachev was getting used to Brussels and looking forward to having dinner that evening with the NATO defense ministers. At the meeting, Perry and Grachev reached agreement to propose to their respective presidents that NATO and Russia establish a "permanent consultative mechanism." It would be a forum for NATO and Russia to discuss how the Bosnia operation was going and also a wide range of other shared post–cold war problems where they could be partners, not adversaries. The consultative mechanism that we devised with Grachev in Brussels eventually came to be called the NATO-Russia Permanent Joint Council.[8] It was established by the "Founding Act on Mutual Relations, Cooperation and Security between NATO and the Russian Federation," signed in Paris by Boris Yeltsin and the heads of state of the NATO members on May 27, 1997.

The Founding Act proclaimed a new NATO-Russia relationship, but if it is to fulfill the spirit of the Perry-Grachev arrangements over Bosnia, this diplomatic document must be implemented through concrete deeds, especially military-to-military cooperation between NATO and Russia. If Preventive Defense is to be successful in Europe, the experience of working with Russia in Bosnia needs to be extended, deepened, and made a permanent part of the security structure of an undivided Europe. In the rest of this chapter, we explain why, and how.

Preventing "Weimar Russia"

The most important application of Preventive Defense in today's international security environment is avoiding what we call "Weimar Russia," in which a former enemy, isolated by the rest of the world, could fall prey to its worst tendencies.

For eight years, Russia's leaders under Boris Yeltsin have sustained a vision of Russia as a "normal" or mainstream European state both in its internal development and, especially crucial for the United States, in its foreign and defense policy. But the path they have chosen entails a complete transformation of both their political system and their economic system. Accompanying these changes is a profound reconfiguration of Russia's security policies and institutions, particularly its armed forces, and its external perspectives and linkages. This transformation in particular has the deepest significance for U.S. security. The scope of these reforms is unprecedented, so it is not surprising that the going is tough and the outcome uncertain.

We draw our lessons, and the tag "Weimar Russia," from the parallels to the period earlier in this century when, after World War I, European statesmen spurned a former enemy, the fragile democracy known as the Weimar Republic in Germany. The result was a chaotic and isolated Germany, xenophobic, hypernationalist, and aggressive, in which Adolf Hitler rose to power and dragged his country, and the world, into global war.

Events in Boris Yeltsin's Russia were beginning to bear disquieting similarities. A decade and a half passed between the founding of the Weimar Republic in 1919 and the rise of Hitler in 1933. Post-Soviet Russia is in just its seventh year, and the revolution is far from over. The Russian economy has shrunk each year since the Berlin Wall fell. A fledgling democratic government with only a narrow base of popular support rules over a restive, frustrated population. The foreign policy elite of Moscow, long accustomed to being consulted on every foreign policy issue in every corner of the world, now feels slighted and ignored as Russia's power contracts drastically.

Of the four possible outcomes for Russia's security outlook, three hold serious dangers for U.S. security, giving the United States a profound interest in developments in Russia. In the best outcome, Russia would continue the tendency it has followed during the first years of the post–cold war era, taking a cooperative, "integrationist" approach in its international behavior and seeking to establish itself as a normal mainstream European nation. This external disposition might persist, irrespective of whether the democratic reformers who led Russia in the years of the first post–cold war era are able to prevail in their domestic policy of establishing Russia as a successful free-market economy, as promoted by western nations and international financial institutions (which appears increasingly unlikely); or whether a more statist and uniquely Russian approach to economic affairs wins out; or whether Russia just "muddles along." Whichever form its internal political and economic life takes, it is possible that Russians could remain largely focused on their internal development, and the integrationist idea could remain dominant in Russia's foreign policy.

In a second possible evolution, however, Russia's frustrations would be channeled outward; it would rearm, turn again against the West, and rekindle a kind of cold war. It could not achieve full power to threaten its neighbors for a decade or more, but in the meantime its nuclear arsenal and still formidable conventional forces could menace its neighbors, and it could mount a broad challenge to the United States on the world stage.

In a third path, Russia would not attempt to challenge the West frontally, but would emphasize Russian "uniqueness" rather than integration in international affairs. This Russia would seek international respect and leverage through its ability to act as a spoiler of western security objectives rather than through partnership. It could become the "bad boy" of Eurasia, arming rogue states like Iran and Iraq, abetting proliferation, and disrupting peace processes from the Middle East to the Balkans by backing extremist factions.

On a fourth path, Russia would simply collapse from internal discord, with chaos reigning from the Baltic and Ukrainian borders to the Pacific Ocean. Regional warlords would capture and seek to exploit all the resources at their disposal, including nuclear weapons.

Western statesmen cannot control which of these futures Russia will follow. But they do have influence, and history demands that they exercise it. Moreover, while Russia's fate holds deeply troubling possibilities for international security, the converse is also true: Russia has the potential to be a uniquely valuable security partner for the United States. Moscow has good reason for its own security to be opposed to the proliferation of weapons of mass destruction, terrorism, international crime and drug trafficking—the era's new security problems. In these and in many other areas, U.S. and Russian interests coincide much more than they diverge. Most of Russia's foreign policy leaders have inherited from their Soviet past the instincts of a world leader with a stake in preserving stability and world order, not challenging it. They therefore have the potential to join the relatively small number of countries besides the United States that continue to take an active role in world affairs. Moreover, Moscow's global outlook, international contacts, and substantial technological and military expertise equip it to make a large positive contribution to international security. Naturally, Russia's interests and those of the United States will not always coincide. But where they do, Russia can be a valued partner, and where they do not coincide, differences can be resolved peacefully as they are between other countries.

Like Russia's influence on the world, America's influence on Russia can be strongly positive or strongly negative. At the end of the cold war, the U.S. government understood the Weimar analogy and has since attempted to assist Russian economic and political reform broadly. Public funds for this purpose have been limited— certainly nothing close to the Marshall Plan, which sought to prevent a replay after World War II of the tragic collapse of democratic Weimar Germany. The largest and most crucially important support to the Russian economy during the period of reform has come from the International Monetary Fund, strongly backed by the United States, although even that funding has been curtailed lately as evidence mounted that much of this funding was diverted from its intended purposes of economic reconstruction in Russia. But the Bush and Clinton administrations have given consistent political support to Russia's reformers. Through the novel mechanism of the Gore-Chernomyrdin Commission, the U.S. government has also stimulated cooperative intergovernmental projects of mutual benefit in such fields as environment, space, and health.

Private funds in the form of U.S. investment in Russia have, like public funds, been quite limited, and so the effect of American policies on the destiny of the Russian economy will probably remain modest and indirect. The idea that Russia could vault from seventy years of socialism to the mainstream of the world's market economy, an idea promoted by both internal reformers and western governments, has generally been discredited in Russian minds by bitter experience and political rhetoric. Western economic models, like western assistance, will play a smaller role in Russia's quest for internal economic stability.

But the scope is much wider for American policy to make a difference in Russia's external outlook in the security sphere, if it is used vigorously and wisely. The benefits for both Russia and the United States would be direct. The first key to reaping these benefits is a recognition by both countries that their security interests in the twenty-first century will have a great deal in common. The second key is adapting "partnership" to the realities of the new era.

Partnership in the Second Post–Cold War Era

In the immediate aftermath of the end of the cold war, during what might be termed the first post–cold war era, the objectives of U.S.-Russian security "partnership" were rooted in the confrontation just ended. The focus was to solidify the end of a half-century of confrontation and to dismantle its most dangerous vestiges. The emphasis was still on the symmetry of the situations from which they were emerging and the similarity of the adjustments each needed to make to put the cold war behind them. Important progress was made.

Although there is unfinished business from the first post–cold war era, it is important to recognize that today we have entered a second post–cold war era very different from the first, and the basis for U.S.-Russian partnership must accordingly be adapted. For while "the two sides" were then emerging from past circumstances that were in many ways similar, they are now entering very different futures.

While the U.S. defense budget has fallen by 40 percent in real terms from its cold war peak, this is nothing like Russia's experience of near free-fall in its defense budget, to say nothing of the complete withdrawal of its forces from Eastern Europe and the amputation of the military holdings of the non-Russian republics of the former Soviet Union. Accompanying the loss of Moscow's military power has been an undeniable loss of its influence around the world. The influence it has lost is all the more a source of chagrin for Russian security policymakers because it was voluntarily surrendered in the most peaceful transition of power in history. Russia deserves much credit for the transition, which now poses for Russians the problem of defining a new security identity for their country.

The second post–cold war era is therefore characterized by an asymmetry in the situations of the United States and Russia. It is also characterized by problems that cannot be solved and opportunities that cannot be seized by the joint action of the two powers alone, as was frequently the case during the cold war and in the first post–cold war era. Increasingly, each finds its dealings with third parties as important as its dealings with the other.

For both of these reasons, the easy "us and them" or "Joe and Ivan" conviviality of the early years after the Berlin Wall came down increasingly rings hollow. Partnership now needs to be given a new basis that takes these realities into account. It can no longer be a nostalgic extension of bipolarity.

Needed: A New Russian Security Concept

Preventive Defense in the second post–cold war era has the same goal as it did in the first post–cold war era: effective U.S. partnership with Russia in the security sphere. But a new set of policies and programs must be created that are suited to the problems and opportunities of the second era. Russian security leaders understand this quite clearly: it is the principal topic of discussion and debate in the Moscow foreign policy elite. Just as international security will hinge on the outcome of reform in Russia and the avoidance of a "Weimar collapse," so also the success of "integrationists" within Russia's foreign policy elite will depend in important measure upon their ability to define for their country a self-respecting place in the world order.

Therefore a central challenge for Preventive Defense is to assist Russian foreign policy leaders to conceive of a post-Soviet security concept that matches Russia's national interests to the interests of international stability. This problem obsesses the Russian foreign policy elite. Frustrated by Moscow's loss of power, they fear the political implications if such frustration builds in their own people. They are challenged by domestic political forces that promise the Russian people greater prestige in the world if Russia breaks from the international mainstream and security partnership. It is a vital U.S. interest to help Russia resist these urges and find constructive means of forwarding its international interests.

Preventive Defense in the second post–cold war era must therefore focus on the determinants of Russia's security concept, helping to shape them cooperatively: first, on the Russian security establishment's internal reform, which is the key to its outlook on the world and Russia's place in it; and second, on its external linkages, especially bilaterally to the U.S. security establishment and to Europe, particularly NATO. In these endeavors, practical military-to-military cooperation plays a key role and, like the Perry-Grachev work on Bosnia, can lead the way to a renewed Pragmatic Partnership.

Working with the Russian Military on Reform

The military is a central institution in Russian society. Although it no longer commands as much of the state budget as it did in Soviet times, a large fraction of the new Russia's industry, technology, and talent is still associated with the defense sector. Myriad "armies," from the Russian Army to border troops, interior troops and intelligence organizations, continue to employ millions.

Reform of this vast structure is crucial to Russia, the United States, and the world. Many Russians have commented that overall reform of their society cannot succeed unless military reform succeeds. A military in material and morale decline is a potent source of instability and a lightning rod for the emotions of rejection and isolation that carry the threat of "Weimar Russia." A reformed security structure, on the other hand, will be more confident and more competent to cooperate in international affairs and will free up resources and creative talent for the new Russia.

Reform of the Russian military entails moving from the large standing formations of Soviet times to smaller, more mobile forces. Force restructuring must be accompanied by a change in the military's definition of threat to encompass the new problems of regional instability, proliferation, and terrorism. Reform also entails developing new mechanisms of civilian control. These adaptations will make the Russian military both less threatening to its neighbors and better able to work with them in combined operations toward common goals. It would also become a better partner for the United States military in common pursuit of common interests.

Military reform is the commanding preoccupation of Russian military leaders. It forms a lens through which these leaders increasingly view all security issues, including those of most importance to American policymakers. Whenever U.S. objectives in arms control, regional conflict, arms sales, counterproliferation, or counterterrorism can be made complementary or compatible with the Russian military's reform agenda, they will have a much greater chance of fulfillment. Conversely, U.S. proposals that run counter to the needs of reform are likely to fall on deaf ears in Russia. Therefore it is imperative that the United States be a partner in, and assist, Russian military reform through a robust bilateral military-to-military program.

On occasion, this assistance might be material, as in the case of U.S.-provided housing for the Russian officers retired as their nuclear missile units and other military units are dismantled. In other cases the assistance will take the form of sharing experience and techniques for accomplishing reforms that the United States has also faced or is facing now, such as making the transition from a conscript force to an all-volunteer force, developing military doctrine and tactics for peacekeeping, closing unneeded bases, and managing a contracting defense industry. Most valuable will be joint exercises and joint activities that are mutually and professionally rewarding to militaries on both sides and that prepare them for the possibility of combined operations in pursuit of common interests. Bilateral U.S.-Russian cooperation is central and is the most important external linkage to the Russian military.

Russia's External Military Linkages and the Importance of NATO

The external linkages of Russia's military to the outside world will also shape Russia's security concept over time. A key linkage is the U.S.-Russian military relationship, which must be greatly enriched, as we urge above. Beyond the bilateral relationship, however, a dilemma arises for Russian security leaders. The puzzle for them is, "What clubs do we belong to?" In the economic sphere, the Yeltsin government has made association with the G-7 a key objective because it connotes acceptance into the family of "normal" industrialized nations.

In the security sphere, a similar quest is on, but with fewer promising prospects from the Russian point of view. The Warsaw Pact has dissolved, the Soviet Union has broken into fifteen states, and the Commonwealth of Independent States (CIS) has not won strong allegiance from its members. The Organization for Security and Cooperation in Europe lacks a strong security arm and a distinguishing role for Russia. Attention in Moscow, in the other CIS states, and in the West has therefore focused on NATO. This attention is appropriate, as NATO is Europe's leading security institution. It is also the world's leading combined military organization, while Russia is one of the world's largest and best armed militaries.

NATO expansion, however, provoked a crisis for Russia's security identity. Indeed, this event can be said to mark the end of the first post–cold war era and the beginning of the second for most Russian foreign policy leaders. Russia's exclusion from Europe's main security "club" grew more painful as the club began to grow in membership and in importance. Russia's difficult relations with NATO illustrate not only the dangers of "Weimar Russia" but also the role of Preventive Defense in overcoming them.

The Question of NATO's Own Future

Russia's relationship to NATO is inseparable from NATO's own evolution. A Preventive Defense vision of European security and the NATO-Russia relationship must therefore begin with NATO itself.[9] NATO serves a vital purpose in post–cold war Europe. Some argue, especially in Russia, that NATO should be dismantled now that its founding purpose of deterring attack from the Warsaw Pact has been fulfilled.

We strongly disagree. On the contrary, NATO provides much of the security framework for realizing, at last, George Marshall's vision of a Europe united in freedom, peace, and prosperity. NATO anchors the United States in Europe to the benefit of both Europe and the United States. It constitutes the world's only standing, readily usable coalition military capability, a capability that was crucial to defeating Iraq's Saddam Hussein in Desert Storm and establishing a peacekeeping operation in the Balkans. It exercises a stabilizing influence on current and future members as their militaries learn to plan together rather than against one another, avoiding the nationalization of defense across Europe. NATO is the expression of the shared values and interests of a community of member nations.

As a matter of principle, NATO's membership rolls have never been closed and never should be closed. But while enlargement of NATO's membership has benefits, it also carries costs and risks. Adding members is a grave matter and should not become automatic or routine. When the U.S. Senate ratified the addition of Poland, Hungary, and the Czech Republic to NATO, it recognized that to do otherwise would have been a major setback to U.S. credibility and to the U.S. position in Europe. Even the most pessimistic estimates of the risks and costs of expansion portrayed in the vigorous Senate debate preceding enlargement could not justify such a setback. But the next steps in NATO's adaptation to the post–cold war world should be analyzed and debated thoroughly and publicly in advance, and a clear course with broad bipartisan and international support should be charted.

Adding new members is not the only, or even the most important, adaptation of NATO to the new security environment. A much larger issue looms for the alliance: what is NATO's purpose? In fact NATO serves, not a single purpose, but three, the first two military and the third politico-military. First, and originally paramount in urgency, is territorial defense, enshrined in the pledge of Article V of the NATO Charter that an attack on any member "shall be considered an attack against them all." Second, deriving from Article IV as well as Article V, is NATO's mechanism for the rapid formation of combined military forces with prearranged patterns of command and control and a practiced habit of working together. These forces can be mobilized to protect common interests of NATO members within Europe, as in the Bosnian peacekeeping force; or outside Europe, as when the U.S.-led coalition that defeated Iraq in 1991 drew upon the forces and habits of cooperation forged in NATO. Third is NATO's historic role of drawing members together, encouraging them to resolve disputes peacefully, causing them to plan and work with rather than against one another, and fostering respect for democratic values and institutions.

The relative emphasis previously given to NATO's first two military roles is changing in response to the changing security environment of Europe and the needs of its members for combined military capabilities. The need for the first role—territorial defense—has decreased, while the need for the second role—coalition operations in pursuit of common interests—has increased.

NATO must adapt its military strategy accordingly: the primary danger to the security of NATO's members in this historical era is not potential aggression to their collective territory, but rather threats to their collective interests even when these lie beyond NATO territory. These threats require attention to preventing deadly conflict, restoring and preserving peace, preventing regional conflict, stemming the proliferation of weapons of mass destruction, ensuring the supply of key resources such as oil, and responding effectively to transnational dangers such as terrorism. NATO's principal strategic and military purpose in the post–cold war era is to provide a mechanism for the rapid formation of militarily potent "coalitions of the willing" able to project power beyond NATO territory. In NATO parlance such a power projection force for "out-of-area" operations is called a combined joint task force (CJTF). Shifting the emphasis in an evolutionary manner from defense of members' territory to defense of common interests beyond NATO territory is the strategic imperative for NATO in the post–cold war era.

Such a shift in military mission would not supplant territorial defense. Defense of members' territory according to Article V of the NATO treaty would remain a solemn commitment of allies. From a military point of view, the same mobile forces and command and control that are suitable for CJTFs are also best suited to territorial defense under the conditions of modern warfare. But NATO territory—including the territory of its new members—is not threatened today, nor is it likely to be threatened in the foreseeable future. Neither Russia nor any other country has the intention or the potential military capability to threaten the alliance. In the absence of imminent threat, American and allied publics will not continue to support an alliance—whether enlarged or not—that appears to focus on nonexistent threats of aggression in Europe rather than on today's security problems.

Neither will a shift in strategic emphasis from territorial defense to power projection supplant NATO's important politico-military role: fostering good relations among its members, inducing their militaries to plan with rather than against one another, inculcating democratic and free-market values, encouraging the rule of law, and fostering civilian control of the military. Indeed, these functions deserve strong emphasis in the next phase of NATO's history.

The evolving change of emphasis in NATO's mission, from homeland defense to coalition operations, has two important consequences for NATO's relations with Russia. First, since territorial defense is not currently at issue, it should be clear to all that NATO is not drawing new lines across Europe or directed at Russia. Second, since "coalitions of the willing" organized by NATO will include some—but not necessarily all—NATO members, and will generally include nonmembers drawn from the Partnership for

Peace (as in Bosnia's peacekeeping force), the distinction between full membership and partnership will be less important in the new NATO. In particular, Russia can be and should be expected to be a partner in future coalition operations, as it has been in Bosnia.

Further NATO Expansion?

NATO should in principle remain open to membership by all PFP members without exception, contingent on their meeting NATO's stringent standards for admission. But no additional members should be designated for admission until Poland, Hungary, and the Czech Republic, the states already offered membership, are fully prepared to bear the responsibilities of membership and have been integrated into the alliance. The reason for NATO to take a "deep breath" before admitting more members is not only, or even principally, to permit more time to improve NATO's relations with Russia. The reason is to protect the military integrity of the alliance in a period of rapid internal transformation and novel external challenges in the Balkans, and during the task of absorbing Poland, Hungary, and the Czech Republic. Adding more members to this mix too quickly would not be healthy for NATO.

Therefore other security relationships and structures designed to extend stability to non-NATO members are of the highest importance and require more attention than they have received. This is particularly true of the Partnership for Peace.

NATO-Russia Relations I: Enhancing Partnership for Peace

We argued in 1995 that NATO's Partnership for Peace was the best foundation for NATO's eastward policy, and we continue to believe this today. But the implementation of PFP, in practical military terms, continues to fall short of its promise. For the great majority of former Warsaw Pact and former Soviet states—and even, indeed especially, for Russia—PFP can and should be their central military linkage westward. But attention was diverted from PFP in 1995 by the question of NATO membership. It is essential to restore PFP's momentum.

The objective of a renewed Partnership for Peace should be to make the experience of partnership as close as possible, in practical military terms, to the experience of membership in NATO. Partner militaries should be prepared through PFP activities to interoperate with NATO militaries in "coalitions of the willing," such as the one that went into Bosnia. On a day-to-day basis, the relations among PFP militaries should be shaped toward peaceful relations, in the way that Germany and France, or Greece and Turkey, have been brought closer together over time by NATO membership.

This is the vision for the Partnership for Peace: the original vision, not yet realized, as well as the vision for the future. Much is needed to realize this vision. PFP has been starved of the resources, human and financial, that it merits. NATO nations, including the United States, should acknowledge that for most PFP members, including Russia, participation in PFP's exercises and other activities competes with other exigencies in tight defense budgets. U.S. and NATO financial help is crucial. PFP-combined exercises and other military-to-military activities should advance from the partnership's early focus on peacekeeping and humanitarian operations to true combat operations. These are the activities that engage partner military personnel at their professional core. PFP activities—exercises, joint training, discussion of tactics and doctrine—should also begin to address the new problem-set of proliferation, terrorism, and other transnational security problems.

Most important for Russia itself, the Russian military should be encouraged not only to participate in PFP but to adopt a leading role. After all, PFP-inspired military-to-military activities are occurring around Russia's periphery. A combined battalion of the Baltic countries has been formed, the so-called Baltbatt. A similar Centrasbatt of Central Asian states (Uzbekistan, Kazakhstan, and Kyrgyzstan) and a Polish-Ukrainian combined battalion have also been established. All this was unthinkable a decade ago. Through such linkages, PFP brings the new states of the former Soviet Union together and contributes to the prevention of future "Bosnias" in the former Soviet space. But Russia has only seldom and reluctantly joined in these activities, and it has not taken the lead in forging relationships with the militaries that have taken the place of its former Warsaw Pact allies. It is in Russia's own interest to do so; standing aside is not in Russia's interest.

NATO-Russia Relations II:
Implementing the NATO-Russia Founding Act

The NATO-Russia Founding Act provides the other vehicle for enhancing the NATO-Russia relationship. Implementation of the political provisions of the Founding Act will require responsible actions on both sides. Up to now, the Permanent Joint Council, established in the wake of the Perry-Grachev talks on Bosnia and in the shadow of Russia's protest over NATO enlargement, has been more of a diplomatic debating society than a catalyst for practical NATO-Russia cooperation. But implementation of the Founding Act's military provisions is less problematic and can provide strong benefits in both the long and short terms. Moreover, military implementation is, in effect, already under way in Bosnia. The objective of implementing the military provisions of the Founding Act should be the establishment of military-to-military relationships modeled on those forged between the NATO and Russian contingents in Bosnia. Practical cooperation dealing with real-world problems of mutual concern is more valuable than meetings and councils. Military-to-military cooperation changes attitudes by creating new, positive shared experiences to supplant the historical memory of dedicated antagonism between NATO and Russia. Military-to-military cooperation also engages critical constituencies in the formation of the new Eurasian security order: the Russian and NATO militaries.

In order to make the NATO-Russia military cooperation forged in Bosnia broader, deeper, permanent, and institutionalized, the following steps need to be taken:[10]

— finish posting Russian liaison officers at each of NATO's major headquarters, especially at the planning cell for Combined Joint Task Forces, with NATO sharing the cost of such postings with the Russian government;

— establish reciprocal postings of NATO liaison officers at corresponding Russian headquarters;

— continue efforts to involve Russia in Combined Joint Task Forces, as appropriate, using the Bosnia experience as a model;

— deepen cooperation in the fields of hastening nuclear reductions, ensuring safety and control of nuclear weapons, counter-proliferation, and emergency planning;

— initiate cooperation in new areas of common concern to Russia and NATO, including counterterrorism, counternarcotics, and international security problems of all sorts outside of Europe;

— coordinate support for and assistance with Russian military reform, using western experience and example where applicable;

— establish an initiative to work with Russia on enhancing the competence of the Organization for Security and Cooperation in Europe in resolving regional conflicts, such as the struggle over Nagorno-Karabakh;

— enhance links with the Russian defense industry where mutually beneficial and ensure an "open door" policy for Russian arms and spare parts sales to Central and East European states;

— encourage Russia to participate more vigorously in the Partnership for Peace, with NATO assistance to help defray the costs of Russian participation in PFP exercises and other activities.

NATO's Relationships with Other Nonmembers

While Russia's struggle for a new security identity is the most portentous for the United States, similar struggles are occurring throughout the post-Soviet space. From Central Asia to the oil-rich Caspian littoral, and from the Balkans to the Baltics, more than two dozen states in this region, released from cold war, are defining their threat perceptions and building new militaries. In this fluid, formative period, the United States has a substantial opportunity to shape cooperative relations and promote a stable Eurasia. Only three of the twenty-seven members of the PFP are being admitted to NATO; a way must be found to address the security of the other twenty-four states.

The U.S. effort to open security relations with the eastern European and former Soviet states, both bilaterally and through the Partnership for Peace, has already borne fruit. The denuclearization of Ukraine, for example, was accomplished in large part because the United States demonstrated through a vigorous program of defense cooperation and assistance that Ukraine's own future was more secure with strong friendships than with nuclear weapons. Ukraine is now developing a special relationship with NATO, as befits a major European state.[11]

Defying many predictions made at the end of the cold war, the states of the former Soviet bloc are at peace with one another. Most share a desire to shape their security futures in partnership with the United States and its principal allies, and most are undergoing military reform and establishing civilian control of their militaries. Thus, much benefit has been had for a relatively modest U.S. investment.

But the United States can and should do much more. The potential of Preventive Defense for the other states of the former Soviet bloc, as with Russia, is far from fully realized. The security concerns of the great majority of the new Eurasian states will need to be addressed outside the context of NATO membership. As with Russia, military-to-military cooperation is a central mechanism by which stability can be extended eastward to states and regions not designated to join NATO. NATO's principal mechanism for military-to-military cooperation is the Partnership for Peace. PFP's "reinvention" needs to receive attention at least comparable to that devoted to NATO enlargement.

The NATO-Ukraine Charter, like the NATO-Russia Founding Act, should be vigorously implemented with an emphasis on practical military cooperation. NATO should continue to encourage and support regional military cooperation among PFP members, such as the Baltbatt, Centrasbatt, and the Polish-Ukrainian joint peacekeeping battalion.

The United States should strengthen its bilateral programs of military-to-military cooperation with PFP members who are not members of NATO. These relationships were inaugurated with great vision, but the resources devoted to their implementation have not been commensurate with the stakes the United States has in Eurasia.

Conclusion: Preventive Defense and the NATO-Russia Relationship

Russian exclusion from the Bosnian peace implementation would probably have added materially to "Weimar Russia" tendencies in Moscow and quite possibly would have fueled disruption of the Bosnian peace itself. This outcome was averted by Preventive Defense: the negotiation by U.S. and Russian defense officials of a command and control arrangement that made possible Russian participation in the multinational peacekeeping force in a manner that was militarily and politically acceptable to both NATO and Russia. The success of these negotiations was itself a product of close relations between civilian and uniformed officials developed in the early post–cold war years and enhanced by the joint peace-keeping exercises held by U.S. and Russian troops. The Bosnian cooperation is building further trust and confidence as U.S., Russian, and other NATO and non-NATO contingents enter their third year of shoulder-to-shoulder operations.

Military-to-military relations constitute a powerful tool of Preventive Defense. Vexing political dilemmas sometimes yield to practical military-to-military problem solving. Joint experience in joint operations displaces the historical memory of cold war, and joint operations engage the institutions that matter most in the task of constructing the post–cold war security system and Russia's place in it.

Defense cooperation with Russia should be both bilateral and multilateral. Particularly important are the implementation of the military provisions of the NATO-Russia Founding Act and Russia's participation in the Partnership for Peace. The objective of these activities should be to broaden, deepen, institutionalize, and make permanent the practical cooperation first experienced in Bosnian peacekeeping. Doing so will require renewed effort and additional resources by the United States and NATO, and especially by the

Department of Defense. But the reward can be a Russia that will be an enduring security partner of the United States.

The historian Gordon A. Craig wrote of the lost opportunity of democratic Weimar Germany:

> While totalitarian regimes were consolidating their power in Russia and in Italy [after World War I], an experiment was being conducted in Germany to determine whether a democratic Republic could be made to work in that country. After fifteen years of trial and crisis, it failed, and the ultimate consequences of that failure were a second world war and the deaths of millions of men, women, and children. If some benevolent spirit had granted the peoples of Germany and the neighboring states even a fragmentary glimpse of what lay in store for them in the 1940s, it is impossible to believe that they would not have made every possible sacrifice to maintain the Weimar Republic against its enemies. But that kind of foresight is not given in this world, and the German Republic always lacked friends and supporters when it needed them most.[12]

The historical parallels give us, this time, the necessary foresight if we are wise enough to heed it. Russia's tendencies toward an integrationist foreign policy, fragile as they may be, desperately need the international "friends and supporters" whose absence in the interwar years Craig lamented. The United States is in a unique position to be both a major source of support and a major beneficiary if Russia succeeds in remaining on the path toward becoming a normal member of the international community.

CHAPTER 2

Project Sapphire, the Nunn-Lugar Program, and Arms Control

In the early morning hours on a wintry day on the steppes of Central Asia, U.S. and Kazakhstani technicians departed in a highly guarded convoy from a metallurgical facility near the remote town of Ust-Kamenogorsk, Kazakhstan, headed for a nearby airport. Their cargo was 600 kilograms of bomb-grade highly enriched uranium packed in specially constructed steel drums. Waiting at the airport were giant U.S. Air Force C-5 transports. As the sun rose, the drums were forklifted onto the planes. At 11 a.m. on November 23, 1994, the C-5s took off from Ust-Kamenogorsk, heading for the United States.[1]

As the C-5s passed over the Persian Gulf, the Mediterranean, and the mid-Atlantic, they were refueled in the air by U.S. Air Force tankers, to avoid environmental concern at stops along the way and to keep the operation secret. While they were in the air, Carter quietly took Senator Richard Lugar aside at a White House dinner to tell him that the top-secret operation, known to its few familiars as Project Sapphire, was almost complete. Later that night, Carter telephoned Senator Sam Nunn with the welcome news. They agreed that the operation came just in time: the CIA believed that

Iranian agents were on the trail of the uranium at Ust-Kamenogorsk. If the material had ended up in Iran, it would have spelled instant nuclear proliferation to a regime that was hostile to the United States and to several of its neighbors in the Middle East. The highly enriched uranium that had just been spirited out of Kazakhstan would have been enough to make sixty bombs as powerful as those that destroyed Hiroshima and Nagasaki—enough to satisfy the wildest ambitions of Iran, North Korea, Iraq, and Libya put together. But now it was in safe custody.

The C-5s did not touch down again until they reached Dover Air Force Base, Delaware, where the uranium was loaded onto "safe and secure transports" (SSTs). From the outside, these special trucks look like any other tractor-trailer rigs on the highway. But they are heavily armored; they carry radio beacons so their location can be tracked at all times; and they are a veritable funhouse of violent tricks that immobilize, stun, or kill anyone who tries to hijack them or tamper with them.

The SSTs, in a convoy with heavily armed escorts disguised as civilian vehicles, sped to Oak Ridge National Laboratory in Tennessee. Just forty hours after it had left the ground at Ust-Kamenogorsk, the uranium from Kazakhstan was slipped into armored, guarded bunkers on the Oak Ridge reservation, site of the Manhattan Project plant that had made uranium for the first atomic bombs.[2]

By Washington standards the secret of Project Sapphire was well kept; it did not leak to the press until shortly before the heavy doors swung closed on the storage bunkers at Oak Ridge. For months, Project Sapphire—the first major operation under the Nunn-Lugar program to reduce the dangers arising from "loose nukes" in the former Soviet Union—had been kept secret. Indeed, Project Sapphire was only one of many such projects, some of them still secret.

But the main contribution of the Nunn-Lugar program was not simply the millions of dollars it provided to carry out the operation and compensate Kazakhstan for its uranium. And the most extraordinary thing about Project Sapphire was not the secrecy, nor was it how smoothly the planning and implementation went, nor was it the cooperation of Kazakhstani officials with the sometimes-fractious Washington bureaucracy.

What was truly extraordinary, and what was an enormous credit to the Nunn-Lugar program, was the fact that when President Nursultan Nazarbayev—Kazakhstan's former Communist party boss and its first president after the Soviet Union disintegrated—discovered that there was a huge quantity of bomb-grade highly enriched uranium on the territory of his new central Asian state, he called the president of the United States half a world away and asked to have it taken away to safekeeping.

That request was historic, but it was no accident of history: Nazarbayev's call was a testament to his commitment to associate his new country with the West and his trust in the sincerity of American goodwill and cooperation. That trust, and the phone call that launched Project Sapphire, had been earned by the United States through its exercise of Preventive Defense under the Nunn-Lugar program. For months, scores of cooperative projects throughout Kazakhstan, Russia, Ukraine, and Belarus had been under way between the United States and its former cold war enemies to eliminate and safeguard the lethal legacy of the cold war. Kazakhstan had already experienced proof of American sincerity in direct and tangible ways. Nazarbayev's officials knew their American counterparts well; they knew whom to call and what kind of help they could expect. And their trust was justified; Project Sapphire was carried out and the uranium placed where it could do no harm.

Delighted with the news of the project's success, we hosted a press briefing at the Pentagon later that morning. There Perry, Secretary of State Warren Christopher, and Secretary of Energy Hazel O'Leary jointly described Project Sapphire and announced the successful completion of the operation. The costs of the operation to remove a proliferator's treasure trove from Central Asia were borne by the defense budget, but Project Sapphire generated plenty of credit to go around: the project involved the close collaboration of the Department of Defense, the Department of Energy, the State Department, and the Central Intelligence Agency. The government of Russia as well as the government of Kazakhstan had shared in the operation from the beginning. Moscow authorities were aware of the uranium's existence from Soviet days, and they were as eager as the Americans and the Kazakhstanis to have it removed.

Project Sapphire was Preventive Defense at work in the most direct possible way, all made possible by the Cooperative Threat Reduction program. That was its official bureaucratic name, but almost everyone referred to it as the Nunn-Lugar program, after the far-sighted senators whose legislation in 1992 had given the Pentagon the money and mandate to try to safeguard the huge nuclear arsenal of the disintegrating Soviet Union.

Under the Nunn-Lugar program, the U.S. military had advised and assisted Kazakhstan's military with the units that, when the Soviet Union broke up, were on Kazakhstan's territory, reforming and reshaping them into the kind of independent, civilian-controlled force appropriate to an independent state. Nunn-Lugar technicians and equipment had been busy dismantling the silos, bunkers, and bases that housed the SS-18 ICBMs. The SS-18, the largest Soviet ballistic missile, had been the fearsome inspiration for President Reagan's "Star Wars" missile defense program. But now, rather than trying to destroy SS-18s in space as they flew to targets in the United States, the U.S. Department of Defense and its Kazakhstani and Russian partners were destroying them on the ground.

Kazakhstan had also been home to other Soviet facilities for weapons of mass destruction. At Semipalatinsk, for example, the Soviet Union had tested its nuclear weapons, exploding them aboveground on the open steppes, and later in tunnels underground. DOD provided sophisticated medical diagnostic equipment to the hospitals at Semipalatinsk to screen the local populace for cancer induced by the aboveground testing. It set about plugging up the testing tunnels so they could not be used again. The nuclear scientists and engineers who had worked on Semipalatinsk's nuclear weapons tests were offered research grants through Nunn-Lugar to begin new scientific projects, turning their technical talents to building the economy of their new country.

Kazakhstan was also home of the once super-secret Baikonur Cosmodrome, where Soviet cosmonauts and military satellites were launched into space. Early in his career, Perry had studied the pictures and telemetry signals from Baikonur as they were captured by U.S. spy satellites. Many years later, in March 1994, he and Carter would travel to Kazakhstan to inaugurate the Nunn-Lugar projects there and stand next to a "Proton" space booster at Baikonur, looking up at the real thing rather than down at a satellite photo. Kazakhstan was converting some of the military rocket facilities at Baikonur to peaceful commercial purposes, with help from the Nunn-Lugar program. Another factory being converted with Nunn-Lugar assistance at Stepnogorsk had made the biological warfare agent anthrax for the Soviet Union; it would now make pharmaceuticals.

DOD's Nunn-Lugar program was Preventive Defense at its best, and Project Sapphire was the Nunn-Lugar program at its best. What might have been history's biggest and most devastating case of "loose nukes" was averted.

Loose Nukes: The Lethal Legacy of the Soviet Nuclear Arsenal

The collapse of the Soviet Union in 1991 left vast stocks of nuclear weapons, fissile materials, and chemical and biological weapons in the midst of an ongoing political and economic revolution that continues to this day. The Soviet Union had made tens of thousands of nuclear weapons during the cold war. It had enriched enough uranium and reprocessed enough plutonium for tens of thousands more. Its chemical weapon stocks figured in the tens of thousands of tons. The full extent of its biological warfare program, conducted in violation of the Biological Weapons Convention it had signed in 1972, is still not known, though President Yeltsin has acknowledged that it existed. The nuclear weapons were spread not only throughout most of the fifteen republics of the USSR that became independent countries after the breakup, but throughout Eastern Europe as well. By the time the Soviet Union came to an end, Soviet nuclear weapons remained on the territory of four new states: Russia, Ukraine, Kazakhstan, and Belarus.

The theft, sale, or diversion of the tiniest fraction of this lethal trove would satisfy the most dangerous of the ambitions of Iraq, Iran, North Korea, or other nuclear aspirants. It could fulfill the most gruesome fears of what terrorists, radical political factions, insubordinate military officers, or messianic cults might do in possession of such destructive power.

However cleverly designed the Soviet nuclear command and control system was, and however flawless its performance through a half-century of cold war, apparently never losing control of any of the thousands of the USSR's nuclear weapons, it is at bottom a human system designed for normal times. Like its U.S. counterpart, it was meant to function against a backdrop of general social order, when most nuclear custodians—numbering many thousands of uniformed and civilian personnel located at hundreds of sites throughout the Soviet Union's vast nuclear weapons complex—could be expected to behave predictably. This expectation is unrealistic in a period of social unrest. Despite technical safeguards and the strong sense of duty felt by most of the military and civilian custodians of this lethal lode, it is no insult to them to assert that loss of control of these weapons posed in 1991, and continues to pose today, a potential "A-list" danger to the United States and the world.[3]

Birth of the Nunn-Lugar Program

Senator Sam Nunn and Senator Richard Lugar began to worry about loose nukes long before the Soviet Union disintegrated and Russia, Ukraine, Kazakhstan, and Belarus were born.[4] For years Senator Nunn had worried about the United States and the USSR stumbling into nuclear war by accident in a cold war crisis. From his position as chairman of the Senate Armed Services Committee he had urged both sides to negotiate arms control agreements that would make the nuclear standoff more stable. With Senator John Warner, he had championed the establishment of Nuclear Risk Reduction Centers in Washington and Moscow to smooth communications and prevent misunderstandings that could trigger a

nuclear exchange. By the late 1980s, Mikhail Gorbachev was ending the cold war and with it the likelihood of crises. But the August
1991 putsch awakened a whole other set of concerns. Nunn had
visited Moscow in August 1991 and met with Gorbachev shortly
after the Soviet leader was released from house arrest. He came
away shaken. Who had control of the Soviet nuclear arsenal during the attempted putsch? What if the coup had split the military,
some siding with Gorbachev and others with the plotters? What if
the Soviet Union were to descend into revolution and chaos?

When Senator Nunn returned to Washington, he found that
Senator Lugar had the same concerns. Together, they began to consider what could be done to contain the loose nukes danger.

On November 19, 1991, David Hamburg, president of the
Carnegie Corporation of New York, invited the two of us and our
colleague John Steinbruner of the Brookings Institution to a meeting in Nunn's office. Hamburg had a knack for bringing the right
people together at the right time to work on the right problems,
stimulating common thoughts and common action. Through the
Carnegie Corporation of New York, a foundation devoted to
peace and education, Hamburg and his associate Jane Wales had
for many years supported exchanges and discussions between
Soviet and American scholars and officials, even through the dark-
est days of the cold war. We had participated in many Carnegie-
sponsored meetings and had frequently met with Senator Nunn
and Senator Lugar through these meetings.

We were then both outside of government, Perry leading a
research team at Stanford, and Carter a research team at Harvard,
both studying national security problems. Perry's group at
Stanford had been studying the giant military-industrial complex
of the Soviet Union and the opportunities it presented to be the
engine of recovery for the Soviet Union's backward economy once
the cold war ended. Carter's team at Harvard had just completed
a study of the Soviet nuclear arsenal.[5] This study predicted that the
breakup of the Soviet Union posed the biggest proliferation threat
of the Atomic Age and outlined a new form of "arms control" to
stop it: joint action by the two former cold war opponents against
the common danger. Carter briefed the senators on the Harvard

study. It turned out that Senator Nunn and Senator Lugar and their staff members, Robert Bell, Ken Myers, and Richard Combs, were working on a similar scheme for joint action. After the meeting broke up, Carter, Bell, Myers, and Combs stayed behind to draft what became known as the Nunn-Lugar legislation.

Two days later, Nunn and Lugar convened a bipartisan group of senators at a working breakfast. Carter repeated his briefing, warning of the potential dangers of the Soviet nuclear arsenal as the state that had controlled it fell apart. Nunn and Lugar asked the senators to support legislation that would authorize the Pentagon to initiate U.S.-funded assistance to stem the "loose nukes" problem of the former Soviet arsenal. In the ensuing discussion, the needed support was garnered from the senators in attendance, not all of it motivated strictly by the problem at hand. (Nunn swore Carter to secrecy; not many outsiders get to witness democracy's horse trading at work.)

On November 28, 1991, just nine days after the legislation had been drafted in Lugar's office, the Nunn-Lugar amendment to the annual defense bill passed the Senate by a vote of 86 to 8. Les Aspin gathered the necessary support in the House of Representatives, and the legislation passed the House shortly thereafter on a voice vote.

In March 1992, after the legislation had gone into effect, we joined Senators Nunn, Lugar, Warner, and Jeff Bingaman, as well as David Hamburg and staffers Bell, Myers, and Combs on a trip to look at the problem firsthand. By then, however, we were visiting not the Soviet Union, but the newly independent states of Russia and Ukraine. Leaders in the new states were eager to learn more about the program and to meet the two senators whose names were soon known throughout the weapons of mass destruction archipelagos of the former Soviet Union.

Working Nunn-Lugar from inside the Pentagon

A year later we had both gone to work in the Pentagon, Perry as deputy secretary of defense (becoming secretary of defense in

February 1994) and Carter as assistant secretary of defense with specific responsibility for the Nunn-Lugar program. Having observed Nunn-Lugar in the making, we were determined to implement the senators' vision.

This was easier said than done. The staff structure Carter inherited, which would be responsible for spearheading implementation, had a branch that targeted the Soviet Union and another that had negotiated arms control agreements with the Soviet Union. But no one had ever *assisted* the Soviet Union; a whole new organization had to be set up for Nunn-Lugar.

The key officials in the new organization were Gloria Duffy, Susan Koch, Laura Holgate, and the policy chief for the region, Elizabeth Sherwood. They set about crafting a set of objectives and identifying facilities and officials in the new countries who could serve as working partners for the new programs. These four officials made scores of visits to the former Soviet Union, frequently to remote sites under very difficult conditions. They all happened to be women, a matter of no particular note in the Pentagon; however, in the former Soviet Union it took a while before the disbelieving generals in Moscow, Kiev, Minsk, and Almaty realized that these women really did carry the authority of the secretary of defense.

Our team at the Pentagon needed not only to identify appropriate objectives for the Nunn-Lugar program, but also to engage the cooperation of the countries whose weapons were to be dismantled or safeguarded. The objectives of the program had to be shared objectives. This necessitated some lengthy negotiations over a number of issues. For example, our partners in the former Soviet Union were understandably intent on receiving social assistance for their people, not just help in dismantling weapons; suspicion lingered that the Americans were pursuing their own security at the expense of their former opponents; and the Russians had a legitimate need to shield their military secrets from our eyes. All these barriers had to be overcome.

In addition, the governments of the Soviet successor states bridled under the legal restraints of the program. Assistance would be largely in kind, rather than cash, which we feared might disappear amidst the shrinking economies and growing crime in what were, after all, countries in profound social revolution. Onerous audits and inspections were required by the Pentagon legal office. Pentagon lawyers were terrified at the prospect that some of the taxpayers' money might be misspent; one of the lawyers explained to Carter and his staff that, if this were to occur, they could all expect to spend the rest of their natural lives testifying about the diversion.

The Pentagon acquisition bureaucracy is justly fabled for its ponderous procedures, endless paperwork, and slow workings. Now the acquisition system that seemed able to purchase airplanes in California and computers in Massachusetts only with difficulty was being asked to conduct multimillion-dollar engineering projects in places like Pervomaysk, Ukraine; Engels, Russia; and Semipalatinsk, Kazakhstan—on the homeland of the former enemy, in places where U.S. industry had never done business. Contracting and project engineering were the responsibility of the Pentagon acquisition system, led by John Deutch and Harold Smith. They found it necessary to set up a whole new organization to contract for Nunn-Lugar programs and to staff this organization with personnel who could be inspired by the challenge of doing something that history had never before permitted.

Congress sometimes also made implementation difficult. It was not hard to understand why many senators and representatives found breathtaking the very notion of providing assistance to the former Soviet enemy, and in particular to units with custody of nuclear forces. Once the program was explained, however, most saw that it advanced U.S. security as well as the interests of the cooperating countries and gave their support. But even though many voted enthusiastically for weapons dismantlement projects, some still balked at the social programs that were essential to getting the job done. Examples of such programs were housing for officers whose bases were being closed and defense conversion assistance for weapons factories that had no orders, both of which were crucial for success at Pervomaysk and elsewhere. And, finally, some members of Congress clung to the idea that the Pentagon's job was simply to fight and that its money should be spent only on tanks, planes, and ships.

We argued that Nunn-Lugar was "defense by other means." Its contribution to U.S. security was at least as great as any other program in the defense budget. The Department of Defense was the correct agency to manage the program because the parties with which the United States needed to work to get the job done were, for the most part, the militaries of the former Soviet countries. Moreover, the expertise to dismantle weapons resided in the DOD and the defense industry.

Most frustrating to us, however, was the fact that far too many people, both inside and outside of Congress, seemed to assume that nuclear dangers belonged to the cold war and now that the cold war was over, the dangers would disappear by themselves. The lack of public and press attention to the nuclear danger in the former Soviet Union, as opposed to, say, events in Bosnia or Haiti, made it much harder to overcome congressional and bureaucratic barriers.

The initial ambivalence in Congress had a result that we faced immediately in 1993. The original Nunn-Lugar legislation did not actually appropriate money from the Treasury to spend on forestalling loose nukes. It only authorized the secretary of defense to take money from other Pentagon programs and "reprogram" it to Nunn-Lugar. One can easily imagine the lack of enthusiasm for the Nunn-Lugar program within the Pentagon bureaucracy when it came time to pass the cup for Nunn-Lugar. One of our top priorities, therefore, was to secure for the Nunn-Lugar program its own congressional appropriation, so we would not have to raid other parts of the Pentagon. The first budget DOD submitted after we took office contained a dedicated appropriation for Nunn-Lugar.

Elsewhere in the U.S. government, it was difficult to shake the grip of the old-style arms control bureaucracy. Officials used to the glacial pace of arms control during the cold war sought endlessly to form "interagency negotiating teams" and send them to foreign capitals, rather than sending the engineers and technical specialists who were essential to action on the ground. These and other well-intentioned "helpers" around Washington's other agencies and the White House needed to be discouraged from impeding the program, a process which sometimes caused hard feelings.

Nunn-Lugar's Achievements

These false starts were, in a sense, testimony to the ambition of the vision of Nunn and Lugar. They asked the Pentagon, the rest of the U.S. government, and the new governments of Russia, Ukraine, Kazakhstan, and Belarus to put aside fifty years of mistrust and to do things they had never dreamt of doing before. The effort had the constant support and intervention of President Bill Clinton and Vice President Al Gore. The president once even found himself discussing the technical details of the disposition of rocket fuel with the president of Ukraine. In the end, we overcame the barriers, and the senators' vision became reality.

Nunn-Lugar has, as of mid-1998, provided $2.4 billion in DOD funding for programs to reduce and control weapons of mass destruction in the successor states of the former Soviet Union. The program has designed and funded more than forty large and complex engineering projects to safeguard, dismantle, or convert the lethal legacy of the cold war. More than 4,800 nuclear weapons designed to destroy the United States have been eliminated. All nuclear weapons have been eliminated from the non-Russian successor states to the Soviet Union, avoiding what would otherwise have been the biggest burst of proliferation in Atomic Age history. Proliferation in Ukraine and Kazakhstan, with their crucial locations in Europe and Asia, would have been disastrous for stability in their regions and for the global nonproliferation norm. Belarus, under its first, strongly reformist post-Soviet government, was the first to begin most Nunn-Lugar programs with the result that nuclear weapons were soon removed from its territory. The fast work of Nunn-Lugar in Belarus proved to be crucial: the current government of Belarus, under the erratic and autocratic President Alexander Lukashenka, espouses a longing to return to the Soviet past, including basing nuclear weapons on Belarusian territory. Within Russia, nuclear reductions continued, despite a five-year stalemate in traditional arms control, at a pace that would have been impossible without Nunn-Lugar. A large program to safeguard weapons remaining in the hands of the Russian Ministry of Defense has been initiated. Caches of fissile material like that secretly removed from Ust-Kamenogorsk in Project Sapphire have been safeguarded. A grant program funded by Nunn-Lugar has paid weapons scientists to turn their talents to peaceful pursuits.

Thus the danger of loose nukes has been contained and reduced during the first post–cold war era. In truth, we never expected this astounding degree of success. When we took office in 1993, it seemed to us entirely unlikely that Ukraine, Kazakhstan, and Belarus would all stay on the path to become nuclear-free states; that Russia would continue to safeguard and dismantle weapons amidst its titanic social upheaval; that somewhere, sometime, there would not be a sale, diversion, theft, or seizure of these weapons or nuclear materials by disgruntled military officers or custodians somewhere across the eleven time zones that had been the Soviet empire. Every morning we would open the daily intelligence summary fearing to read that nukes had broken loose and hoping that at least U.S. intelligence sources would have detected the break. But so far, nukes have not broken loose. Much of the credit must go to Sam Nunn and Dick Lugar and their timely vision of Preventive Defense.

What Next for the Nunn-Lugar Program?

The Nunn-Lugar program has been a success, but it will have to change to be as effective in the second post–cold war era as in the first, transitional era. The revolution continues in Russia, and history shows that a profound revolution like the one that brought an end to the Soviet Union is likely to continue for decades. The worrisome fact is that Russia still possesses enough plutonium for 25,000 to 50,000 weapons and enough highly enriched uranium for 40,000 to 80,000 weapons. Add to that the ineluctable technical fact that the half-life of plutonium (the relevant isotope, Pu-239) is 24,400 years and the half-life of highly enriched uranium (U-235) is 713 million years. The result is a danger that will persist through many turns of the wheel of history. Without a continuing, vigilant effort we must still judge the odds of disaster very high indeed.

Unfortunately the required level of effort is not assured. It will require a renewed and "reinvented" Nunn-Lugar program attuned to the changing times, augmented by a fundamentally different type of arms control. In the remainder of this chapter we sketch the ingredients of the needed effort, beginning with the reinvention of Nunn-Lugar and a new conception of arms control.

First, Nunn-Lugar must continue to be funded by the U.S. Congress and in fact should grow. One result of congressional ambivalence about the Nunn-Lugar program in the first post–cold war era is that funds available in the program continue to fall short of the opportunities to reduce the threat to the United States. Existing programs could be accelerated and expanded to good effect. Whether or not U.S.-Russian arms control makes further progress and reaches further agreements, Nunn-Lugar can play a role in continuing reductions of the strategic weapons that threaten the United States. And there are many aspects of the threat not yet being addressed at all because funds are lacking. Another unfortunate result of congressional attitudes toward the program is that Nunn-Lugar managers must labor under burdensome restrictions. Congress has looked skeptically on aspects of the program such as defense conversion and officer housing, which are useful and sometimes necessary to jump-start and hasten the process of weapons dismantlement, as at Pervomaysk. Congressional skepticism forces program managers to adopt an especially conservative approach to contracting and to "audits and inspections" of assistance for fear that a single mishap in any individual project would bring all of Nunn-Lugar under attack. Safeguards are necessary when spending taxpayers' money anywhere, especially in foreign countries. But excessive emphasis on controls slows programs and creates a distrustful "arms control verification" atmosphere that hinders cooperation. Program managers should be freed of unnecessary obstacles, both those written into law and those unwritten restric-

tions that grew up under congressional ambivalence in the first
post–cold war era. We believe that Nunn-Lugar's successes in its
first half-decade justify such expanded latitude.

Such latitude will be needed, because if Nunn-Lugar is to
expand its scale and scope to continue its successful application of
the principles of Preventive Defense, it will have to adapt its established patterns of cooperation to the realities of Russia at this stage
of its continuing revolution. The program was launched when
Russia's opening to the West was in full flower and offers of U.S.
"assistance" were eagerly accepted. But the political backdrop and
economic motivations for Russia's leaders today are totally different. Therefore money, good intentions, and strong will on the part
of the U.S. government will not be enough. These are not our
countries nor our weapons, and cooperation could well be the
scarce resource when it comes to getting results. Russian politics is
making distinctly greater demands that cooperative programs satisfy Russian needs as well as American needs. Russian military and
industrial managers, and the troops and guards at weapons store-
houses, have problems and preoccupations that, understandably,
take precedence in their minds over the costly weapons dismantlement efforts and security improvements that are Nunn-Lugar's
highest priority. These must, as a practical matter, be acknowledged and dealt with if Nunn-Lugar is to make more progress.

The most successful Nunn-Lugar programs to date have
involved nuclear weapons and weapons delivery systems, where
great progress has been made, but progress has been much slower
in the other three categories of weapons of mass destruction: fissile
materials, chemical weapons, and biological weapons. Three specific technical thrusts are needed in the "reinvented" Nunn-Lugar
program:

First, it is crucial for Nunn-Lugar to extend its successes with
nuclear weapons themselves to the still-faltering programs for
safeguarding fissile materials. The United States enjoyed superb
cooperation from all involved agencies in Ukraine, Kazakhstan,
and even Belarus when establishing programs to eliminate nuclear
weapons systems. Within Russia, both of the agencies that control
nuclear weapons and delivery systems—the Ministry of Defense

and the Ministry of Defense Industry (now incorporated into the Ministry of Economy)—have formed strong cooperative relationships with their U.S. counterparts. But this is not true of Russia's Ministry of Atomic Energy (MINATOM), which has the vital job of producing and safeguarding fissile materials and of fabricating and dismantling nuclear warheads. MINATOM has been much more reluctant to cooperate with U.S. officials, with the result that progress has been much slower in the area of safety and security of highly enriched uranium and other fissile materials.

One concept that has great merit is to place excess fissile materials into secure long-term storage in Russia, creating a "fissile material repository."[6] Similar repositories could be established in other countries containing bomb-usable fissile materials, including the United States. The material would not necessarily have to be moved to new facilities. Instead, existing facilities would be upgraded to internationally approved standards of safety and security, as is already being accomplished at Mayak, Russia, in one Nunn-Lugar program. But upon formal deposit, the material would become the property of an international consortium, consisting of Russia, the United States, European countries, Japan, and perhaps others, which would operate the repository. The land on which the repository stood would enjoy the same protections as diplomatic premises, and an international guard force would provide perimeter security. Inside the fence, the depositing nation could maintain its own guard force and protect its own nuclear weapon design secrets. For each kilogram of material deposited, the depositing country would be paid an agreed sum from a fund capitalized by the international consortium. Material could later be withdrawn from the repository for approved peaceful purposes—for example, if highly enriched uranium was to be blended into reactor fuel, or plutonium into "mixed oxide" reactor fuel—upon payment back to the consortium of a per-kilogram sum. The result of establishing an international fissile material repository would be prompt upgrade of the security for the material, cash payment to the depositing country, and a boost for the global nonproliferation regime, without disruption in long-term plans to use the material for reactor fuel. For the repository concept to work, a fund of several billion dollars would be needed. The bulk of the funds would have to come from the United States, Europe, and Japan, with Russia paying little into the fund in the near term but withdrawing a substantial sum as it placed its excess materials in safe storage. The effect would be "purchase" of the dangerous Russian excess bomb material by the countries paying most into the international consortium, including the United States through the Nunn-Lugar program.

Nunn-Lugar can also be a powerful tool for reducing the danger from chemical and biological weapons. Russia has a chemical weapons stockpile that it must eliminate under international agreements, but elimination of chemical weapons is costly. Without the catalyzing effect of Nunn-Lugar, it is unlikely Russia will undertake the task on a reasonable schedule. Russia also inherited chemical industry facilities expressly designed to be easily converted from production of ordinary chemicals to production of warfare agents. A future will need to be found for these facilities and their work forces, either converting them permanently to civilian pursuits or destroying them. While Nunn-Lugar cannot and should not take on the entire multibillion-dollar task of eliminating the USSR's chemical weapons stock, it can jump-start the process by sharing and developing technology for neutralizing chemical agents and by building pilot elimination plants. A Nunn-Lugar program of this type has been launched but has only fitful support in Congress and limited funding. If Russia's chemical weapons inheritance is truly to be eliminated, a new livelihood will need to be found for the facilities and the chemists who staff them. Otherwise they will replicate the pattern found elsewhere in the old state-owned industries, where factories stay open because the work force has no other employment opportunity. Or worse, they will seek employment by foreign proliferators. Nunn-Lugar can sponsor the search to find commercial outlets for safe products of the chemical weapons infrastructure.

Biological weapons are an even more serious matter. Russian President Boris Yeltsin has acknowledged that the Soviet Union maintained a biological warfare capability and industrial plant in violation of international agreements. Nunn-Lugar has only recently begun to design projects to dismantle this germ warfare complex and turn its fearsome capabilities to peaceful purposes. If Russia agrees to these projects, Nunn-Lugar will need additional funding to carry them out. Some officials in Russia appear to believe that biological weapons can still contribute to Russian military security, or at least that a research program into offensive uses for germ warfare is necessary to craft defenses against them. But, as with chemical weapons, there is also a strong element of economic self-preservation in the stubborn persistence of Russian germ warfare facilities. Discussions between American and Russian officials over Russia's implementation of its multilateral and bilateral agreements to open these facilities to inspection have been largely fruitless. Because of Russian intransigence in these talks, some in Congress oppose Nunn-Lugar initiatives in the biological warfare area. But Nunn-Lugar programs directed at the economic conversion of germ warfare facilities to peaceful purposes and to new scientific pursuits for their technical work force might provide leverage by addressing directly those in the Russian program whose motivations are predominantly economic survival. This approach deserves a larger and less hesitant effort.

Larger and bolder Nunn-Lugar programs, and new initiatives in further arms control assistance, fissile materials safeguarding, and chemical and biological weapons, can make Nunn-Lugar as effective in the second post–cold war era as it has been in the first. Launching a new and different Nunn-Lugar program for the future must be a top priority of Preventive Defense.

Arms Control at an Impasse

Just as Nunn-Lugar needs to embark on a new phase, so does arms control, which has shown none of the dynamism in the past five years that Nunn-Lugar has shown. Traditional arms control is at an impasse. Nuclear arms control negotiations took a back seat in the first post–cold war era. This was necessary: urgent attention had to be given to the emergency posed by the first-ever disintegration of a nuclear superpower. Simply implementing the agreements previously concluded with the USSR as it broke up was an ambitious prospect by itself. The Soviet government that had signed START I and negotiated START II now had multiple successors. All were struggling to define themselves and their security, and all had political and economic problems that occupied their attention much more than arms control. Their decisions could not be predicted and could certainly not be taken for granted. Their actions were not shaped by the old canons of bipolarity and strategic stability, but instead by internal politics, economic exigencies, and the brand new security dilemmas of new post-Soviet states. This situation required action, not more documents.

As the uncertainties increased, so did the stakes. The issue was no longer the size and shape of the arsenal of a stable superpower, but the possibility of multiple new nuclear states, each with enough nuclear weapons to qualify as a superpower. Ukraine, for example, was born with a nuclear arsenal on its territory larger than those of Britain, France, and China combined. Within each state, moreover, desperate economic conditions and tumultuous political conditions threatened the secure control of weapons and materials.

To deal with the new problems of nuclear control, new tools were needed, and new opportunities opened up. Traditional arms control negotiation was no longer the most effective tool. In Ukraine, for example, three alternative types of policy action were applied instead. One was trilateral diplomacy, in which the parties were the United States, Ukraine, and Russia, and the issues were largely economic rather than strategic. Another was Nunn-Lugar assistance in the denuclearization process. The third and fundamentally important approach was a policy to address Ukraine's broader security dilemma. The United States, especially the Pentagon, made it convincing to the leaders and people of Ukraine that they would be more secure with friends and no nuclear weapons than with nuclear weapons and no friends. DOD accordingly initiated training and exercising with Ukrainian forces, drew Ukraine into the activities of NATO's Partnership for Peace and the NATO-Ukraine Charter, and advised the Ukrainian Ministry of Defense on how to transform the conventional forces it inherited from the Soviet Union into a capable defensive force. In these actions and others crafted to meet the urgent needs of the first post–cold war era, traditional arms control negotiations played no part. This transitional period, however, is now over.

It is once again time to return to negotiated arms control, this time between Russia and the United States. But the new phase of arms control will differ fundamentally from the last phase of arms control between the United States and the Soviet Union. To achieve its full rewards, the new phase will need to have some ambitious new features. In the spirit of Preventive Defense, the new arms control should emphasize less the bolstering of deterrence (the objective of START I and START II) than keeping loose nukes from becoming a new threat.

Whether and when this phase begins depends on ratification of the START II agreement by the Russian Duma. As of this writing, the prospects for Duma ratification are unclear. The Duma has balked at ratification for over five years. No single reason predominates. The relatively few arms control experts in the Duma have raised such issues as the pace and cost of the dismantlement of Russian weapons required by the agreement, and U.S. interpretation of the Anti–Ballistic Missile (ABM) Treaty as it applies to missile defenses. The United States has taken steps, notably at the Helsinki summit in March 1997, to address the experts' concerns. At Helsinki the United States agreed to extend the time to implement START II from 2003 to 2007, which would permit Russia to "stretch out" dismantlement costs over a longer period. Russia and the United States also agreed to a framework for distinguishing theater missile defenses against short-range missiles, which are not covered by the ABM treaty, from national missile defenses against strategic missiles, which are.

But for most members of the Duma, the problems with START II are broad and political. START II was negotiated between 1990 and 1993; many Russians believe that during this period the Soviet Union and Russia were overly accommodating to the United States. Other legislators cite NATO expansion as a sign that the United States does not take Russia's strategic interests into account. Some note that ratification is desired by the Yeltsin government and the U.S. government, and this alone seems basis enough to withhold ratification.

The Duma continues to withhold ratification despite the fact that Russia intends to reduce its nuclear forces anyway, and despite law and policy adopted by the United States that would freeze U.S. forces at START I levels until Russia undertakes comparable reductions. In short, START II ratification would appear to be strongly in the national interest of Russia, just as it is in the interest of the United States. The Yeltsin government has been steadfast in pursuing ratification, but there seems little else it or the United States can do that would decisively improve the chances of early ratification.

If ratification of START II does eventually take place, a new vista for arms control will open up for the first time in the decade. A new agreement to follow START II can be negotiated, the first truly post–cold war arms control agreement. What should it contain?

Needed: An Entirely New Type of Arms Control

The principles and objectives of a new phase of arms control after START II should be fundamentally different. The goal will be less to stabilize a balance of nuclear terror than to move beyond it. Ultimately, the nuclear reduction process should be broadened to include the other nuclear powers. However, Russia and the United States still possess arsenals many times larger than those of China, France, or the United Kingdom, and thus it makes sense to take the next step bilaterally.

The U.S. position with respect to its own nuclear forces should reflect the changes wrought by the end of the cold war. In the 1994 Nuclear Posture Review we conducted in the Pentagon, the Clinton administration stated that with the cold war over, nuclear weapons play a smaller role in U.S. defense than at any time since the nuclear age began.[7] The U.S. approach to its own strategic forces should no longer be governed by the old cold war calculus reflected in the famous Single Integrated Operational Plan.[8] U.S. officials have already indicated that U.S. strategic forces could be reduced to about half their START II levels without an impact on U.S. security.

A new agreement should codify Russia's desire to reduce and simplify its strategic forces for budgetary reasons. From the U.S. perspective, the agreement should address U.S. security concerns over problems of custody and control of the entire Russian arsenal, and not just the military potential of its intercontinental forces. This new focus would have several important consequences for the scope of the next arms control agreement.

First, the new agreement should encompass not just strategic nuclear weapons, but all nuclear weapons. It makes little sense to debate whether deployed strategic weapons should number 1,000, 2,000, or some similar number when the number of tactical and nondeployed warheads and fissile cores, all with the potential to become "loose nukes," is many times as large. If the next arms control agreement were only a version of START II with smaller weapons limits on strategic weapons exclusively, we would miss the opportunity to make a decisive advance in nuclear safety. Russia maintains a nonstrategic nuclear arsenal several times as large as that of the United States. These weapons are deployed at too many locations, in too many hands, for secure control. Their continued existence, moreover, encourages some in the Russian military in the view that nuclear weapons, rather than military reform, are the solution to the poor state of Russia's conventional forces. The United States concluded in the Nuclear Posture Review that its own security needs and commitments to allies can be fulfilled with a nonstrategic arsenal of 1,500 to 2,000 tactical bombs and submarine-deployable cruise missiles, and Russia's needs surely do not require a nonstrategic arsenal several times larger than this. Both sides also maintain a large reserve of strategic and nonstrategic weapons that are not deployed. These weapons would not play a part in nuclear strikes, but their safe custody and ultimate elimination are still a concern.

Second, the new agreement should account for and require reduction not just of delivery systems, but of nuclear warheads themselves. Past arms control agreements have focused on submarines, missiles and silos, and bombers because only limitations on these items were verifiable under cold war conditions. The new relationship between Russia and the United States should now permit progressive steps toward warhead accountability. The needed technologies have been developed, but the procedures required to carry them out will be difficult to craft. Looking to a future when more countries may be brought into nuclear arms control, the United States and Russia will both benefit by pioneering these techniques now.

Third, the new agreement should attempt to go beyond warhead limits to accounting for the fissile materials from which the warheads can be made. This feature, even more than nonstrategic weapons and warhead limits, will necessitate technical and procedural innovations. Together with warhead controls, fissile material controls imply a system of mutual transparency for nuclear establishments that goes well beyond the "from the outside looking in" style of verification pursued during the cold war. The fissile material repository described above might figure in this aspect of an agreement, also pointing the way to future multinational agreements covering fissile materials.

A fourth step is sometimes mentioned as an appropriate goal for future arms control. It is argued that reduction in numbers should be accompanied by measures to "de-alert" nuclear forces, taking them off the hair-trigger posture that each side adopted to maximize deterrence during the cold war. The objective was then to make it clear to the other side beyond any possible doubt that swift and massive retaliation would follow any first nuclear strike. The new political relationship permits a less dangerous deterrent posture, and we believe operational matters are as important to safety as numbers.

However, we do not believe that such de-alerting steps should be the subject of post–START II arms control negotiations. While de-alerting is clearly desirable in principle, three practical factors counsel caution when it comes to making it a central feature of arms control. For one thing, the technical implementation of de-alerting usually involves relatively subtle changes in missile systems and command and control procedures. If an agreement requires each side to satisfy the other that it has taken the specified de-altering steps, the level of transparency needed will exceed even that required for verification of warhead and fissile material controls. For example, the most dangerous aspect of Russian strategic forces from the U.S. point of view is the apparent Russian practice of maintaining submarine-based strategic forces in a launch-on-warning posture when they are tied up at pierside (as they usually are now, for budgetary reasons), where they are vulnerable to a hypothetical U.S. first strike. It is difficult to see how the Russian Navy could give the United States assurance that such submarine missiles could not be launched quickly or could not be returned shortly to a posture where they could. Second, de-alerting steps can generally be reversed rather quickly, whereas dismantlement cannot. Third, protracted and complex negotiations over de-alerting might distract negotiators from the more fundamental tasks of permanent dismantlement. For the time being, therefore, de-alerting steps are probably best left to the separate initiatives of each side, encouraged by the other. Other informal cooperative approaches are also promising, such as sharing data from missile warning radars and satellites to avoid mistaken alerts, a step that has recently been agreed between Russia and the United States and is being implemented.

The extensive cooperation and new technology demanded by an agreement addressing the "loose nukes" problem incorporating the three ingredients described above will require a new wave of joint implementation programs funded by an expanded Nunn-Lugar program.

If There Is No More Arms Control

The prospect for post–START II arms control sketched above is attractive and extremely ambitious, but it hinges on ratification of START II by the Russian Duma. Suppose more months and years go by without ratification? This prospect is distinctly less promising, but it is time to begin to think through its consequences. A starting point is to imagine a scenario in which there is no arms control beyond START I, and the arsenals of the two sides are determined solely by unilateral constraints, based on budgetary and technical trends, together with reasonable restraint on both sides.[9]

It seems clear, according to Russian experts and spokesmen, that in this scenario Russia would reduce its strategic arsenal anyway. A straitened budget climate and the evident end of strategic competition with the United States dictate this course. The result will be a Russian arsenal with the same size that START II would require (or considerably smaller), but with a different shape. In particular, Russia is unlikely to turn all its land-based missiles into single-warhead versions, "de-MIRVing" them. Instead, Russia would maintain the heavily MIRVed missiles it possesses as long as possible, extending their service life. There are technical limits to how long this can be done, especially considering that many of its heavily MIRVed missiles were built in Ukraine, and Russia lacks the industrial facilities to maintain and refurbish these types. Russia might also equip its new, smaller ICBMs (the SS-27s), built in Russia, with multiple warheads, perhaps three. This ICBM force would be the backbone of Russia's strategic forces, complementing a small submarine force and a very small intercontinental bomber force.

In this scenario, the United States would be wise to continue to assist reductions and eliminations through Nunn-Lugar even when they are not called for by an arms control agreement.

Budget pressures are much less severe in the United States, but they will still apply a downward pressure on U.S. strategic forces. Spending on strategic forces has declined from 10 percent of the total defense budget in the mid-1980s to less than 4 percent today, while the budget itself has declined by about 40 percent. Strategic nuclear forces will continue to compete for funds with readiness and current operations like peacekeeping in Bosnia, needed counterproliferation and modernization programs for non-nuclear forces (described in chapters 4 and 6), and quality-of-life programs to ensure recruitment and retention of top-rate military personnel (described in chapter 6).

Least susceptible to budget pressures are the B-52H and B-2 bombers, which have important non-nuclear roles that would cause them to be retained whatever the dynamics of nuclear arms control will be. The Trident submarine force would probably be converted entirely from the C-4 to the D-5 missile to avoid the costs of extending the service life of the C-4. As a result, the United States would not need to develop a new submarine missile force for many years. The total number of Trident submarines on which these missiles were deployed, however, would probably be reduced to avoid the costs of refurbishing their nuclear reactors. START II requires each submarine missile to be "downloaded" to a less highly MIRVed configuration, but if it is not ratified, downloading would probably be forsaken in the interest of "more bang for the buck," given the smaller number of submarines and crews.

U.S. ICBMs consist of Peacekeeper (MX) missiles carrying ten warheads and Minuteman III missiles carrying three warheads. Current plans call for Peacekeeper to be retired, and these plans would probably be carried out even if START II is not ratified. Minuteman III is supposed to be downloaded from three warheads to one warhead under the START II treaty. Plans to download are well advanced, but the cost of keeping three warheads on each Minuteman III missile is small. Thus, without START II ratification, the Minuteman might or might not be de-MIRVed. A larger question about the U.S. ICBM force is whether it would be retained at all in this scenario. Keeping the 500 Minuteman III missile force healthy requires replacing its guidance and propulsion systems, an expensive proposition. Since it carries far fewer warheads than the SLBM force, the ICBM force might be retired, reducing U.S. strategic forces to a dyad rather than a triad.

The sacrifices to security under the no–START II scenario are therefore considerable. Russia would retain MIRVed ICBMs, though the remaining missiles would have three rather than six or ten MIRVed warheads. But the concept of eliminating MIRVs entirely was a major goal of START II; this benefit to U.S. security would be sacrificed if START II is abandoned. U.S. forces would consist of bomber and submarine missile forces, without, perhaps, retention of ICBMs; the advantage of having the additional diversity in U.S. forces represented by a triad would be sacrificed.

To these sacrifices must be added the forgone advantages of the ambitious program of post–START II superpower arms control described above and, more important, the opportunity to address through arms control the central problem of loose nukes. It is therefore much to be desired that START II is ratified by the Duma and enters into force, or that some other route to another round of

U.S.-Russian arms control is found. On the other hand, the situation is much less serious than it would be if the cold war were still under way. In those days, strategic competition and unbridled spending on strategic nuclear arms would have produced ever larger and more sophisticated—and dangerous—nuclear postures. While certainly not desirable, this scenario is not catastrophic either. It would, however, place new emphasis on the patterns and structures created by the Nunn-Lugar program to keep a spirit of cooperation and restraint alive in U.S.-Russian nuclear relations. And another route to a more global system of nuclear arms control would have to be found that did not pass through another round of U.S.-Russian agreement.

The Danger of False Comfort

During the mid-1980s the danger of nuclear war hung over the world like a dark cloud. Analysts argued over the probabilities and the methods for reducing this danger, but everyone agreed on the urgency of the problem. It was an "A-list" threat, and nearly every day the media carried the story of the effort to meet it. But when the cold war ended, a strange calm descended. Relieved that a nuclear exchange had been made decisively less likely by a change in politics, many seemed to forget that the technology had not changed nearly as fast. The cold war's A-list risk continues in a sense, in the persistence of the means of destruction and the continuing revolution in the former Soviet Union, but an imminent threat to be deterred has transformed into a different, but still serious, danger of "loose nukes." Indeed, many would argue, and we would agree, that the probability of nuclear use has increased, not decreased. Without a forceful "reinvented" effort at cooperative programs like Nunn-Lugar, and a clear new direction for arms control, the subject of nuclear terror might again return to the headlines. The job of Preventive Defense is to keep it off the front pages.

CHAPTER 3

Dealing with a Rising China

On the evening of March 7, 1996, I joined Secretary of State Warren Christopher and Anthony Lake, the president's national security adviser, in the State Department's small conference room for a meeting with Liu Huaqiu, vice minister of foreign affairs of China. It was a tense occasion. Earlier that day the Chinese had conducted what they called a "missile test" in the Taiwan Strait.[1] They had fired three missiles only eighteen miles from a port city in Taiwan's north, and just over twenty miles from a port city in its south. At the same time, the People's Liberation Army (PLA) was massing 150,000 troops along the Chinese coast opposite Taiwan and planning to conduct live-fire military exercises in the Strait of Taiwan over the next two weeks. These provocative military actions were taken just before Taiwan's first democratic presidential election, only two weeks away, and had provoked an international crisis.

Carter was not present for the events described in the first part of this chapter, so Perry tells this story himself.

We believed that China's leaders had misread the American position on Taiwan and wanted to deliver a crystal-clear message to Vice Minister Liu so that he could immediately pass on this message to the highest levels in the Chinese government. We had therefore decided to transform a scheduled dinner meeting between Lake and Liu into an opportunity for all three of President Clinton's primary advisers on American security policy in the Western Pacific to deliver a strong and unambiguous message.

It was particularly important that the secretary of defense be present at that meeting to demonstrate U.S. military resolve. I believed that the Chinese leaders' actions had created a dangerous situation and that the danger was magnified by their misunderstanding of our policy.

I also believed that my statements on this issue would carry particular weight with the Chinese because many senior Chinese officials had long been acquainted with me. In 1980, as undersecretary of defense, I had led the first U.S. military delegation to the People's Republic of China and had established a military-to-military relationship with the People's Liberation Army. Our delegation had visited China's most modern defense laboratories, plants, and test ranges, including the missile test range in Western China. My host then had been General Liu Huaqing; now as the vice chairman of the Central Military Commission, he was effectively the senior military leader in China.

I had visited China a half-dozen times during my later association with Stanford University, and I had maintained my acquaintance with General Liu Huaqing and other leaders of the PLA. During these visits, I had also begun to develop relationships with civilian leaders in China including Jiang Zemin, who at the time was the minister of the electronics industry (he later became mayor of Shanghai and rose in the party to become its general secretary in 1989 and president of China in 1993).

As a result of these contacts, when I became secretary of defense I believed that I could play a leading role in the administration's efforts to reestablish a constructive engagement with the Chinese government, including a military-to-military relationship with the PLA. But that relationship was very slow in getting started. During the presidential campaign, candidate Clinton had criticized President George Bush for not reacting more strongly to the Tiananmen Square incident and to the Chinese government's abuses of human rights. As president, therefore, Clinton was not initially receptive to the position of those in the administration, including myself, who argued that the only way to influence China in a positive direction was by engaging it.

By the second year of the administration, however, President Clinton had begun to accept this position and had, with Secretary Christopher's strong endorsement, given his approval for me to plan a trip to China. The engagement was to be developed in stages. Assistant Secretary of Defense Charles Freeman, a seasoned diplomat and a scholar of modern Chinese politics, was to visit first; when that visit went well, planning began for my visit a few months later.

Thus, I did not make my first visit to China as secretary of defense until nearly two years into the administration, in October 1994. The visit had been very productive and cordial, and I had met with China's president, premier, and foreign minister, as well as all of China's senior military officials. A high point was the opportunity to present my views on security to an audience at China's National Defense University that included virtually every senior Chinese general.

This visit led us to issue a reciprocal invitation to the Chinese minister of defense, General Chi Haotian, to visit the United States. His return visit was scheduled for June 1995, but just a week before that visit, President Lee Teng-hui of Taiwan had traveled to Cornell University, his alma mater in New York State, to receive an honorary degree. Lee's acceptance speech had been quite political and had outraged many in China. The Chinese government charged that the United States, by allowing the speech, had violated its "One-China" policy, and the Chinese government canceled the proposed visit of Minister Chi. By the end of 1995, however, that crisis seemed behind us, and the minister was again authorized to visit the United States in late March 1996.

Thus, despite my intention to pursue a vigorous program of constructive engagement with Chinese defense officials, I had managed only one meeting in three years. Now, with Minister Chi's visit only a few weeks away, a new crisis was upon us, and our program of contacts was in doubt again. I joined the meeting with Vice Foreign Minister Liu, therefore, with a real sense of frustration, but I was intensely interested in what spin the vice foreign minister would put on the missile firings.

Speak Softly . . .

We assembled that evening in a somber mood in the State Department's small, plain conference room. The Chinese delegation, consisting of Vice Minister Liu, an assistant minister, and an interpreter, sat on one side of the table. The American delegation, consisting of Secretary Christopher, National Security Adviser Lake, and myself, sat on the other side. A few others sat on chairs along the wall. We made our greetings and got right down to business. Secretary Christopher invited Vice Minister Liu to speak. He began by repeating the official Chinese government position about that day's missile firings and the military exercises in the Strait of Taiwan. These were, he said unconvincingly, "routine exercises," and we should not be concerned by them. Any American concern, he argued, should be directed to Taiwan, where at least one presidential candidate had been running on a platform of independence from China. Moreover, he said, President Lee Teng-hui had been flirting with this same theme on his international trips, especially his trip to the United States the previous year.

Warming to his argument, Vice Minister Liu said that the United States should focus instead on the consequences of the U.S. policy of selling arms to Taiwan and especially the decision of the Bush administration to sell Taiwan a fleet of F-16s, due to be delivered in less than a year.

Secretary of State Christopher responded by spelling out the tenets of the U.S. "One-China" policy. It had been formulated several decades earlier, during the process of normalizing U.S. relations with China, and it had, he pointed out, been honored by all six presidents since then. The United States was continuing to honor its end of the agreement by recognizing that there was only one China and that Taiwan was a part of China. But Secretary Christopher insisted that China must honor its end of the agreement, which was that it would not use military force to achieve the "One China." He said that the military maneuvers and missile firings amounted to military coercion of a democratic election and that these actions raised our concern that China was prepared to use its military power to create "One China" forcibly. He emphasized that U.S. national security officials were of the unanimous view that these coercive military actions should be stopped. To underline this point, he said, he had invited the secretary of defense to the meeting to convey a message directly to the People's Liberation Army.

At this point, then, I spoke very plainly to the minister so as not to be misunderstood. I told him that his assertion that these missile firings were routine military exercises was simply not credible. "As a former artillery officer," I said, "I understand very well, and the PLA understands very well, the symbolism of 'bracketing' a target. And as a technologist, I understand the very real possibility that a missile guidance system can malfunction. As a senior official in the Foreign Ministry, you should understand that if any of these missiles were to land on Taiwan, there would be grave consequences." I told him that I believed that aggressive military actions directed against Taiwan could be seen as a threat to American interests, and I reminded him that "the United States has more than enough military capability to protect its vital national security interests in the region, and is prepared to demonstrate that." Finally, I told him that I believed that a repeat of the missile firings would be a political blunder and in time would come to be seen as such even in China.

The vice foreign minister listened intently and soberly to my words. I had the impression that he had not known that the missile firings would be so close to Taiwan or that they would occur on the very day of his meeting. He was struggling to put the best possible face on an action that had surprised and possibly shocked him.

Lake then repeated the essential message in clear language: the United States had vital national security interests in the Western Pacific, and the recent Chinese military actions threatened those interests. Then, however, he shifted to a problem-solving mode; he suggested that the Chinese government should cease its provocative military activity in the strait and work to resume dialogue, travel, and trade between Taiwan and the mainland. Anticipating that the current crisis would be solved peacefully, he began to discuss a prospective trip to China and the possibility of dealing in depth with some of the problems that had led to the current crisis.

The vice foreign minister was visibly relieved at this turn of the conversation, and the meeting ended on a cordial note. I have no doubt that he immediately conveyed our message to the highest levels in the Chinese government. However, our words were not heeded. The Chinese announced on March 9 that they would hold live-fire military exercises in the Taiwan Strait between March 12 and March 20, and during that period they conducted one more missile firing. Our diplomatic approach, although uncommonly blunt, had not been effective. We speculated that while the message was heard and understood in the Foreign Ministry, the military leadership may have thought that we lacked the will to act. It was clear that we needed a stronger way to communicate our concern and our resolve.

. . . But Carry a Big Stick

Accordingly, I met with Chairman of the Joint Chiefs of Staff General John Shalikashvili to consider what response would be most effective, and particularly what form of military response would be best understood by the PLA. We considered the alternatives open to the U.S. government at this point. First, we could send another diplomatic message. However, we believed this would continue to be interpreted by the PLA as a lack of will. Second, we could deploy one carrier battle group (CBG) to the region. This, however, we considered too weak, since we routinely kept one CBG in the general vicinity anyway. Third, we could steam two CBGs into the area where the Chinese were conducting their exercises, but this, we believed, would be unnecessarily provocative. We concluded that we should send two carrier battle groups to patrol off Taiwan, but that they should not go into the exercise area. We believe that this would send a message of capability and firmness, without undue provocation.

Our next concern was to find the carriers. General Shalikashvili made urgent calls to his commanders-in-chief and to the acting chief of naval operations, Admiral Jay Johnson, for their views. He quickly determined that the *Independence*, based in Japan, could shortly be in Taiwan along with its escorts.

Getting the second carrier was not so easy. The *George Washington* was deployed in the Mediterranean, but it was actively involved in supporting the "no-fly" zone in Bosnia, and NATO Commander General George Joulwan was understandably reluctant to release it without an alternative. The *Nimitz* was deployed in the Gulf of Arabia, but Saddam Hussein was again stirring up trouble, so we were reluctant to weaken our military capability there. The *Kitty Hawk* was undergoing "work-up" tests off San Diego, preparatory to deploying to the Gulf in two months. Admiral Johnson was reluctant to break its training cycle, since this was a key factor in maintaining the fleet's high level of readiness.

Within a few hours, General Shalikashvili was back to me with a plan of action. We could direct the *Nimitz* to leave the Persian Gulf immediately and steam at high speed to Taiwan; it would get there in ten or twelve days. At the same time the *George Washington* would steam from the Mediterranean to the Gulf to maintain carrier coverage there. The U.S. Air Force would assign additional ground-based fighters to carry out that part of the Bosnian "no-fly" mission that had been the job of the *George Washington* battle group. This was a plan that satisfied General Shalikashvili, General Joulwan, and myself. I called a hasty meeting to present our plan to Secretary Christopher and National Security Adviser Lake; we reached immediate agreement with the plan and the urgency of implementing it.

Before the day was over, General Shalikashvili and I met with President Clinton and his national security advisers to present our recommendations. I received the president's authorization to deploy the two CBGs and to delay the visit of the Chinese defense minister, which was just a few weeks away.

President Clinton also authorized Secretary Christopher to announce to the Chinese government and to the Taiwan liaison office in Washington that we would continue to maintain a "One-China" policy. We did not want either the Chinese government or the Taiwan government to misunderstand our actions.

CBG Diplomacy

The results were as we had hoped: the Chinese wrapped up their naval exercises in the Taiwan Strait and sent the ground troops back to their barracks. The rhetoric on all sides cooled off. The CBGs stayed in the area a few weeks and then returned to their home bases. We had no intention of initiating a military action with our naval forces, nor did we believe that there was a serious likelihood of these forces being challenged. But the presence of the CBGs had effectively communicated to China how seriously the U.S. government viewed their action.

In retrospect it seems clear that Chinese government officials had misunderstood the seriousness with which the United States viewed unprovoked military actions directed against Taiwan. The CBG deployment straightened out the misunderstanding. It also communicated to other countries in the region our commitment to maintaining stability in the region.

Following Through

Throughout my time in office, I believed that the U.S.-Japan security alliance was the linchpin of security and stability in the Asia-Pacific region. I also believed that this alliance was in no way incompatible with building a constructive engagement with China. However, that China did not yet see things quite this way was brought home to me in my last meeting as secretary of defense with the leadership of the Chinese government.

I was finally able to meet with General Chi Haotian, the Chinese minister of defense, later that year in Washington. I was disappointed that in four years we had been able to arrange only two meetings; these were not really enough to develop a strong working relationship such as I had established in a dozen meetings with Russian Defense Minister Pavel Grachev. Moreover, I expected that events during the Taiwan Strait crisis, including the carrier deployment I had ordered and the postponement of our meeting, would create a strain when we did finally meet. To my surprise, however, our meetings were cordial, and they were relatively productive on a wide range of topics.

The most sensitive issue for the Chinese was the recent reaffirmation in April of the U.S.-Japan Security Alliance. The Chinese government saw this strengthened alliance as being directed at China—an attempt to isolate or encircle their country. The Chinese view was reinforced by the timing of the reaffirmation, which had taken place just one month after the Taiwan crisis. As I explained to General Chi, however, the timing had been coincidental: long before the crisis, I had proposed the main outlines of the reaffirmation agreement to Japan's Prime Minister Tomiichi Muruyama during a November 1995 meeting in Tokyo, and President Clinton had essentially settled the agreement when he met with Prime Minister Ryutaro Hashimoto in a February 1996 meeting in California.

My explanation did not seem to ease Minister Chi's concern, and I redoubled my efforts, taking advantage of this opportunity to explain our views of the future of Pacific security. I pointed out that the U.S.-Japan alliance and the concomitant deployment of U.S. troops in Japan and Korea were the two most important contributors to the stable environment in the Western Pacific that had made possible the extraordinary economic growth there. This alliance provided the "oxygen" for the engine of economic growth in the Pacific, as the former assistant secretary of defense for international security affairs, Joseph S. Nye Jr., often put it. In response to my question, Minister Chi conceded that his own country had been a principal beneficiary of this economic growth during the last decade.

I asked Minister Chi if he thought that China's security would be improved if there were no U.S.-Japan alliance, and if instead Japan had to provide for its own security. I pointed out that this would be likely to result in an arms buildup in Japan and in neighboring countries as well—an arms race that could not possibly be in China's interest. I argued that if I were the Chinese minister of defense, I would encourage the U.S.-Japan security alliance, on the grounds that it promoted rather than harmed China's national security interest.

I thought the arguments were convincing, and I could see that Minister Chi was listening intently. But I must confess that I do not believe that I brought him around to sharing the view that the U.S.-Japan security alliance is beneficial for China. The historical baggage is simply too great; China's leaders do not trust Japan and think that the United States is naive to do so. I believe that this view will be a drag on security relations in the Pacific as long as the current generation of leaders is in power in China. It may, indeed, take a generational change in China before positive trilateral security relations are possible among the United States, China, and Japan.

Nonetheless, the U.S. relationship with China is as crucial as the U.S.-Japan relationship to the future of stability in the Asia-Pacific region. We must look for opportunities to strengthen and reconcile our relationships with both countries in order to assure security in this region, whose importance to U.S. security and economic health will only continue to grow in the coming decades.

Preventive Defense to Assure Stability in the Asia-Pacific Region

For the last two decades the Asia-Pacific region has enjoyed a period of unprecedented economic growth and importance to the U.S. economy and security. Even with the current economic downturn, U.S. trade with the Asia-Pacific region exceeds its trade with Europe. A necessary condition for this healthy state of economic affairs has been security and stability in the region and the confidence that it will continue.

The stability of the Asia-Pacific region depends on a strong forward deployment of U.S. military forces in the absence of a regional collective security institution that would parallel NATO's role in Europe. The U.S. forward deployment would not be possible without the U.S. alliances with South Korea and Japan. Their friendship with the United States is the cornerstone of U.S. policy in the region. This combination has maintained the peace and reduced the perceived necessity for regional arms races.

The principles of Preventive Defense remind us not to be complacent about this generally favorable state of affairs, but instead to look ahead and ask what the challenges to this stability might be. There are several areas of risk, including a decline in U.S. willingness to support the forward deployment and the alliances that underlie the stability, growing out of pressure to lower the U.S. defense budget. A second area of danger is the possibility that our allies might become unwilling to carry their share of the costs of sustaining the forward deployment of American forces. That issue has already arisen: in 1995, the U.S.-Japan alliance and basing came under serious criticism in Japan. The differences at that time were resolved by the security affirmation that President Clinton and Prime Minister Hashimoto signed in April 1996. The issue could arise again, however, if the economic problems that Japan and South Korea are now facing were to reduce their ability or willingness to share the expenses of basing U.S. troops on their territory.

Third, a destructive regional war would destabilize the region. Although the United States has major forces deployed in and around Korea to help the Republic of Korea deter such a war, this uneasy balance could be upset if North Korea acquired nuclear weapons, or if its regime "imploded" due to the collapse of the North Korean economy.

A fourth potential source of regional instability would result if a major military power were to emerge in the region and begin to threaten its neighbors. Some in the West believe that China is headed inevitably in this direction and point to the March 1996 crisis as evidence.

The more general fear is that China could go the way of Japan in the 1930s: as Japan increased its economic, political, and military power in the Pacific, this created inevitable conflicts of interest with other Pacific powers, especially the United States. This conflict was not managed well, and the result was a bloody Pacific war.

Indeed, China is today increasing its economic, political, and military power in the Pacific, and this has led and will continue to lead to conflicts of interest with other powers in that region, especially the United States and Japan. We believe that this path poses special dangers for American security but that it also provides rich opportunities. A U.S. policy of Preventive Defense is needed to help manage the U.S.-China relationship so that it does not lead to military conflict, but instead serves to strengthen the present stability in the Asia-Pacific region.

Why the U.S. Should Engage More with China

As China unfolds from the introverted crouch of the Maoist period and becomes more powerful, it is defining a wider role and a new identity for itself in international security. China's emergence is the most portentous geostrategic development in America's westward vista, as important as, to the east, Russia's search for a post–cold war security concept. An increasingly important objective of Preventive Defense is to promote the likelihood that China will emerge as a security partner rather than an adversary of the United States in the twenty-first century.

The United States cannot steer China's course, but, as with Russia, it can exercise an influence. Chinese strategic thinkers themselves rate actions of the United States the most important factor they need to take into account, for better or worse, as they chart their country's future.

Americans, for their part, eye China's growing power warily. Comfort can no longer be taken, as it was during the cold war, from the fact that China's power was an offset to Soviet military power. Now China must be assessed on its own terms. Some Americans have already concluded that China is destined for competition and conflict with the United States. But such a conclusion rashly pre-judges the outcome of a process that is only beginning. Fatalism would likely prove a self-fulfilling prophecy. If China is treated like an adversary, it will surely become one.

U.S. policy has wisely chosen to reject fatalism, as well as its prescription, a strategy of containment that would seek systemati-cally to limit China's power and role. Instead of containment, U.S. policy recognizes the malleability of China's future course and the potential for America to influence it through engagement. For now, the weight of American political opinion appears to support engagement.

Any program of engagement must recognize the reality that China's rapid rise as an economic, political, and military power inevitably poses challenges to other Pacific powers, and in particu-lar to the United States and Japan and to their security alliance. This alliance, and its concomitant deployment of American troops, has provided the security and stability underlying the remarkable economic growth these past two decades in the Asia-Pacific region. But even though China has itself profited from this stability, China believes that this alliance and these troops are directed against it and constitute an American policy of containment.

In fact, however, America's policy under its last six presidents has consistently been one of engagement with China. This policy began with the signing of the Shanghai Communiqués in 1972 by President Nixon. Since then, it has had its ups and downs: up with the recognition of China in 1979 by President Carter; down with China's suppression of the Tiananmen demonstrations in 1989 and the subsequent sanctions by the United States; up with President Clinton's resumption of engagement in 1994; down with China's firing of missiles bracketing Taiwan in 1996 and the deployment of two American carrier battle groups in response; up again most recently with the meetings in the United States and China of President Jiang Zemin and President Clinton.

The successful visit by President Jiang Zemin to the United States in October 1997 and President Clinton's reciprocal visit to China in June 1998 signaled a thaw in China-U.S. relations after their post–cold war low of 1995 and 1996. This new rapprochement, while welcome, remains highly contingent and fragile on both sides. The question of Taiwan still dominates the bilateral relationship, and miscalculation by either party could easily shatter the fragile stability. There is still much U.S. dissatisfaction with China over such issues as human rights, proliferation, Tibet, and the trade deficit. The fragility of the present improvement in relations is why the United States must seize this moment to lay a more solid foundation by creating understandings and linkages that will provide for greater stability and predictability in the future bilateral relationship.

How to Give Content to U.S. Engagement with China?

Seizing the opportunity presented by the present period of improving relations means developing specific policies and activities that, together, form the content of future engagement. It is not sufficient merely to proclaim a policy of engagement. Once we are talking to China, what shall we say? What understandings should we seek, and what programs of cooperation should we foster? Engagement is a process, not an end. Engagement requires substance to be sustainable. The content of engagement should be a Preventive Defense strategy: a focused, forward-looking program to shape the U.S.-China security relationship to mutual benefit. We believe that the most crucial opportunities are in these areas:

— First, the United States should work to deepen and broaden the defense-to-defense relationship;

— Second, the United States should work with China to stabilize the Taiwan question;

— Third, the United States should seek to engage China's neighbors;

— Fourth, the United States should encourage China to greater participation in counterproliferation and other global security regimes.

Forging a security partnership with China will be very different from forging one with Russia and in some ways more difficult. Russia has been a global power for half a century. But China's isolation has been profound, and its strategic perspectives are still regional, not global. Russia is accustomed to world responsibility; China will be assuming new responsibilities. Whereas Russia easily thinks of itself as an advanced industrial peer of the western nations, China thinks of itself as a developing country. China also harbors a substantial sense of historical grievance and dissatisfaction. China's region of the world possesses no security institutions like the Organization for Security and Cooperation in Europe, NATO, or the Partnership for Peace that could provide a ready-made security framework for resolving East Asia's unresolved animosities. But despite these differences, the opportunity for Preventive Defense with China is easily as great as the opportunity with Russia. The risk if Preventive Defense is not successful is the prospect of an A-list threat in East Asia in the twenty-first century.

Deepen and Broaden the Defense-to-Defense Relationship

Our first recommendation for a U.S. policy of engagement with China is to seek more and better military-to-military contacts and exchanges. That relationship should not only deepen but also broaden over time to become a comprehensive defense-to-defense relationship. The Chinese People's Liberation Army has a strong hand in China's national security policymaking. The generation of officers now assuming senior positions has had few if any opportunities for international experiences, because they have served most of their careers deep in China's interior. As these PLA officers now form their own views of the international scene and China's role in it, in important measure they will be influencing China's views.

As the debate over engagement continues in the United States, it also continues in China. Chinese military strategists fear that "engagement" is a trap for China, a trap that will contaminate it with ideas of transparency and cooperation, which will eventually undermine its interests. More dangerously, the PLA appears to share the Chinese government's overall preoccupation with the Taiwan question: over the past decade the PLA has been shifting its war plans and weapons-buying programs from general war with its northern neighbor, the former Soviet Union, toward acquiring the capability to coerce Taiwan. The 1995–96 missile crisis intensified this focus. The Taiwan question is now driving PLA reform and modernization programs.

All sides will benefit if the views of PLA officers and Chinese military strategists are formed within a context of dialogue with the U.S. military and, when possible, joint efforts. Some progress has already been made toward engagement between the PLA and the U.S. Department of Defense, including exchange visits by senior officials, reciprocal visits of warships to one another's ports, an agreement spelling out steps to avoid incidents at sea, discussion of mutual approaches to humanitarian relief, agreements to observe one another's exercises, and an agreement to "de-target" strategic missiles.

The United States and China will inevitably have different objectives in such military-to-military exchanges. The United States is interested in influencing the political-military outlook of PLA officers in a manner that will be beneficial to U.S. security over the long term. The U.S. military must also demonstrate its proficiency, professionalism, and will to the PLA, particularly in light of some apparent Chinese misperceptions about U.S. willingness and ability to use force when its interests are threatened. The deployment of the CBGs to Taiwan in 1996 was necessary precisely because the PLA had misperceptions either about how America viewed its national security interests in the region or about the American will to use force to protect those interests. A U.S. goal for these exchanges will be to develop relationships and mechanisms to avoid any such misunderstandings, miscalculations, and dangerous incidents in the future; intentions are likely to be better understood if each side has a network of contacts on the other side. The United States will want the exchanges to provide some transparency into the capabilities and intentions of the PLA, but at the same time it will wish to avoid activities that would significantly strengthen the Chinese military's power-projection capabilities.

For the PLA, objectives of defense-to-defense contact with the United States are likely to focus on improving capabilities, including acquiring technology and weapons; these objectives are not consistent with U.S. interests. The PLA will also be interested in concealing weaknesses that may come to light as a result of these contacts and will thus resist rapid progress toward a great deal of transparency.

While these differing objectives can be accommodated to some extent, each side must also acknowledge the other's goals and assume a certain degree of risk. The challenge to both is this: in order for exchanges to be effective at meeting both sides' goals, they must be substantive and meaningful.

We believe that specific actions to deepen the China-U.S. military-to-military relationship should include continuing and intensifying regular high-level talks, joint activity, functional exchanges, military educational exchanges, familiarization briefings, confidence-building measures, nuclear weapons safety and security, and biological and chemical weapons defense.

The first action we propose is that the U.S. military and the PLA should sustain a regular program of high-level talks. Such contacts should have a wide-ranging agenda and should occur at all levels between uniformed and civilian Defense Department officials and their Chinese counterparts. An important element of such relationships is an operational channel that can be employed in incidents and crises. Such discussions should also extend to the civilian strategic studies communities in each country, and efforts should be made to expand bilateral, informal (often referred to as "track two") security and defense dialogues.

Second, the relationship between the Department of Defense and the PLA should now begin to evolve from visits to joint activity: planning and carrying out combined exercises and training. China has long-standing policies that prohibit the PLA from engaging in joint military exercises with any country. The United States should encourage China to relax these prohibitions in the case of humanitarian and disaster relief (if not combat) field exercises and to conduct such exercises jointly with U.S. forces.

Third, midlevel, substantive functional exchanges should be held in areas of military art in which both countries would benefit from the sharing of techniques. Military justice and environmental security are examples of two such areas.

Fourth, more Chinese and American personnel should attend one another's professional military education institutions, so that each country can develop a cadre of true experts on the other's military. Exchanges that involve younger officers are especially important for the future, as a generational transition is under way in the PLA.

Fifth, the United States should encourage mutual transparency through briefings and familiarization tours covering such topics as force structure, military doctrine and requirements, modernization, defense reform, threat perception, national security decision-making, and civil-military relations.

A sixth set of activities should involve confidence-building measures. The Military Maritime Accord, signed in January 1998 by Secretary of Defense William Cohen and Defense Minister Chi Haotian, can serve as an example for a broader set of confidence-building measures such as communications links and notification of major weapons tests and exercises.

A seventh area for military-to-military engagement is in the area of nuclear weapons, arms control, and security of fissile materials. We believe that it is time for the United States to begin discussions with China about nuclear weapons. These discussions should involve personnel from the U.S. Strategic Command and the PLA's Second Artillery Corps. The safety and security of weapons and fissile material is of long-term interest to both countries and should form a major topic of discussion, along with the command and control of nuclear weapons systems.

Future nuclear arms control agreements might begin reducing the U.S. and Russian arsenals to levels near that of China and the other nuclear powers. The United States should begin to discuss now the question of China's inclusion in future multilateral nuclear arms reduction negotiations. The United States can also work with China to develop more effective procedures for administering export controls over nuclear proliferation–sensitive exports.

A beginning has been made in developing exchanges with Chinese weapons laboratories on safety and security issues, in much the same way that U.S. weapons laboratories have had significant interaction with their Russian counterparts. This is a positive development and the effort should be stepped up. Since we have a common interest in the safety and security of nuclear weapons, Chinese experience and expertise can be useful as the international community seeks to enhance the effectiveness of the International Atomic Energy Agency and other safeguards of nuclear material. The U.S. and Chinese weapons labs can also work together in the development of technologies applicable to verification of the Comprehensive Test Ban Treaty, to which both countries are signatories.

Finally, we believe that an important focus for deepening U.S.-China military-to-military relationships is in the area of biological and chemical weapons defense. Both the United States and China have forsworn biological and chemical weapons, but each might face their use by others, including terrorists. Discussion of techniques and technology for protection of military personnel and the civilian populace from these weapons would be mutually beneficial.

The U.S.-China relationship should also begin to move beyond military-to-military contacts to embrace a wider security dialogue, and it should include other countries in the region. The Department of Defense should not be the only part of the U.S. government developing such linkages with the Chinese military and strategic establishments or with the Chinese government and people more broadly. We urge specific steps to broaden the military-to-military relationship to a comprehensive defense-to-defense relationship. First, we believe that the United States and China should develop a series of meetings that bring together corresponding cabinet officials of the two governments twice a year to discuss cooperative projects. This would create a network of high-level relationships, and it would also help to situate the security relationship in a wider context. A similar process, begun in 1993 by Vice President Al Gore and Russian Prime Minister Viktor Chernomyrdin, has been fruitful in its pursuit of cooperative projects and solutions to bilateral problems between Russia and the United States.

We also urge regular meetings for members of the U.S. Congress, especially from the Armed Services, Foreign Affairs, and Intelligence Committees, with China's National People's Congress.

This would give members of the U.S. Congress a chance to interact with, and better understand the functioning of, the Chinese government as well as gain perspective on U.S. long-term strategic interests in China. Just as important, it would give Chinese legislators a better understanding of the functioning of democracy and how it is conducted in the United States.

Third, the United States and China should establish dialogue on their shared interests in a wide range of transnational security issues such as countering organized crime, drug trafficking, the smuggling of illegal aliens, piracy, environmental contamination, and terrorism, including terrorism involving weapons of mass destruction.

Fourth, we believe that it is time for defense-to-defense exchanges to move beyond the bilateral to include other key countries in the region. A set of triangular or quadrangular exchanges combining U.S. and Chinese defense officials with Japanese, Korean, and Russian officials would develop security and military dialogue with regional states and would also solidify and clarify the U.S. presence and role in the future security of the Asia-Pacific region.

A more robust defense-to-defense program that includes such activities would give the United States an opportunity to influence a critical audience at a formative moment in China's development as a player on the global scene; it is an opportunity that will not last forever and should be seized while it is available.

Stabilize the Taiwan Question

Taiwan has been the touchstone of improved U.S.-China relations since President Nixon signed the Shanghai Communiqués of 1972. But Taiwan is also the flash point in the relationship, as shown in 1996 when China's missile firings and live-fire military exercises in the seas surrounding Taiwan compelled the United States to send two carrier battle groups to the area. The Chinese missile firings were themselves a reaction to the government of Taiwan's pursuit of more "international space" in which to represent its people and economy, as well as to the 1995 visit of Taiwan's leader, Lee Teng-hui, to his American alma mater, Cornell University. Chinese leaders tend to interpret the pursuit of international space by Taiwan as the pursuit of independence in disguise. In this regard we believe they are unreasonably suspicious.

Taiwan is prosperous and democratic. Its growing opposition Democratic Progressive Party (DPP) has advocated independence, or at least self-determination, in contrast to the ruling Kuomintang Party's (KMT) policy, dating from 1949, that Taiwan is part of China and must be reunited with it. To outflank the DPP, even some KMT leaders have moved away from the One-China stance, maintaining instead that the Republic of China is a de facto state (and thus has no need to declare independence). Thus China sees Taiwan drifting away. But reunification is the highest priority of Chinese national security policy, reflecting a widely and emotionally held view that Taiwan's separation is one of the last unmended instances of China's historical dismemberment by foreign powers.

In the face of this volatile and changing situation, the United States probably cannot improve on its long-standing policy toward the two parties. This One-China policy is laid down in the three communiqués negotiated bilaterally with Beijing by Presidents Nixon, Carter, and Reagan, and in the 1979 Taiwan Relations Act sponsored by Senator Robert Dole. The One-China policy maintains that Taiwan is part of China and recognizes Beijing and not Taipei as its capital. But the policy also holds that the final resolution on Taiwan should be peaceful and on terms worked out by both sides. The act further commits the United States to help Taiwan maintain the military means to prevent coercion by Beijing.

The One-China policy correctly leaves to the parties the task of working out the terms of reunification, allows for plenty of time to do so, and discourages provocation by either side, while allowing the United States to have good relations with both. The United States should not adopt a direct mediating role between Beijing and Taipei, which it has prudently refrained from doing since 1972. But within the framework of the One-China policy, the United States can and should take additional actions to avert conflicts between China and Taiwan that would catch the United States in the middle.

The danger arises from a scenario like the one that led to the 1996 missile-firing crisis: Taiwan's politicians, either vying for the approval of that portion of the island's electorate that favors independence or seeking more international space for its people and economy, take actions interpreted in Beijing as a bid for independence. Beijing uses force—missile firings, blockade, or other steps—to try to intimidate Taipei. The United States government finds itself caught between two strands of American opinion, one unwilling to see a prosperous market-oriented democracy attacked by its giant communist neighbor, and another unwilling to go to war with mainland China over Taiwan.

The way to avoid such a Hobson's choice is to encourage stronger practical linkages across the Taiwan Strait. Better relations between Beijing and Taipei would provide both with a greater stake in nonviolence, better means to avoid dangerous miscalculations of each other's intentions, and a shared understanding of just how much international space is appropriate for Taiwan. The U.S. One-China policy, which supports neither the use of force by Beijing nor independence for Taipei, forms the necessary backdrop for an improvement in cross-strait relations. The United States should emphasize that neither Beijing (through force) nor Taipei (through the pursuit of independence) should try to change the status quo.

The United States should, however, go beyond reaffirming the One-China policy. Now that the cross-strait talks that were suspended by Beijing in 1995 are resuming, the United States should encourage an agenda that can lead to early and specific agreements. The agenda should be concrete and should focus initially on three topics: increasing cross-strait contact; agreement on the degree of international space for Taiwan; and development of confidence-building measures.

First, the two parties should come to agreement on ways to increase cross-strait intercourse in areas such as business and cultural contacts, communications and transport links; antidrug, antismuggling, and anticrime initiatives; customs cooperation; and air traffic control. The establishment of direct flights between the mainland and Taiwan would be a good start, improving cultural contacts and allowing easier access for cross-strait business and investment. An agreement on this matter and greater contact across the Taiwan Strait in the other areas of trade and communications—including the establishment of direct shipping links—would have near-term, tangible benefits for both sides.

Second, the two parties should also seek agreement on a practical and appropriate measure of international space for Taiwan. This agreement should be a balance between the extremes of diplomatic recognition, which is still sought on some occasions by Taipei, and the tendency sometimes exhibited by Beijing toward total isolation of Taiwan. In particular, a formula should be explored whereby Taipei is represented in a wide range of intergovernmental organizations in which statehood is not required for membership, an arrangement that has been adopted successfully with the Asian Development Bank and the Olympic Games.

It appears that some key agreements could be reached in the near term. A reasonable beginning would be for Beijing to relax its opposition to financial contributions by Taiwan to the Korean Peninsula Energy Development Organization (KEDO). KEDO provides funding for the North Korean light-water reactors that the United States, together with South Korea and Japan, agreed to provide North Korea in exchange for the latter's freeze and eventual dismantlement of its nuclear weapons development program.[2] The Asian financial crisis has put this crucial program at risk, and Taiwan is both willing and able to provide assistance. Allowing Taiwan to participate in KEDO would not constitute diplomatic recognition, but it would give Taiwan as an economy an opportunity to play a role in a regional nonproliferation effort. The two sides should also begin to come to agreement on Taipei's participation in international economic organizations such as the International Monetary Fund (IMF) and the World Bank. There is precedent in this area, since the two were able to agree on Taiwan's participation in both the Asian Development Bank and the Asia-Pacific Economic Cooperation Council. The IMF is playing a strong role in trying to facilitate Asia's recovery from the 1998 financial crisis. Taiwan, which was affected by the crisis but not as severely as other countries in the region, could contribute to the IMF's efforts and thus take part in an organization dealing with a serious regional issue. Taiwan's participation in the IMF and the World Bank would also give due recognition to the strength and importance of Taiwan's economy, without taking a position on the political aspects of Taiwan's existence vis-à-vis mainland China.

Finally, Beijing and Taipei should develop a formula to allow Taiwan to participate in international counterproliferation regimes and technical organizations such as the Missile Technology Control Regime and the International Atomic Energy Agency. Such participation by Taiwan would enhance international oversight of Taiwan's nuclear and weapons-related activities and would provide a useful opportunity for Taiwan to achieve some international space that also serves the broader interests of the international community.

Third, confidence-building measures between the militaries of Taiwan and China should be developed. At present, in the event of a crisis the two sides have no designated means of communicating with one another. Development of contacts and confidence-building measures can reduce tension levels and provide a means to avert a crisis and avoid dangerous miscalculations. In addition, even under Beijing's current proposals for unification, Taiwan would maintain control of its military forces after reunification with the mainland. Thus, the two militaries should begin to build a long-term relationship and lay the groundwork for future cooperation and coordination.

In encouraging the parties to pursue this three-part agenda, the United States should urge them to set aside their sterile disputes over a "formula" describing the status of Taiwan before unification. It should also stress that they should defer premature consideration of the terms upon which the "two systems" might ultimately reunite to become one China. Unification will seem both more plausible and less urgent to people on both sides of the strait if they have working economic, cultural, and political relationships. In addition, the people of Taiwan will enjoy greater international representation and dignity. Only much later might the discussions evolve into talks on political topics such as a formula

covering Taiwan's relationship to mainland China before unification and the nature of the eventual relationship of Taiwan to mainland China after reunification. Beijing favors discussion of these
latter topics, but Taipei is wary of allowing the cross-strait discussions to stray into such areas. The United States should encourage
dialogue on the functional issues, while supporting an evolution
toward discussion of the more contentious political issues as the
linkages increase and improve.

The U.S. government is constrained when it comes to the issue
of Taiwan and, therefore, unofficial (track-two) dialogue can play
an important role; track-two representatives can contribute more
to cross-strait relations than the U.S. government is willing or able
to do. Track-two efforts should endeavor to create working relationships with Taiwan's military and begin to encourage the development of confidence-building measures and military contacts
across the Taiwan Strait. The steady reduction of tensions across
the strait would remove obstacles to greater cooperation between
Washington and Taipei.

Engage China's Neighbors

The United States needs to begin to promote with China a
shared vision of an East Asian security system for the coming
decades. In this shared vision, the United States and its allies
would not seek to contain China, but neither would China seek to
undermine the U.S. forward military presence or its alliances. The
U.S. presence reassures China's neighbors in the region that
China's emergence can proceed without threatening them.
Conversely, the U.S. presence also serves China's interests by
greatly reducing the incentive for regional powers to rearm
against it. One sign of the success of Preventive Defense in East
Asia would be open recognition by China of the benefits of the
U.S. presence in East Asia, just as the European powers have wel-
comed U.S. forces there for fifty years. An explicit statement by
China to this effect would be a step in the right direction, and U.S.
policy should work toward this end. The United States can do so
with attention to a number of areas, including multilateral mili-

Top: At the edge of an underground silo holding an SS-24 intercontinental ballistic missile on the authors' first trip to Pervomaysk, Ukraine, in March 1994. The nuclear warheads have been removed for shipment to Russia for dismantlement. William Perry is third from left. Above, U.S. and Ukrainian officials at Pervomaysk, March–April 1995. U.S. officials, from left, Nunn-Lugar Program coordinator Gloria Duffy, Deputy Assistant Secretary of Defense Elizabeth Sherwood, interpreter (in front of Smith), Assistant to the Secretary of Defense Harold P. Smith, Undersecretary of Defense for Acquisition and Technology Paul Kaminski, Perry, Ashton Carter. The Ukrainian defense minister, Valeriy Shmarov, stands to Perry's left.

Second trip to Pervomaysk, March–April 1995. The authors in front of an SS-19 missile silo as the missile is removed for dismantlement.

Third trip to Pervomaysk, January 1996. The missile silo shown on previous pages is destroyed with high explosives. Officials examine the remains of the silo.

Third trip to Pervomaysk, January 1996. Perry joins hands with his Ukrainian and Russian counterparts, Valeriy Shmarov and Pavel Grachev, on a viewing stand above the demolished silo. Carter is at left.

Fourth trip to Pervomaysk, June 1996. Top, Perry and Defense Ministers Shmarov and Grachev plant sunflowers at the site of the demolished SS-19 silo. Carter is at right. Below, the authors visit housing for retired officers from the former Pervomaysk missile base built by the United States under the Nunn-Lugar program.

Top, NAOC arrives to an honor guard at Moscow, April 1995. Perry is escorted by Deputy Defense Minister Andrei Kokoshin, who later became national security adviser to Russian President Boris Yeltsin. Above, strategy session in the conference room aboard NAOC en route to Geneva for the first meeting with Russian Defense Minister Pavel Grachev to discuss the participation of Russian troops in the Bosnia peacekeeping force, October 1995. From left, Deputy Secretary of State Strobe Talbott; Perry; Undersecretary of Defense Walter B. Slocombe; Slocombe military aide Colonel K. C. Brown; Acting Deputy Assistant Secretary of Defense Brigadier General Tip Osterthaler; Joint Chiefs of Staff Director for Strategic Plans and Policy (later Supreme Allied Commander, Europe) Lieutenant General Wesley Clark; Carter; National Security Council Senior Director for Europe Alexander Vershbow

Top, Perry at joint U.S.-Ukrainian exercise, Lviv, Ukraine, May 1995. Above, "Peacekeeper-95" joint U.S.-Russian exercise, Fort Riley, Kansas, October 1995. From left, Russian Brigade Commander Col. Veryanov, Russian Division Commander Gen.-Maj. Sokolov, Grachev, Deputy Assistant Secretary of Defense Elizabeth Sherwood, Perry, Carter, Senior Military Assistant to the Secretary of Defense Lieutenant General Randy House.

Top, Perry and Carter brief Russian senior officers en route to joint U.S.-Russian peacekeeping exercise at Fort Riley, Kansas, October 1995. Russian officers, seated from left, Defense Minister Grachev, Russian General Staff Chief of Main Operations Directorate Gen.-Col. Barynkin, General Staff Chief of International Affairs Directorate Gen.-Col. Kharchenko. Above, Chairman of the Joint Chiefs of Staff General John M. Shalikashvili and Perry display the detonator used by Perry and Grachev to trigger demolition of U.S. Minuteman missile silo, Whiteman Air Force Base, October 1995.

Top, Perry and Grachev in the cockpit of the B-2 stealth bomber, Whiteman Air Force Base, October 1995. Grachev was the first Russian defense official allowed to approach the once-secret plane. Above, "NATO + Russia = Success." From left, Supreme Allied Commander in Europe General George Joulwan; Perry; Grachev; Russian Bosnia commander Colonel-General Leontiy Shevtsov. Carter at left rear. Brussels, November 1995.

Top, "The Turning Point." Secretary of State Warren Christopher, Perry, and Shalikashvili at the London conference during which NATO moved toward intervention in Bosnia, July 1995. Above, U.S. forces enter Bosnia over a pontoon bridge constructed by army engineers, January 1996. The bridge had to be doubled in length when winter rains caused the Sava River to flood.

Top, Perry presents the Legion of Merit to Gen.-Maj. Lentsov, commander of the Russian brigade in Bosnia, June 1996. Above, Perry, NATO Secretary General Javier Solana, Shalikashvili, Carter, and U.S. Ambassador to NATO Robert Hunter at the Pentagon, June 1996.

Top, a Russian nuclear missile submarine is dismantled at Severodvinsk shipyard, Russia, with assistance from the Nunn-Lugar program, October 1996. Above, Senators Joseph Lieberman, Sam Nunn, and Richard Lugar hold submarine models while visiting Severodvinsk with Carter and Perry. On the far right is Laura Holgate, DOD's special coordinator for the Nunn-Lugar program.

Top, Perry with President Jiang Zemin of China, October 1994. Above, the demilitarized zone between South and North Korea, April 1994.

Top, Perry examines damage from terrorist attack on Khobar Towers barracks, Saudi Arabia, July 1996. Above, Perry and German Defense Minister Volker Rühe are briefed on training for Bosnia at Hohenfels, Germany, November 1995. The commander of the training base wished the weather had been even more severe to prepare the troops adequately for a Bosnian winter.

tary engagement and China's relations with Japan, Korea, South Asia, Southeast Asia, and Central Asia.

The United States conducts a variety of multilateral military contacts with other nations in the region. China has generally declined to participate in these activities, but it should be encouraged to send observers and ultimately participants to them.

The relationship between China and Japan is one of the key relationships that will have the greatest impact on the future security of East Asia. Mutual distrust is fueled by underlying historical grievances. Bad China-Japan relations make U.S. bilateral relationships with both states more difficult. A contentious relationship between Japan and China is also destabilizing for the entire region. The United States should, therefore, encourage the policies begun in 1998 by China and Japan to develop confidence-building measures and dialogue on security matters in East Asia that will enhance mutual trust and transparency and encourage them to engage in direct military-to-military exchanges.

The United States and Japan jointly should attempt to come to an understanding with China on how this relationship could be mutually beneficial. The U.S. presence in, and relationship with, Japan is the cornerstone of U.S. security policy in the Asia-Pacific region. The Chinese have viewed the U.S. alliance with Japan as a means for the United States to maintain its dominant role in Asia and to limit Chinese ambitions for regional influence. There was great dismay in China when the U.S.-Japan Defense Guidelines were renewed in 1997, as Beijing saw in the guidelines a prescription for a U.S.-Japanese effort to contain China while protecting Taiwan. The United States and Japan should engage China jointly, rather than independently, to explain the importance of a continued U.S. presence to present and future regional stability and security. This "joint engagement" serves to underscore the strategic relationship between the United States and Japan and to enhance the dialogue between China and Japan.

The United States should also seek China's cooperation in maintaining peace on the Korean peninsula. The United States and China are already working together in the four-party talks to stabilize the situation on the peninsula and ultimately create a final peace settlement. The United States and China share a desire to avoid war on the peninsula and to stabilize the demilitarized zone, and they also share a sentiment that reunification should not be rushed.

The United States and China should also continue to work together, along with South Korea and Japan, to ensure that the freeze on North Korea's nuclear program is sustained. China's political and diplomatic support, as well as its understanding of the internal workings of North Korea, can be useful in helping to ensure that this freeze continues. At some point, the question of U.S. forces on the peninsula will be addressed in the four-party talks, and the United States must be ready to discuss what the future security provisions for a reunified peninsula will be. In the process of discussing the presence of U.S. troops, the United States should once again underscore the stabilizing influence of U.S. forces in East Asia. Cooperation on Korea can serve as a "success" for China-U.S. relations and a model for future cooperation on East Asian security issues more broadly.

Among the reasons, both international and domestic, that impelled India to conduct nuclear weapons tests in May 1998, prompting Pakistan to follow suit, was New Delhi's troubled relationship and nascent strategic competition with Beijing. The United States and China view the specter of an arms race on the subcontinent from very different positions. Nevertheless, they share an interest in preventing further escalation or fatal miscalculation by India and Pakistan and in preserving the nonproliferation regime, and there is an opportunity for close consultation and cooperation. In addition, the United States can encourage better relations between India and China, including resolution of their long-standing border dispute. In particular, China should be encouraged not to return to its pattern of strategic cooperation with Pakistan directed against India, a policy "tilt" that China had been leveling throughout the decade preceding the 1998 Indian and Pakistani nuclear tests.

A major concern often cited for the future stability and security of Asia is the long list of remaining territorial disputes, particularly those involving the Spratly Islands, which are thought to contain significant oil and gas deposits. Chinese moves in the early 1990s involving these islands caused concern in Southeast Asian capitals. While it would be an overstatement of the case to attribute the Asian arms buildup exclusively to concerns over Chinese aggression, it seems clear that these outstanding territorial disputes and the hostility with which claims are pursued do not promote regional stability and confidence. The United States should maintain its current policy and take no position on the question of which country or countries the islands belong to. But the United States should encourage China to pursue multilateral efforts to reach agreement on joint exploration of the oil and gas deposits in the area. The removal of these bones of contention would help to assure the states of Southeast Asia that China could be a good security partner and neighbor, rather than a regional bully against which they must arm.

There are substantial energy reserves in Central Asia and the Caspian region, to which China, along with most of the rest of the world, will require access in coming decades. The stability of this region will become increasingly important as its role as an energy supplier increases. There are potential sources of instability in this region, placed as it is at the nexus of nearly all the major Asian powers. Further, the breakup of the Soviet Union resulted in several new states that are striving to establish independent security strategies. The United States and China both have a strong interest in the future peace and stability of this region. The United States could begin to discuss with China, and with states of the region such as Kazakhstan, Uzbekistan, and Turkmenistan, the future security of that region and the future role of China as both neighbor and energy importer.

Encourage China to Participate in Global Security Efforts

In addition to encouraging China's greater involvement in regional security matters, the United States should encourage China to play a stronger and more constructive role in global security. China's development has benefited from a stable global order; China should increasingly contribute to creating and maintaining that order. Chinese leaders recognize that global interests carry global responsibilities, but Chinese rhetoric still often criticizes U.S. leadership as "hegemonism." In reply, the United States should point out that U.S. leadership more often involves catalyzing cooperative action among countries with common interests than a unilateral exercise of power, and that it is being used to defend precisely those interests that China will share with the United States in the next century. U.S. policy should be to promote China's entry into the organizations and institutions that make up the global order and to urge China to play a role in strengthening and creating them. The latter, a policy of preventive defense, is clearly distinct from a policy of containment, because it encourages Chinese participation and influence while containment would discourage it.

An example of global order is the nonproliferation regime. In decades past, Maoist ideology kept China outside the major agreements that counter nuclear, chemical, biological, and ballistic missile proliferation. Then, in 1984, China acceded to the Biological Weapons Convention, and it has gradually joined or otherwise indicated adherence to a growing number of such norms. In 1992 China acceded to the Nuclear Nonproliferation Treaty. It also agreed to abide by the Missile Technology Control Regime (MTCR) in 1992 (a commitment it reaffirmed in 1994), signed the Chemical Weapons Convention in 1993, signed the Comprehensive Test Ban Treaty in 1996, and joined the Zangger Committee in 1997.[3]

China still stands outside of some key regimes, and the United States should continue to urge its membership. For instance, though it agreed to abide by MTCR provisions, China is not a formal member of the MTCR. It is also not a formal member of the Nuclear Suppliers Group or the Wassenaar Arrangement.[4] Efforts should be made to bring China into all three regimes.

Even while China has begun to join such regimes, however, it has continued to make troubling transfers of weapons and technology to two states, Pakistan and Iran. There is evidence that China sold Pakistan ring magnets that can be used in a gas centrifuge to enrich uranium for a nuclear weapon, as well as other nuclear weapons–related equipment.[5] There is evidence that China has transferred M-11 short-range missiles and components to Pakistan, raising serious questions about China's 1992 and 1994 commitments to abide by the MTCR. There is also evidence that China has transferred materials and equipment for uranium enrichment to Iran, as well as other nuclear-related technology, anti-ship cruise missiles, ballistic missile technology, and chemical weapons precursor materials.

More recently, however, China has undertaken to stop these transfers. It has done so in part to improve its relations with the United States, but China no doubt also acknowledges its own future dependence on Middle East oil and the direct risk to itself of destabilizing the region.

The next step in this evolution would see China not only abide strictly by its undertakings regarding Pakistan and Iran, but also become not just an adherent of global nonproliferation norms but a codesigner and enforcer of such norms and regimes. China has objected to joining regimes that it had no role in shaping. The United States should, therefore, seek appropriate opportunities for China to lead and to play a shaping role in international regimes.

U.S. pressure on China regarding its fidelity to global regimes is likely to have only partial success in affecting its proliferation behavior. U.S. policy must also focus on what is driving Chinese proliferation behavior, which has been selective and directed primarily toward Pakistan and Iran. Therefore, U.S. policy must turn its attention to the regional policies and strategic imperatives that influence China's proliferation behavior. The United States should begin to discuss with China how it views the future security of each of these states and regions, including the potential for nuclear war in South Asia or a further destabilized Middle East, with all that the latter implies for world oil prices and China's own growing need for imported oil. Further, the United States should urge China to recognize and acknowledge that the overall development of U.S.-China relations depends on progress in the area of proliferation, an issue of great importance to Americans.

Finally, U.S. sanctions policy should be rationalized, and the United States should be less ready to resort to sanctions when evidence of Chinese proliferation comes to light. Sanctions tend to be seen in China merely as reflections of American domestic politics, not as part of any consistent international policy. The current honeycomb of uncoordinated sanctions laws is ineffective and a burden on policymaking. Although the United States needs to rationalize its sanctions policy, it should continue to maintain control of the transfer of munitions to China, since it is not now in the U.S. national interest to strengthen Chinese military capabilities. Careful review of controls on dual-use exports is warranted in order to give appropriate balance to national security and economic objectives.

Conclusion

As the most portentous geostrategic development in America's westward vista, the emergence of China is a development that calls for a Preventive Defense strategy. The United States now has an opportunity to influence how China comes to define itself and its role in the international system of the twenty-first century and to influence in which direction China-U.S. relations will evolve.

"Containing" China is not a viable option. Such a strategy could produce precisely the adversarial kind of China we would like to avoid, and both the American public and America's allies in the region are unlikely to support the kind of expense and effort that would be required to pursue such a risky and difficult strategy. Instead, the United States should grasp this moment of improving relations with China and use its strong position of power and influence to build a solid foundation for U.S.-China relations and to shape that relationship to both countries' present and future mutual benefit.

CHAPTER 4

Standing at the Brink in North Korea: The Counterproliferation Imperative

It was June 16, 1994, and Joint Chiefs of Staff Chairman General John Shalikashvili and General Gary Luck, who ably commanded our forces in Korea, had joined me in the Cabinet Room where we were waiting for President Clinton. I had been in office as secretary of defense just four months, and I was deep in the crisis that would prove to be the most serious during my tenure. I went over the "talking points" prepared by my staff, which sketched out how we should explain to the president the difficult choice he had to make. As I reviewed them, however, I decided that they did not capture the seriousness of the situation. I modified them to start with a pungent statement attributed to John Kenneth Galbraith: "Politics is not the art of the possible. Rather it consists of choosing between what is disastrous and what is merely unpalatable." We were about to give the president a choice between a disastrous option—allowing North Korea to get a nuclear arsenal, which we might have to face someday—and an unpalatable option,

Carter was not present for the events described in the first part of this chapter, so Perry tells this story himself.

blocking this development, but thereby risking a destructive non-nuclear war. How had we gotten to this position?

North Korea's Weapons of Mass Destruction Programs

North Korea, a desperately poor nation with a population just over 20 million, is the last Stalinist nation remaining in the world. More than four decades earlier, it had been defeated in its attempt to take control of South Korea by force, but its leaders had never given up on this goal. North Korea maintains one of the largest armies in the world. Its million-man ground force is outnumbered only by the armies of Russia and China and is more than twice the size of the U.S. Army, which has 450,000 active-duty troops. For the last few decades, the North Koreans have maintained their army in a state of combat readiness, including a menacing "forward deployment," with two-thirds of their ground forces based less than 100 kilometers from the border with South Korea.

Twice in the last year I had visited Korea. In 1993 I met with General Bob RisCassi, then commander of the Combined Forces in Korea, and in 1994 with his successor, General Gary Luck. General Riscassi had taken me to the DMZ, the demilitarized zone that had been established as a part of the armistice agreement that ended the fighting in the Korean War. I had come to think that every American should visit the DMZ for a firsthand understanding of the danger posed by the North Korean military, which has staged repeated incidents there during the years; several of them had resulted in the deaths of American or South Korean soldiers. Just as the North Korean government is the last remnant of Stalin's influence, the DMZ is the last remnant of the cold war. My visit there felt truly surreal. The North Korean flag just across the border was huge, having grown through the years to stupendous proportions to ensure that it was always larger than the South Korean flag flying on the other side of the border. The North Koreans had installed monstrous loudspeakers to barrage the South Korean and American troops with inane propaganda. I stared at North Korean troops through binoculars from our defensive positions, and soon they were staring right back at me through the windows of the DMZ conference room. This room has, for forty years, been the scene of literally thousands of contentious but sterile and inconclusive meetings. Americans assigned to the armistice team are mercifully rotated out of these frustrating assignments every year, lest they lose their sense of reality. But I was told that one man had been head of the North Korean armistice team for more than thirty years.

Aside from staging bad political theater at the DMZ, the North Korean Army was posing a truly dangerous threat to South Korea and American forces based there. Through the years, these North Korean forces had been deterred by a Republic of Korea force about half their size, a small but powerful U.S. force comprising 37,000 troops of all three services, and the capability to reinforce U.S. troops rapidly in a crisis. In a day or two, we could dramatically increase our air power in South Korea using fighter aircraft ordinarily based in Alaska, Japan, and Hawaii. A small but important part of our ground reinforcements also could be available in a number of days, because we had pre-positioned tanks and other heavy equipment in South Korea so they could be "married up" quickly with troops flown in from the United States. But most of the ground reinforcements would have to be sent from the United States by sea and would take about a month to get into position. Thus, defending South Korea from a surprise attack from North Korea would depend on a well-planned and well-executed reinforcement of American troops, which we practiced and demonstrated convincingly every year in one of the military's largest overseas deployment exercises, called Team Spirit.[1] This tense face-off of military forces in Korea was certainly not a desirable situation, but for a long time it appeared to be stable. Deterrence appeared to be working.

Then, about a decade before, North Korea initiated a nuclear reactor program near the town of Yongbyon. Eventually the program encompassed a small test operating reactor, larger reactors under construction, and a large processing facility that could convert the spent fuel from the reactors into weapon-usable plutonium. The entire Yongbyon facility was subject to inspections by the International Atomic Energy Agency (IAEA) under the Nuclear Nonproliferation Treaty (NPT), to which North Korea was a signatory.

However, the North Koreans had constant disputes with the IAEA about access for the inspectors. As a consequence, in 1989, when the North Koreans unloaded some of the fuel rods from the operating reactor, they did so without IAEA supervision. Our intelligence assessment was that the North Koreans had reprocessed some of the spent fuel they had unloaded from the reactor, recovering weapon-usable plutonium, but neither the American team nor the IAEA knew whether they had reprocessed all or only some of the spent fuel. The size of the reactor told us that if all the unloaded fuel had been reprocessed, the North Koreans could have enough plutonium to make one and possibly two atomic bombs.

By the fall of 1993, the operating reactor was nearing completion of its initial fuel cycle, and its entire load of fuel rods would be ready for reprocessing in a few months. If all of this fuel were to be reprocessed, it would yield enough plutonium for another five or six nuclear weapons. Moreover, if the reactor were to move into full-scale operation, it could yield enough plutonium for ten or twelve nuclear bombs a year. When the larger reactors were completed, their total capacity would amount to scores of bombs per year.

We believed that such a development would create intolerable risks. This was not just another nonproliferation issue to be dealt with by our diplomats and the IAEA; this had the potential of dramatically increasing the military threat to South Korea, to the U.S. troops in South Korea, to Japan, our essential ally in the region, and indeed, to nations all over the world. We took a much more serious view of this proliferation issue because the military situation in Korea was dramatically different from any other place in the world, because of the tense military situation on the Korean Peninsula, North Korea's history of extreme behavior, and our concern that North Korea might sell some of this plutonium to rogue nations or terrorists to get desperately needed hard currency.

Therefore, as North Korea prepared to unload the fuel from the reactor in late 1993 and early 1994, U.S. diplomats worked intensively with the IAEA to persuade the North Koreans to allow the reactor and its defueling to be inspected, a normal practice for NPT signatories. The IAEA also pressed North Korea to submit to "special inspections" that would involve digging up the waste from their earlier reprocessing to see if they had obtained the one or two bombs' worth of plutonium we feared they might have.

North Korea's response was to threaten to suspend its membership in the NPT and the normal refueling inspections; it declared that it had no intention whatsoever of allowing special inspections, which it viewed, with some justification, as a novel burden designed by the IAEA just for it.

Initially the U.S. government supported the IAEA position. But beginning in 1993 some in the Pentagon, especially Undersecretary John Deutch, a chemist, and Assistant Secretary Ashton Carter, a physicist, began to have their doubts. They brought their concerns to Les Aspin, then secretary of defense, and to me, then deputy secretary. The IAEA position, Deutch and Carter argued, might be consistent with the NPT and IAEA procedures, but from the point of view of security for our troops in Korea and our allies in the region, it demanded both too little and too much of North Korea. That is, merely inspecting the defueling and reprocessing of the fuel rods was not sufficient security protection; the North Korean nuclear program should be eliminated, not just inspected. After all, the North Koreans could "suspend" their membership in the NPT at any time, take possession of the plutonium they had reprocessed, and build nuclear weapons. They would be just months away from making nuclear bombs out of a growing hoard of plutonium.

On the other hand, Deutch and Carter argued, the special inspections only reinforced the North Koreans' belief that they were being singled out by the IAEA for discriminatory treatment, while offering little security benefit. Aspin and I accepted their analysis and began to argue that the United States should switch from the IAEA position to a new position emphasizing a demand that North Korea freeze all of its future nuclear operations but deferring "special" inspections of its past operations. Regional experts Charles Freeman and Stanley Roth on my staff advised that North Korea was intent on turning its dispute with the IAEA into a dispute with the United States anyway. So it was important, we argued, that the United States have its own policy, supportive of but independent of the IAEA.

By the spring of 1994, I had succeeded Les Aspin as secretary of defense, and time was running out. The fuel was ready to be removed from the Yongbyon reactor, and no agreement had been reached for IAEA supervision to ensure that it would not be reprocessed into weapon-usable plutonium. North Korea had flatly refused the "special" inspections that would look into their previous fuel rod removal. By May the negotiations between North Korea and the IAEA had broken down. North Korea had ordered the IAEA inspectors to leave Yongbyon and had announced that it was preparing to reprocess the spent fuel. We were faced with the highly dangerous prospect that North Korea could, within months, have five or six nuclear bombs and an active weapons program. My senior military and civilian policy advisers all agreed with my assessment that this would pose an unacceptable risk and that the United States had to seek the elimination of the North Korean nuclear program but could forsake special inspections. This view began to gain ground within the administration.

I asked General Shalikashvili and General Luck to update OPLAN (Operation Plan) 5027, our military plan for defeating a North Korean attack. I also asked for an update of a contingency plan, which I had requested earlier, for destroying key components at the reactor site with a military attack.

The plan for an attack on the reactor site had been presented to a small, grim group seated around the conference table in my office. The plan was impressive; it could be executed with only a few days' alert, and it would entail little or no risk of U.S. casualties during the attack. Additionally, it had been designed so that it entailed a low risk of North Korean casualties and a very low risk of radiation release into the atmosphere. The North Koreans, of course, could have rebuilt the facilities destroyed by the attack, but without question it would have achieved its objective of setting back their nuclear program many years.

However, both General Shalikashvili and I had concluded that such an attack was very likely to incite the North Koreans to launch a military attack on South Korea. Even though the North Koreans would surely lose this second Korean War, they could cause hundreds of thousands, perhaps millions, of casualties before being defeated. Therefore, I decided against recommending this option to the president at that time. Instead, I would support Secretary of State Warren Christopher's approach. He favored putting pressure on the North Koreans with a program of tough sanctions. The sanctions strategy, while not without risk, was not so likely to lead to war; moreover, if it failed, the military option could be reconsidered.

As a result of skilled diplomacy conducted by Secretary Christopher and his team, within a few days the Republic of Korea and Japan joined forces with the United States at the United Nations in demanding that North Korea stop its nuclear program or face severe economic sanctions. North Korea responded by threatening to "turn Seoul into a sea of flames." A few days later it announced that it would deem the imposition of sanctions an "act of war." Some viewed these threats as simply bombast and rhetoric, but I thought it would be irresponsible to shrug off the threats, particularly given the enormous military force North Korea had poised on the border, the desperate state of its economy, and its political isolation. The North Koreans were in a corner and might lash out in desperation.

On June 14, 1994, therefore, I called a meeting of the U.S. military leaders who would be most intimately involved if a military conflict broke out. General Luck flew back from Korea to report on his assessment of the situation, how he would execute OPLAN 5027 if that became necessary, and what actions he wanted to take immediately to prepare for that contingency. Besides myself and General Shalikashvili, the small group who participated in that intense meeting in the Joint Chiefs' "tank" included the commander of our forces in the Pacific; the commander of our forces in the Persian Gulf, because we were concerned that once our attention seemed to be diverted, Saddam Hussein would take the opportunity to start trouble in Kuwait; and the commander of the transportation command, because we were considering a massive transportation of troops, weapons, and supplies. General Luck's plan to prepare for the possibility of hostilities was laid out with great care and expertise and, typically, gave the decisionmakers several options.

Our review of General Luck's plans took two long days and resulted in some modifications. In particular, we wanted the plan to fully reflect that nuclear weapons were not the only weapons of mass destruction that North Korea had been working on. They clearly had chemical weapons, and their interest in biological weapons and ballistic missiles was also evident. We enhanced the plans to deal more effectively with the possibility that North Korea might use some of its large stock of chemical weapons to disrupt the airfields and ports upon which our reinforcement depended. The airfields were critical to our reliance on air superiority to stop the invading force; the ports were critical to our ability to bring in more ground forces to throw back the invading force. We had to be sure that we had adequate chemical defense suits to protect personnel from such an attack and procedures that allowed the airfields and ports to continue effective operation even with our personnel so encumbered. As for the one or two nuclear weapons that North Korea might conceivably have built with the plutonium from the first few fuel rods, Luck concluded that although North Korea could use them to add to the carnage of the war, they would not change the eventual result, namely, the defeat of North Korea.

With these modifications, we concluded that we could deal with any contingency that the North Koreans could present us and still not be vulnerable to an opportunistic "second front" started by Iraq. In short, in a few days we had updated the plans for fighting two major regional contingencies (the plan referred to by Pentagon planners as "2MRCs"). I decided to submit the modified contingency plans immediately to the president for his review and approval, along with my recommendation in support of General Shalikashvili's request for a large, immediate increase in our forces deployed in Korea.

A Reprieve

Thus, on that day in June 1994, as General Shalikashvili and I waited in the Cabinet Room to present the military options to

President Clinton and the National Security Council, we knew that we were poised on the brink of a war that might involve weapons of mass destruction. When the president entered the room, he was much more solemn than usual; indeed, everyone there recognized the gravity of the situation.

I reviewed the situation with the president and then told him that we had prepared three options to get ready to defeat a North Korean attack, if that became the only way we could block the North Koreans from getting a nuclear arsenal. I pointed out that none of these alternatives involved our initiating military action against North Korea, but that they all involved increasing our military forces in South Korea, one of them by a very considerable increment. All of these alternatives, I said, were certain to be considered provocative by North Korea: there was no risk-free course of action. We had to choose between an "unpalatable" option and a "disastrous" option. I pointed out that while we had taken all feasible precautions in the proposed deployments, we could not rule out the possibility of a preemptive strike by the North Koreans when they saw us making these deployments. General Shalikashvili then proceeded to give a military analysis of each of the three deployment options.

President Clinton was within minutes of selecting and authorizing one of these deployment options when the meeting was interrupted by a phone call. Former President Jimmy Carter had gone to North Korea at the invitation of Kim Il Sung. His visit was unofficial but had been coordinated with National Security Adviser Anthony Lake. He had just finished two days of meetings with Kim Il Sung, the aging North Korean leader, and was calling to report that Kim was willing to negotiate an agreement on North Korea's nuclear program with the United States. Just as Freeman and Roth had predicted, the North Koreans preferred to deal directly with the United States rather than the IAEA.

This offer from Kim Il Sung was ambiguous and could very well lead into a cul-de-sac. Still, it was a hopeful development, since it averted for the time being the potential provocation of the buildup we had proposed. It was crucial, however, that Kim agree to address our fundamental problem. The United States should not simply seek compliance with IAEA inspection rules while fuel was unloaded and plutonium reprocessed; we should seek a halt and eventual dismantlement of North Korea's capability to build nuclear weapons. On the other hand, special inspections, so offensive to North Korea, were unnecessary.

The president instructed Lake to reply on behalf of the U.S. government to the message conveyed from North Korea by Jimmy Carter. The United States, the message went, would be willing to begin negotiations provided that the North Koreans would freeze all activities at Yongbyon while negotiations were under way, and that negotiations would point the way to a permanent end of the nuclear dimension of the North Korean military threat. Direct U.S.-North Korean negotiations began shortly thereafter and were conducted brilliantly by Ambassador Robert Gallucci.[2] On October 21, North Korea signed the Agreed Framework proposed by Secretary of State Christopher. The Agreed Framework met our immediate objectives of freezing and inspecting the ongoing nuclear program, without insisting on early conduct of special inspections. Specifically, the agreement required North Korea to continue the freeze on its activities at Yongbyon while it dismantled its nuclear facilities there. The United States agreed to provide North Korea with fuel oil as an energy substitute for the nuclear reactor at Yongbyon that would be shut down; and South Korea, Japan, and the United States agreed to construct two power-generating reactors in North Korea that produced not weapons-grade plutonium, but a less dangerous type of fuel that would be sent abroad from North Korea for reprocessing.

The Agreed Framework drew the region back from the brink of conflict. The nuclear program at Yongbyon was frozen. U.S. forces were spared the unwelcome necessity of deterring a nuclear-armed North Korea. But the North Korean chemical and biological weapons and ballistic missile programs have continued, and there is mounting evidence that North Korea may be developing a nuclear program away from the Yongbyon facility. In the meantime, Saddam Hussein continues his efforts to restart his nuclear weapon program, in defiance of United Nations inspectors. The implications for the United States are clear: we cannot count on either of the two ever-present, major regional contingencies to be "symmetric" conflicts in which the aggressor relies only on conventional weapons to attempt to prevail against America's superior conventional forces.

The next major conflict involving U.S. forces will be against an opponent armed with nuclear, chemical, biological, or ballistic missile weapons—or all of them. Therefore, the major regional conflicts that compose the B list of imminent threats are in danger of graduating to include weapons of mass destruction—in short, to graduate from the B list to the A list. Forestalling proliferation of weapons of mass destruction and preparing U.S. forces to counter them on the battlefield are therefore both important tasks of Preventive Defense.

Dealing with the Proliferation of Weapons of Mass Destruction

The story of North Korea's weapons of mass destruction program is still unfolding. So also is the story in the other theater to which U.S. forces are committed on a daily basis, the Persian Gulf. Here recent history has been deeply misleading about the future. Operation Desert Storm, watched on television by millions of Americans, was a purely conventional military conflict. As a result, most Americans suppose that American conventional superiority and the implication that the U.S. military can defend accepted interests in the Middle East and East Asia with conventional military power and with no danger to the American homeland are "facts of nature" unlikely to be overturned for decades. But this is true only with respect to military challengers who choose the same playing field of conventional warfare. Saddam Hussein did this in 1991; his military and its invasion of Kuwait looked like a smaller version of the Warsaw Pact threat against which the United States and NATO had planned for decades. Against the "hammer" of such U.S. and allied forces, Iraq obligingly configured its forces like a nail. The resulting rout in Desert Storm was deeply, though misleadingly, reassuring to Americans.

But beneath the surface of the Desert Storm victory was a sobering array of close calls and surprises involving every category of weapons of mass destruction. Iraq is now known to have made and fielded an array of biological weapons in numbers and variety not known to the U.S. military before the conflict. Its nuclear weapons program was much larger and of a totally different technical character than U.S. intelligence had suspected. Iraq was known before the war to have chemical weapons—it had used them in its war with Iran—but the U.S. military knew little about which Iraqi units had the weapons or how they might use them against coalition troops. Iraq's SCUD ballistic missiles, which ended up defining the war for many television viewers, might have changed the whole character of the war had they succeeded in provoking Israel into entering the fray.

In sum, had Saddam Hussein in 1991 been farther along in his programs to develop and deploy weapons of mass destruction, Desert Storm might well have taken a course far less reassuring to Americans, although the United States would still eventually have won. Likewise, as the story of the Agreed Framework and its sequel illustrates, North Korea has been pursuing weapons of mass destruction. The implication is clear: future military challengers of the United States will heed the lessons of Iraq's devastating defeat and will seek to pose "asymmetric threats" instead, using weapons of mass destruction in an attempt to contend with an otherwise unbeatable U.S. military and as a way of intimidating U.S. allies.

The distressing fact is that nearly all military opponents whom U.S. forces are likely to meet on the battlefield possess chemical and biological weapons and the means to deliver them, including ballistic missiles. If not countered vigorously, these weapons have the potential to transform B-list threats abruptly into new A-list threats. To prevent this, the U.S. Department of Defense needs to take a new approach to proliferation, one commensurate with the energy it normally applies to a serious military threat; it should not continue to treat proliferation as merely a diplomatic problem or an unorthodox, unlikely contingency.

The approach that we believe is needed would have two components. The first would involve developing non-nuclear counters to the use of weapons of mass destruction against U.S. forces in regional conflicts, through development of defensive protections and specialized attack and intelligence capabilities. Second, the Department of Defense would place a higher priority on contributing its resources and technical expertise to the U.S. government's overall effort to prevent weapons of mass destruction from spreading in the first place. The Nunn-Lugar program is an example of this effort, as is DOD's essential role in administering export controls that restrict the flow of dangerous technology outside of the United States.

The Counterproliferation Initiative

Early in the Clinton administration, the approach of the Defense Department to dealing with proliferation in both these dimensions— prevention and military counters—was strengthened and given a new name—"counterproliferation"—to go with a new focus.[3] Under the "Counterproliferation Initiative," much has been accomplished, but much more remains to be done. In the main, the U.S. military, like the population at large, still tends to view the "major regional conflicts" that dominate planning and budgeting as purely conventional contests. For such contests the United States is successfully continuing to lead the information technology–based "revolution in military affairs," or RMA. This revolution began in the 1970s with the development of satellite reconnaissance, smart weapons, cruise missiles, stealth aircraft, and other breakthroughs whose design and functioning would not have been possible without the microchip.[4]

Superior U.S. military technology first deterred a Warsaw Pact invasion of Europe and then handily defeated a Soviet-like conventional aggressor in Desert Storm. RMA remains the main concept propelling modernization and innovation in the U.S. military. It shows every sign of continuing to give the U.S. military a decisive edge in symmetrical warfare. But an accompanying "revolution in counterproliferation affairs" is needed to deal with asymmetrical warfare, and that revolution is only beginning.

One reason for the delay is the lingering presence of a dangerously casual reliance on nonstrategic nuclear weapons to deter an enemy's use of weapons of mass destruction in regional conflict. The United States cannot and should not depend on the reliability of such deterrence when dealing with desperate and "rogue" states or with nonstate, terrorist attackers. More important, the United States has not confronted the wisdom of supposing that it would or should ever be the first nation since 1945 to detonate nuclear weapons in anger. If non-nuclear counters to asymmetrical warfare can be devised, surely they are a preferable option to nuclear response.

Non-Nuclear Counters to Weapons of Mass Destruction

Non-nuclear counters to weapons of mass destruction (WMD), especially chemical and biological weapons, are in fact feasible. A revolution in counterproliferation affairs would give counterproliferation weapons a priority equal to the weapons developed under the information technology–based revolution in military affairs. We see such an initiative as having five components. First, U.S. troops should be provided with better protective equipment to render ineffective the direct use of weapons of mass destruction on the battlefield. Such protective equipment would include vaccinations and antibiotics, chemical suits, inhalation masks, decontamination equipment, air filtration systems, and detectors of chemical and biological agents needed to tell the troops when to apply their protection. Second, key vulnerabilities should be eliminated from rear areas, especially the airfields and ports on which U.S. forces depend to reach theaters where U.S. interests are threatened. Third, special weapons and tactics should be devised to destroy weapons of mass destruction before they could be launched, a variation of the cold war's notion of "counterforce."

Fourth, U.S. troops should be provided with more effective defensive systems to intercept aircraft, cruise missiles, and ballistic missiles that might be carrying weapons of mass destruction. Theater ballistic missile defenses are being developed in a manner consistent with the Anti–Ballistic Missile (ABM) Treaty and should be fielded as soon as development is completed. Since the performance of these systems will be less than perfect, however, they are a complement to, not a substitute for, protective suits and other "passive" defenses. A defense from ballistic missile attack of U.S. territory, including Hawaii and Alaska, which are the closest U.S. territory to some potential launch areas, will also become necessary as "regional" threats like Iraq and North Korea develop and deploy intercontinental missiles. The United States should prepare to deploy such systems quickly and should seek the necessary amendment to the ABM Treaty to be sure that deployment of such limited national missile defenses are not misinterpreted as contrary to the intent of the ABM Treaty. However, these defenses are unlikely to offer perfect protection. Thus, friends and allies should be encouraged and assisted to acquire corresponding counter-proliferation capabilities, so that they have the capability to carry out their own roles in collective defense and to protect the lives and morale of their own people in a theater of battle. Important progress has already been made on counterproliferation within NATO, under the U.S.-inspired Defense Group on Proliferation (DGP), which has begun the process of spreading the Counter-proliferation Initiative to our closest allies.

Complementing these new counterproliferation capabilities must be a substantial augmentation of the intelligence and technology base that supports defense against asymmetrical threats. Analyzing foreign WMD programs has long been a priority of U.S. intelligence. However, given the tendency to view proliferation as a diplomatic problem rather than a military threat, the intelligence production effort still focuses on detailing the facilities, scientists, and technology transfers that contribute to a proliferator's WMD program. Instead this effort should focus on the mind-set, doctrine, and specific military characteristics of the WMD arsenals that have already crossed the line from proliferation to threat. Desert Storm showed that this kind of usable military intelligence on proliferators' WMD arsenals was sorely lacking. Because the United States does not have chemical or biological weapons of its own, the research laboratories and

industries that support chemical and biological counterproliferation defensive measures are meager compared to the still-large
nuclear weapons technology base. Yet a strong chemical and biological weapons technology base will be needed to devise new
detectors, protective suits and shelters, vaccines, and other equipment, and to analyze intelligence. However, much of the relevant
expertise resides in the commercial chemical and biotechnology
industries, and ways must be found to enlist that expertise in
counterproliferation protection.

Recently the Department of Defense has formed a new agency,
called the Defense Threat Reduction Agency, to pull together the
department's counterproliferation efforts. This is a good start at
institutionalizing counterproliferation. But further effort and innovation will be required, especially within the combatant commands
themselves, to provide our forces with adequate counters to
weapons of mass destruction.

Defense Department's Role in Preventing Proliferation

Counterproliferation programs of the types we recommend, if
pursued vigorously, can prevent weapons of mass destruction from
catapulting B-list threats onto the A list. But they will not altogether nullify the military and psychological impact of weapons of
mass destruction in aggressive hands.

The Department of Defense, therefore, must enhance its contribution to the government's effort to prevent proliferation from
occurring in the first place. DOD's potential contribution is large.
The international effort to prevent nuclear proliferation has
enjoyed substantial success in the 1990s. U.S. diplomacy was
essential in securing the unconditional and indefinite extension of
the Nuclear Nonproliferation Treaty in 1995. More directly, without specific U.S. interventions, most of them involving Preventive
Defense by the DOD, no fewer than six nations would probably
possess nuclear weapons that today have none: Iraq's program was
stopped by war and the imposition of UN sanctions and inspections. North Korea's Yongbyon program was frozen by the Agreed
Framework negotiated by the United States. South Africa's arsenal

was voluntarily relinquished in the transition from apartheid to majority rule, supported by U.S. policy. Ukraine, Kazakhstan, and Belarus each decided to forgo nuclear weapons inherited from the Soviet Union when the United States undertook to support their independence and assist their new militaries, help them negotiate fair compensation from Russia, and participate directly in the process of weapon dismantlement and cleanup through the Nunn-Lugar program.

On the other side of the ledger, in 1998 India and Pakistan acknowledged their long-standing nuclear capabilities and conducted underground tests of nuclear devices. Chemical, biological, and ballistic missile programs have proliferated widely despite efforts to establish global regimes of restraint through the Chemical Weapons Convention, the Biological Weapons Convention, and the Missile Technology Control Regime.

Global regimes are essential for establishing the norm against weapons of mass destruction and mobilizing international support behind counterproliferation. But the motives to proliferate are usually local, not global. The effort to prevent proliferation therefore needs tools that can be focused locally. U.S. alliances, security relationships, military presence, regional security strategies, and nuclear deterrent forces are not normally thought of as counterproliferation tools, but they are and have been historically. Many nations have found it unnecessary to resort to nuclear weapons or other weapons of mass destruction to ensure their security because of the protection and stability provided by the United States. It is wise to keep in mind not only the "rogue states" that seem now bent on proliferation but also the nations that have elected not to develop weapons of mass destruction. Our goal should be to preserve the conditions that reduce the incentives for possession of weapons of mass destruction.

Attention to incentives is all the more important today because the technological capability to proliferate is now widespread. At the end of World War II and for decades thereafter it was sufficient for the United States to control the export of its advanced technology to foreign nations. Without such technology, proliferation was impossible. But today even backward economies like North Korea can support an indigenous nuclear weapons program and a ballistic missile export business. The rising tide of advancing technology has lifted all boats, and the efficacy of export controls is correspondingly reduced.

Several other factors have contributed to the need to refocus export controls where they can still be effective. For one thing, much of the U.S. export control system was designed to limit transfers to former cold war opponents. These controls need to be reoriented to the security challenges of the post–cold war world, including counterproliferation. Other technologically advanced nations, including long-standing allies, do not always share U.S. views on what items should be controlled or which countries should be denied them. Yet U.S. controls will be of no effect if potentially threatening nations can get the technology they desire elsewhere. Thus it is crucial to secure the agreement of other nations to our export controls standards. Unfortunately, this is not always possible. Additionally, the volume of international commerce in high-technology products is so large that it is increasingly difficult for intelligence and law enforcement to sift through the haystack to find the dangerous needles. For these reasons, the export control system must focus on controlling what can actually be controlled in practical terms.

The U.S. export control system therefore faces very real dilemmas. These dilemmas are obscured when they are characterized merely as a problem of weighing the economic objective of increasing U.S. exports against the security objective of denying advanced military tools to potential opponents. The security side of the balance is itself much more complex in the post–cold war world, and the limits of controllability of dangerous technology must be recognized in crafting controls that can still be effective. The Department of Defense plays a key role in the administration of export controls, contributing its military and technical expertise to decisions about which exports of technology might contribute to military capabilities in foreign hands. It therefore needs to adjust its policies and procedures to take account of the new dilemmas.

Export controls on advanced computers are a good example of the need for adjustment. Computers are obviously helpful, indeed crucial, to proliferators designing nuclear weapons, ballistic missiles, and a host of other threatening weapons. The very fastest supercomputers are made in small numbers by only a few companies in a few countries, all of them friendly to the United States. Denying such computers to proliferators is therefore practical if the United States and its allies can agree to control their export. (If allies will not agree, of course, controls on U.S. exporters alone are of little use.) Laptop computers, on the other hand, are made in large numbers by many companies in many countries and, moreover, are sold retail to millions of buyers whose use of them cannot possibly be monitored by law enforcement. Thus they can easily be diverted to proliferators, and controls on legal exports of such computers would be both cumbersome and ineffective. The result of the march of technology and the globalization of markets on the export control system is that there is no point in requiring a license to export the computing power contained in a laptop: proliferators will get their hands on laptops if they want them. Since laptops have more computational power every year, the control level must be adjusted upward every year if the export control system is to avoid being swamped with superfluous license applications. Progressive upward adjustment of computer export control levels is thus necessary to preserve the effectiveness of the remaining controls. Although sometimes criticized as "relaxation of export controls," this process of progressive adjustment is an unavoidable consequence of technological advance and globalization. Thus while export controls still play a role in reducing proliferation, it is increasingly a less decisive role.

Conclusion

The United States, in concert with the international community, has had some real success in reducing proliferation. The proliferation of nuclear weapons, for example, has been substantially less than many observers predicted at the dawn of the nuclear age. But the United States cannot completely control the proliferation of nuclear weapons, as the recent nuclear tests in India and Pakistan demonstrated. Moreover, controls over the proliferation of chemical weapons and biological weapons and ballistic missiles are far from complete. Therefore, the national strategy is, correctly, to continue to do what we can to slow down the pressure to proliferate through protecting friends and allies, providing incentives to forgo proliferation, promoting multilateral agreements such as the Chemical Weapons Convention, and enforcing vigorously those export controls that are still useful. But because of the fundamental limitations of these actions, they cannot be America's complete strategy for dealing with dangerous proliferation threats. These actions, therefore, must be supplemented by counterproliferation programs that include passive defenses such as defensive chemical suits, active defenses such as theater missile defenses, and counterforce programs. Given the urgency of the problem, these programs should be given high priority and adequate funding.

Prevention and protection will combine to keep weapons of mass destruction from vaulting B-list regional aggressors onto the A list of mortal security dangers. The North Korean example illustrates that this danger is far from hypothetical.

CHAPTER 5

A False Alarm (This Time): Preventive Defense against Catastrophic Terrorism

For decades, the message center for the secretary of defense has been called "Cables," a title that probably dates back to the days when most of the messages to the secretary came in the form of teletypes or telegraphic cables. Today "Cables" is a multimedia message center, but its primary mission remains the same: to inform the secretary promptly, wherever he may be, of important developments that may require his immediate decision or action. Such a development occurred on July 27, 1996.

Secretary of State Warren Christopher and I had just finished a very productive meeting with our counterpart ministers in Australia. I was in my hotel room in Sydney preparing for an airplane ride to the Outback, where Ian MacLachlan, the Australian minister of defense, had invited me and a few members of my team to spend the weekend at his cattle ranch. My packing was interrupted

Carter was not present for the events described in the first part of this chapter, so Perry tells this story himself. We are grateful to John M. Deutch and Philip Zelikow for their considerable contribution to the part of this chapter subtitled "The Specter of Catastrophic Terrorism."

by an urgent knock on the door. It was General Randy House, my senior military assistant, with a message from Cables in his hand and a worried look on his face.

I read the message with a sinking feeling: a bomb had just detonated at the Olympic Games in Atlanta, Georgia. Initial reports were confused, but they indicated that there had been multiple casualties, and there was speculation that this bomb was one of several. The fear was that a large-scale, well-organized terrorist attack was under way.

Terrorism was increasingly becoming a major security concern for the United States. Just a month earlier, on June 26, 1996, a terrorist team had set off a large car bomb a few hundred feet from the Khobar Towers barracks in Saudi Arabia, which housed the American airmen who were enforcing the no-fly zone in southern Iraq. Nineteen were killed in this attack. The fatality toll could have been far worse: it could have been in the hundreds if the terrorists had been able to penetrate the base security and move their panel truck adjacent to the barracks, as terrorists had been able to do in 1983 in Beirut. And the fatalities at Khobar could have numbered in the thousands if the terrorists had attacked with nerve gas or with anthrax.

Why was America facing such an upsurge in terrorism? Could the Atlanta bomb have anything to do with the Khobar Towers attack, had it been home grown, or was it perhaps a mixture of both, like the World Trade Center bombing some years earlier in New York? I pondered these questions and the possible answers.

American military forces in the Arabian Gulf were the most powerful in the region: no nation could seriously plan to challenge them on the field of battle, as Iraq had learned in Desert Storm. But precisely because of that, American military forces were especially susceptible to indirect attacks such as the one at Khobar Towers. The 1983 terrorist attack in Beirut had been successful from the point of view of the terrorists: the U.S. Marines had been withdrawn from Beirut shortly afterward. But the attack on Khobar Towers had, in contrast, been unsuccessful. The Clinton administration did not even consider pulling American troops out of Saudi Arabia, and there was very little pressure from Congress to do so.

Instead, with the cooperation of the Saudis, we undertook to move our air operations from Dhahran, where it had been nearly impossible to protect them from large truck bombs, to a remote base in the desert where we could create a very deep security barrier around the entire operations and living areas. But we feared that whoever had perpetrated that attack would go further, attempting to raise the price to us of maintaining our forces in the Gulf so high that we might bow to political pressure to pull them out. If the terrorists' strategy were to mount ever more serious attacks, even the remote base in the desert was not completely invulnerable; moreover, future attacks could be much more serious if the terrorists were able to get nerve gas, or anthrax, or a nuclear device.

We also worried that future attacks could be directed against our civilian population at home in the United States, which was not as well protected as our military. War is a time-honored means of forcing nations to take actions against their will. Our dominant military force protects the United States against coercion by war, but in this "Brave New World," organized terrorism could become a means of coercing the United States to take actions contrary to our interests.

In addition to politically motivated foreign terrorists, there was the possibility of messianic cults like the Aum Shinrikyo group, which had released the nerve gas sarin into the Tokyo subway in March 1995 and had attempted in June 1993 to spray anthrax spores from the roof of a Tokyo building. American "militias" and other militant groups might also aspire to mass violence. Meanwhile, the tools of mass destruction have been falling into the hands of smaller and smaller groups that are harder and harder to monitor.

Against this background, I was fearful that the Atlanta bomb could be part of a large-scale terrorist attack, possibly even related to the recent attack at Khobar Towers. We simply did not know. I asked General House to activate our worldwide intelligence and communications systems to seek more definitive information on the incident. I reviewed the provisions that the Defense Department had made to assist law enforcement officials in providing security for the Atlanta Olympics. More than six months earlier, I had authorized the use of more than 10,000 National Guard troops to assist with certain security and logistical missions associated with the Olympic Games. That deployment was designed to assist law enforcement officers with routine security issues, including preventing and dealing with the consequences of relatively minor terrorist threats such as pipe bombs.

But we had also worried about the possibility of a much more serious attack, possibly involving chemical or biological weapons, perhaps with the complicity of foreign nations—what we have come to call "catastrophic terrorism." This would be a much more serious matter, beyond the likely capacity of local law enforcement officers. So at the time I authorized the National Guard deployment, I also took several other steps. Director of Central Intelligence John M. Deutch, who had previously been my deputy secretary of defense, had joined me in tasking defense intelligence resources to look for evidence that any foreign nation might be planning such an attack.

In addition, although Atlanta would be swarming with federal marshals, FBI agents, Georgia State Police, and county and city police, we knew that none of these organizations had the capacity that the U.S. Department of Defense had to deal with catastrophic terrorism involving chemical or biological weapons. The difference between prompt detection and treatment or delay might be measured in thousands of casualties. So we sent an elite U.S. Marine unit, which had been formed a year earlier with the dedicated sponsorship of the astute undersecretary of the navy, Richard Danzig (later to become secretary of the navy); this unit had had extensive special training in how to detect a wide variety of chemical or biological agents and how to deal with chemical or biological attacks.

I expected that this elite Marine unit would be among the first military personnel at the scene in Atlanta to determine whether there were any signs of chemical or biological agents in the bomb. They would also scan the area for evidence of other bombs yet to go off. In my Sydney hotel room, I tried to imagine where they were and what they were doing. I wondered how well they were able to coordinate with the local police and the Federal Bureau of

Investigation. Even the FBI can find it difficult to operate in the jurisdiction of a local police force, which sees the prosecution of a local crime as primarily its own responsibility; local police might be even more apprehensive about working with a military unit, untrained in law enforcement and specifically prohibited by the Posse Comitatus Act from carrying out law enforcement.[1] In Atlanta, the Marine unit would have the delicate task of providing assistance in a technical area in which it had unique expertise: responding to the consequences of a chemical or biological attack. But it would have to use that same expertise to determine whether weapons of mass destruction were involved in that particular crisis and thus whether its expertise was needed further. The Marine unit had worked hard in the preceding weeks to create a smooth liaison with law enforcement officials, but tonight it would be testing whether that liaison would work in a crunch.

Within thirty minutes, General House returned to my room with more reports, both from Cables and from Cable News Network. Several conflicting reports further confused issues; some indicated that other bombs had been found, which suggested that this first bomb was part of an organized conspiracy.

Trying to sort out just what had happened, I asked Cables to connect me with my insightful and cool deputy secretary, John White, Joint Chiefs of Staff Chairman John Shalikashvili, and General Denny Reimer, who was then commander of the ground forces based in the United States. I had full confidence in all of them, but I felt that I was in the wrong part of the world if the reports turned out to be true. This could be an example of the catastrophic terrorism that we had begun to fear: it might involve chemical or biological weapons, entailing vastly greater casualties than an attack with high explosives. It might have been perpetrated by a foreign power, and it might be related to the previous attack against U.S. airmen at Khobar Towers. If so, the Atlanta bombing was clearly a national security problem in the traditional sense, in which the Defense Department had special responsibilities and unique capabilities. Although we had only a small crew with special weapons expertise in Atlanta, we could quickly mobilize units with much more capability from other parts of the country. We would need to coordinate all of these possible actions with law enforcement officials and national security officials, and every step we took in this coordination would break new ground.

With these thoughts racing through my mind, I asked General House to find out how long it would take to round up our flight crew and head back to Washington. He had anticipated my request and already had an answer: because of safety requirements associated with maintenance and crew rest, our aircraft would not be ready for a flight back to the United States for another twelve to eighteen hours. This was not the answer that I wanted to hear. Just at that moment, however, Admiral Joe Prueher, the commander of our Pacific forces, stopped by my room. I briefed him on the situation and expressed my desire to get back to Washington as quickly as possible. He graciously offered the Pacific Command plane, on which he had come to Australia, and which could be made ready to return within an hour or two.

I weighed the decision for a few minutes. I knew that the reports of a large-scale attack could very well be wrong: all of my experience with major incidents, accidents, or crimes suggested that the first reports always had significant errors. But if the reports were right, I should be at home helping to deal with the problem, instead of enjoying a social weekend at MacLachlan's ranch. I asked Admiral Prueher to notify his crew that I wanted to leave in two hours. Then I reluctantly called Minister MacLachlan at his ranch to offer my apologies, which he accepted graciously and with understanding.

On the way home, I continued to try to find out exactly what had happened in Atlanta. By the time we landed in Washington the next morning, however, we knew that the early reports had been overblown. The attack was not a large-scale organized attack; it had not been planned in association with a foreign nation; and no chemical or biological agents were used. The explosive was a simple homemade pipe bomb, and as of this writing, the perpetrator has never been caught or identified.

The far more gruesome possibilities that came to my mind and prompted me to leave Australia for home right away are a reflection of the growing vulnerability of the United States to catastrophic terrorism and my judgment that we are still poorly prepared to deal with it. But the preparation we made for the Olympics was also a useful training exercise. It forced the Defense Department and the FBI to work together on a real joint operation, not just a paper exercise. Before the Atlanta Games, we had virtually no readiness to cope with a chemical or biological attack; preparation for potential threats at the Atlanta Olympics was a useful first step, and it highlighted our shortcomings and vulnerabilities. It gave federal law enforcement officials exposure to the problems involved in dealing with the consequences of chemical and biological agents, and it familiarized them with the difficulty they would have in even knowing that such a crisis was upon them.

Some day in the not-so-distant future, Americans will be attacked with these deadly agents, just as the Japanese were in the infamous Tokyo subway attack carried out by the Aum Shinrikyo cult in 1995. We do not know where the first such attack on U.S. soil will take place, and we do not know when. What we do know is that we will want to thwart such an attempt, if possible, and that if we cannot, we will want to minimize the casualties that result from the attack. As we respond to this new and terrible threat to our citizens, we will want to do so in a way that preserves the civil rights first established by the Bill of Rights and reaffirmed and expanded for more than two centuries. We cannot allow the technology of destruction to overturn them.

The Specter of Catastrophic Terrorism

We give the name "catastrophic terrorism" to potential instances of terrorism, that is, attacks outside the context of traditional war, that involve nuclear, biological, or chemical weapons, cyberattack on the computer systems that increasingly support our society's vital infrastructure, exploitation of other critical vulnerabilities of our complex modern societies, or threats to key personnel and institutions of government.[2]

Catastrophic terrorism is different from the bombings, hostage takings, and airline hijackings that, since the Munich Olympics of

1972, have been the stuff of "ordinary" terrorism. It takes to a new level of destructiveness the Oklahoma City bombing, the World Trade Center bombing, the activities of the Aum Shinrikyo cult that spread sarin nerve gas in the Tokyo subway, or the attack on the Khobar Towers quarters of U.S. airmen in Saudi Arabia. Catastrophic terrorism involves damage to life and property that is orders of magnitude more severe and is unprecedented outside of warfare.

Such a jump in destructive quantity brings with it a change in quality. An incident of catastrophic terrorism would abruptly and irrevocably undermine the fundamental sense of security of Americans, their belief that the United States is a safe place to live, to make plans, to raise a family. Americans have not experienced a similar shock of vulnerability in their own homeland since Joseph Stalin exploded the first Soviet A-bomb in 1949. The U.S. reaction to that shock was a huge investment in nuclear weapons, ballistic missiles, and nuclear defenses; widespread fear reflected in the building of backyard fallout shelters and "duck and cover" class-room drills; and the unleashing of a fevered hunt for home-grown "communist sympathizers." In many ways the sudden sense of vul-nerability of the American homeland defined an entire age. For the most part in American experience, security threats have arisen in faraway places, and the violence has taken place there. Cata-strophic terrorism would bring the national security threat home again. The result would be profoundly disturbing to Americans.

More insidiously, were an incident of catastrophic terrorism to take place in the United States, the failure of public authorities to have prevented the attack, and their probable inability to cope with carnage on such a scale, could well undermine confidence in constitutional order. This was the objective of terrorists in Germany in the 1970s and 1980s: to disgrace the established pub-lic order or to provoke the government into actions that would undermine its popular support. In the event of catastrophic terror-ism within the United States, it is easy to imagine the popular out-cry and the demand for drastic measures to ensure that it could not happen again. To some, no price would seem too high for protec-tion, even curtailing the rights and freedoms Americans cherish.

The damage wrought by catastrophic terrorism would not end there. Terror on this scale would be likely to ignite still greater violence, as copycats sought to repeat its "success." And catastrophic terrorism could lead to wider international conflict as an angry search for the parties responsible widened and came to encompass whatever foreign contacts the perpetrators had; with the progress of globalization, even home-grown terrorists are likely to have had such contacts and to have drawn technology, ideology, or grievances from abroad.

The technology and materials required to perpetrate an act of catastrophic terrorism might be obtained in the United States, abroad, or both. The perpetrators could be American or foreign, state or local, or a complex mixture of these. The motives could be domestic or international, or both at the same time. The threat is therefore truly transnational, which is another factor making catastrophic terrorism a new and distinctly different form of national and international security threat.

Though catastrophic terrorism has not struck yet, the probability of its occurrence is likely on the rise. One reason is the growing ease with which modern technology puts destructive power within the reach of smaller and smaller groups of individuals devoted to terror. Another is the increasing vulnerability of complex modern societies, with millions of people dependent on shared networks of energy, sustenance, communications, transport, and public safety. International networks of organized crime, drug trafficking, money laundering, and technology for sale are an emerging feature of twenty-first-century life that provides a ready infrastructure for catastrophic terrorism.

Another development is the existence of groups that have vengeful or messianic motivations that might especially incline them to catastrophic terrorism. They contrast with "traditional" terrorist groups such as Hamas or the Irish Republican Army, which have strictly political motivations and hope eventually to win acceptance for their political agendas; such groups, therefore, tend to limit themselves to relatively small, attention-getting acts of violence. For them, catastrophic terrorism would be overkill that would bring on them lasting opprobrium rather than eventual political acceptance. Thus the source of this type of terrorism might more likely be found among their frustrated splinter groups, or among cults or other groups motivated not by politics but rather by the desire for martyrdom or simple vengeance.

A final reason why catastrophic terrorism might be growing more likely is the United States' current position of unrivaled world leadership and the conventional superiority of the U.S. military. These make Americans a tempting target, while suggesting to those with grievances against the United States that the only way to challenge U.S. power is through unconventional "asymmetric" means such as catastrophic terrorism.

Like the attack on Pearl Harbor, an incident of catastrophic terrorism would divide our past and future into "before" and "after." The effort and resources we have so far devoted to averting or containing this threat now, in the period "before," would seem woefully inadequate when viewed with hindsight after an incident of catastrophic terrorism. Our focus in the balance of this chapter, therefore, is on the challenges that catastrophic terrorism presents, and on a Preventive Defense strategy of prevention and preparation to minimize its consequences for what we value in American life.

Catastrophic Terrorism as a Challenge to Governance

Devising a strategy for dealing with transnational terrorism forces us to confront the deep division between foreign and domestic policy in the U.S. government. The effort to combat catastrophic terrorism is in peril of falling into the chasm between the national security paradigm and the law enforcement paradigm for dealing with destructive threats to society. The national security paradigm emphasizes aggressive intelligence collection, proactive threat identification, campaign planning, deterrence, and anticipatory action. The law enforcement paradigm emphasizes constitutional protection of citizens and suspects, presumption of innocence, post-facto arrests, trials governed by rules of evidence, and punishment of those who have already committed crimes. In the atmosphere of fear and anger that would accompany an incident of catastrophic terrorism, the traditional American balance between protection of freedom and privacy on the one hand, and protection of life and property on the other, might be abruptly abandoned in favor of the latter. Thus there is much, much more at stake than the physical destruction of the act of catastrophic terrorism itself.

An incident of such terrorism would be at once an attack, a crime, a disaster, and a threat to freedom and privacy, and as such would require the concerted action of many parts of the federal government. Thus catastrophic terrorism suggests the need for a third paradigm that bridges the gulf between the national security paradigm and the law enforcement paradigm. It is a problem that requires attention from a much broader spectrum of government than just the Department of Defense or the other national security agencies with which this book is largely concerned. A fully adequate response to the danger of catastrophic terrorism will take years to devise, but we believe that it is important to begin now.

From Awareness to Action

In recent years, awareness of the dangers of catastrophic terrorism has been growing in the executive and legislative branches of the U.S. government. A number of studies detailing the threat and analyzing frightening scenarios have persuasively argued that catastrophic terrorism belongs among the A-list dangers for the twenty-first century to which this book is devoted.[3] The period of awakening awareness is over; now it is time to move to action.

President Clinton announced on May 22, 1998, that the United States must approach the new terrorist challenges of the twenty-first century "with the same rigor and determination we applied to the toughest security challenges of this century." To that end he signed Presidential Decision Directive (PDD)-62 and PDD-63 and appointed a national coordinator for security, infrastructure protection, and counterterrorism on the National Security Council staff to "bring the full force of all our resources to bear swiftly and effectively." The national coordinator and PDD-62 and 63 look to "lead agencies" on one or another issue to "identify a program plan with goals and specific milestones." The national coordinator is charged to produce an annual security preparedness report, offer budget advice, and lead in the development of guidelines for crisis management.[4]

Although we welcome these first steps at addressing the danger of catastrophic terrorism, and see some benefit in the designation of a responsible White House aide, we suggest a different emphasis. The fight against catastrophic terrorism requires solving difficult crosscutting problems of shared powers and overlapping authorities; in such a setting we place no faith in czars. The history of such "national coordinators" is not encouraging overall. Unless they are responding to an actual emergency or are endowed with a rare level of day-to-day support from the president or vice president, such coordinators quickly find themselves unable to direct the activities of cabinet secretaries, who have their own priorities, or to harmonize budgets that are overseen by different congressional committees. We believe that it would be more realistic to give the national coordinator powers that grow as the urgency of the circumstances increases.

In any event, a national coordinator may be necessary but is certainly far from sufficient. A coordinator must have something to coordinate. For better or worse, the real power to get things done resides in the executive departments that actually have people, equipment, money, and capabilities. At present, these agencies lack some key capabilities that will be needed in the fight against catastrophic terrorism. Our recommendations therefore focus on building needed capabilities, rather than dwelling on coordination at the apex.

Guiding Concepts

The devising of new capabilities to combat catastrophic terrorism should be guided by the principles of respect for civil liberties, institutionalized risk analysis and systems analysis, mobilization for imminent emergency, a strong but supporting role for the Department of Defense, and the need to develop counterterrorism technology and tactics.

RESPECT FOR CIVIL LIBERTIES.   Success in the fight against catastrophic terrorism will require bridging the divide between law
enforcement and national security institutions and norms. For
example, because terrorism is transnational in character, an intelligence effort dedicated to detecting preparations for catastrophic terrorism will necessitate the integration of foreign intelligence collected by the intelligence arms of the Central Intelligence Agency
and the Defense Department with domestic intelligence collected by
law enforcement, customs, and border authorities. Such cooperation across the gulf between foreign and domestic agencies will
encounter bureaucratic obstacles. It also raises significant legal and
constitutional issues that will require great sensitivity to civil liberties
and possibly new legislation. The delicacy of this task is an argument
for embarking on it now, since tragic excesses would be extremely
difficult to avoid after even a single incident of such terrorism.

INSTITUTIONALIZED RISK ANALYSIS AND SYSTEMS ANALYSIS.
Catastrophic terrorism will be an A-list national security concern
in the next century, but too little is known about the motives and
methods possible in this type of terrorism and about the tactics
and technology that might be brought to bear by government
against it. Humility and imagination are needed right from the
beginning and require a dedicated, institutionalized analytic effort.
In the 1950s institutions such as the RAND Corporation were
established to struggle with the conceptual issues raised by the new
threat of Soviet military power and the explosion of new military
technology. We recommend a similar deliberate effort to think
about catastrophic terrorism.

Risk analysis for catastrophic terrorism would seek to answer,
"Which of the many potential scenarios are most likely?" and
"Which of the policy tools to cope with them are most effective?"
Systems analysis would look at the entire sequence of steps required to prevent and respond to catastrophic terrorism, including
broad surveillance, threat identification, targeted surveillance,
warning, prevention through denial and deterrence, protective
measures, interdiction and military action, coping with public
health and cleanup in the aftermath of attacks ("consequence

management"), attribution of responsibility and identification of the perpetrator through forensic and other investigation, retaliation or prosecution, and efforts to prevent repeated incidents.

MOBILIZATION FOR IMMINENT EMERGENCY.   Because we have not yet experienced an incident of catastrophic terrorism, there is a natural reluctance to give the problem the priority that such an incident will likely need. An event of catastrophic terrorism will bring with it the danger of precipitous action that is detrimental to other social values, such as civil liberties. The best answer to both of these dangers is to devise—now, before an incident of catastrophic terrorism—special emergency procedures that are meant to take effect when the president determines that a threat is imminent.

It is in the context of such emergency mobilization that a White House czar makes most sense. An overall coordinator should be designated to devise an end-to-end strategy for dealing with catastrophic terrorism, from warning and prevention through response and cleanup. The coordinator would specify the technology, techniques, and institutions required to fulfill the strategy; draw up contingency plans and conduct exercises; and, in an actual emergency, command the national effort. In normal, nonemergency times, the office of the coordinator would consist of a small planning staff, similar to a regional military commander in peacetime. Upon determination by the president that the danger of catastrophic terrorism was imminent, however, the coordinator would take command of designated law enforcement, military, and disaster relief capabilities of the federal government. The coordinator would also be responsible for the survival and continued functioning of the presidency and government against threats or attacks on Washington. The model we draw upon is that of, say, the regional military commander responsible for the Persian Gulf: in peacetime he does not command all the forces he would use in war, nor does he develop and procure weapons, but if war comes, he is in charge. Because everyone knows he will be in charge when forces and weapons are used, his views are taken into account in determining the force structure, even though he does not direct the process of building forces.

STRONG BUT SUPPORTING ROLE FOR THE DEPARTMENT OF DEFENSE. In the magnitude of its threat to U.S. lives, property, and interests, catastrophic terrorism rivals any of the traditional threats to national security from which the Department of Defense has always had the responsibility to defend the country. Some have suggested that catastrophic terrorism be regarded as another "theater of war" and assigned to the military, but we believe that DOD cannot and should not claim the lead role for the nation in combating catastrophic terrorism.

However, as a practical matter the Defense Department possesses most of the nation's technical and organizational capability in the fields of weapons of mass destruction, protection of information systems, detectors and passive and active defenses for chemical and biological agents, intelligence analytical specialties, disaster response, special forces assault, and a host of other assets. These capabilities have been developed to fulfill DOD's core mission of winning wars. The Defense Department now needs to adapt these capabilities to the added mission of combating catastrophic terrorism and to take steps to make them available to the nation in the event of an imminent or actual act of terrorism. DOD has traditionally confined its activities to areas strictly within its mission: protecting deployed military forces, ensuring the national infrastructure necessary for the execution of war plans, and providing for continuity of government in emergencies (a function deeded to DOD during the cold war).

We argue that the Department of Defense should continue and enhance its activities that pertain to catastrophic terrorism. Specifically, DOD must strengthen the technology base for chemical and biological defense, which began to atrophy as the United States eliminated its own arsenals of these types and as the end of the cold war engendered the illusion that future wars would be symmetric and conventional. Second, the National Security Agency's programs to develop protections against cyberattack should be strengthened and an outreach program should be devised for other government agencies and utilities, banks, and other providers of vital computer-dependent services. Third, DOD should develop methods, and seek statutory authority where necessary, to make its capabilities more easily available to civil authorities and law enforcement agencies that generally do not have the resources or technical sophistication that DOD has. An example is the Marine Corps's Chemical-Biological Incident Response Force, designed to assist police, firefighters, and other "first responders" in the event of a catastrophic terrorism incident. Its specially trained troops and equipment, assigned to Atlanta during the Olympic Games, are drawn from the Marines' normal counterproliferation capabilities (including such equipment as decontamination showers and protective suits). Fourth, the Department of Defense should promote a stable, multiyear program and budget (not necessarily in DOD), based on the Nunn-Lugar-Domenici legislation of 1997, which gave the department new legislative authority to contribute to the management of the aftermath of a terrorist attack by weapons of mass destruction. Last, but not least in our list, the Department of Defense as well as Congress should support the Nunn-Lugar program and the counterproliferation programs described in chapters 2 and 4 of this book, since they also contribute directly to the fight against catastrophic terrorism.

However, DOD's capabilities can be developed and applied usefully only in the context of an overall national program for catastrophic terrorism directed by the White House and carried out through the concerted effort of the national security, law enforcement, and disaster relief agencies.

NEED TO DEVELOP COUNTERTERRORISM TECHNOLOGY AND TACTICS.   Just as, during the cold war, the threat of Soviet air and missile attack spawned a major effort to devise protective technology against homeland attack, and Soviet numerical superiority in Europe led the United States to develop high-technology weapons such as stealth and precision-guided munitions, a substantial effort in technology and accompanying tactics will be needed in the fight against catastrophic terrorism. No single counterterrorism technology program in the U.S. government now has the critical mass necessary to be fully effective, nor is there presently a first-rate institution offering a "center of excellence" in technical work in this field.

The Department of Defense excels at this sort of technology development, systems engineering, and procurement program, and it is appropriate for DOD to serve as executive agent and a principal, although not exclusive, funder of the national program that is needed. A program to develop a multiagency long-range spending plan and to encourage joint efforts and technology sharing among agencies should pool the existing efforts of the DOD, the CIA, the FBI, and other agencies.

Elements of an Initial National Strategy

Based on these guiding principles, we urge several specific new mechanisms for immediate implementation. We organize them according to an end-to-end strategy with four elements: intelligence and warning, prevention and deterrence, crisis and consequence management, and a process for coordinated acquisition of needed technology.

Intelligence and Warning

Since 1945 the United States has focused intense attention on any potentially hostile entity that might deliver weapons of mass destruction against its territory or its allies. The intelligence objectives were straightforward, the orientation was toward foreign governments, and the task was the monitoring of weapons development, testing, and deployment. The parallel intelligence task for catastrophic terrorism is complicated by the potential involvement of nonstate (including domestic) actors, concealed weapons development, and unconventional deployments. In cyberattacks, the deployment and delivery of weapons might be entirely electronic, further complicating the tasks of intelligence and warning.

We believe that the U.S. government should acquire the legal authority and the capability for physical and electronic monitoring of any group and its potential state sponsors that might justifiably be considered to have a motive and capability to use weapons of mass destruction. The U.S. government should acquire additional capabilities to detect any use or deployment of such weapons anywhere in the world, both by utilizing remote-sensing technology and by strengthening and evaluating worldwide sources of information such as clandestine collection, open sources such as foreign newspapers and journals or the Internet, and better organized exchanges with key allies and other like-minded states.

Today the U.S. intelligence community lacks a place to perform "all-source" planning for collecting information on potential catastrophic terrorism. It needs a place where the yields from overhead reconnaissance, electronic surveillance, clandestine agents, law enforcement databases and informants, and reports from foreign governments can be sifted and organized for maximum complementary usefulness. There are some problems with establishing such an institution, based on fundamental differences between the goals and philosophies of national security agencies and of domestic law enforcement agencies. Domestic law enforcement officials focus their efforts on investigating suspected criminal actions, with the objective of criminal prosecution. Civil liberties concerns properly discourage them from going out and looking for criminals before they have evidence of crime. In contrast, national security agencies have much more freedom to initiate action. However, they lack some of the capabilities of domestic law enforcement for gathering data, including lawful wiretaps and grand jury investigations, and much of the yield from such efforts is closed off to the national security community by law or regulation to safeguard constitutional rights.[5]

We believe the United States needs a new institution to gather and sift intelligence on terrorism, with particular attention to the threat of catastrophic terrorism. It should combine the proactive intelligence-gathering approach of the national security agencies, which are not legally constrained in deciding when they may investigate a possible crime, with the investigative resources of law enforcement agencies.

We propose a new institution that we call the National Terrorism Intelligence Center. This center would be responsible for collection, management, analysis, and dissemination of information and warning of suspected catastrophic terrorist acts. The center would:

— monitor and provide warning of terrorist threats to relevant agencies of the U.S. government and support defense or intelligence operations, as well as law enforcement;

— establish integrated collection requirements for information gathering by all the intelligence agencies or bureaus of the U.S. government;

— receive and store all lawfully collected, relevant information from any government agency, including law enforcement wiretaps and grand jury information;

— analyze all forms of relevant information to produce integrated reports that could be disseminated to any agency that needed them, while appropriately restricting dissemination of underlying domestic wiretap and grand jury information;

— review planned collection and intelligence programs of all agencies directed toward terrorist targets to determine the adequacy and balance among these efforts in the annual preparation of the president's budget submission to Congress;

— facilitate international cooperation in counterterrorism intelligence, including the bilateral efforts of individual agencies;

— be exempt from motions for pretrial discovery in criminal trials.[6]

We recommend that the center be located in the FBI. Because it would have constant access to considerable domestic law enforcement information, we believe this center should not be located at the Central Intelligence Agency. The highly successful Counterterrorism Center established under the director of central intelligence in the mid-1980s has a narrower mandate than the national center we propose, and it would be incorporated into this new body.

The center would be responsible to an operating committee, chaired by the director of central intelligence and including the director of the FBI, the deputy secretary of defense, the deputy attorney general, the deputy secretary of state, and the deputy national security adviser. The budget would be included within the national foreign intelligence program, which already provides support for the FBI's National Security Division. Unresolved disputes would go to the National Security Council. The director of the center would come alternately from the FBI and CIA. The major intelligence organizations would all be required to detail a specified number of professionals to the center, and this number would be exempt from agency personnel ceilings. The center would not manage operational activities or take on the task of general intelligence about the proliferation of weapons of mass destruction, a job now coordinated in the Central Intelligence Nonproliferation Center.

Such an entity could use our formidable but disparate national security and law enforcement resources to analyze transnational problems including catastrophic terrorism. This combination should be permitted, consistent with public trust, only in a national center that has no powers of arrest and prosecution and that establishes a certain distance from the traditional defense and intelligence agencies. The center would also be subject to oversight from existing institutions, such as the federal judiciary, the president's Foreign Intelligence Advisory Board, and the select intelligence committees of Congress.

There are precedents for creating interagency operating institutions that work, such as the National Reconnaissance Office and the Counterintelligence Center, recently reformed as a result of spectacular spy cases to strengthen FBI and CIA cooperation. We are not eager to create new government institutions, but the problems in information sharing about terrorism are not just products of petty bureaucratic jealousy. They stem from a real dilemma: how to reconcile the practices of foreign intelligence work with the restrictions that properly limit domestic law enforcement. We believe our proposal offers a possible answer.

Prevention and Deterrence

We suggest three measures to contribute to prevention and deterrence of catastrophic terrorism: an international legal initiative to make any development or possession of weapons of mass destruction a universal crime; a National Information Assurance Institute to develop tools against the threat of cyberterrorism; and stronger federal support for strategic risk analysis of the catastrophic terrorism problem.

OUTLAWING TERROR WEAPONS.   Prevention is intertwined with the concept of deterrence. The United States has finally developed a sound, firm, and increasingly credible declaratory policy that criminalizes terrorist activity and supports sanctions, or even the use of force, to thwart an attack or to respond to one. We believe that the United States must also work with other countries to extend the prohibitions against development or possession of weapons of mass destruction.

Matthew Meselson and others have recently proposed a convention that would make it a crime for any individual to be involved intentionally in biological weapons work, prosecutable anywhere, as is the case for pirates or airplane hijackers.[7] (Work on defenses against biological warfare agents would be exempt from this criminal prohibition.)

There are already international treaties by which governments promise to restrain their weapons developments, such as the Nuclear Nonproliferation Treaty, the Biological Weapons Convention, and the Chemical Weapons Convention. Governments breaking such treaties violate international law. We are pressing a different idea: prohibited weapon development would become a universal individual crime, subjecting individual offenders to prosecution and extradition wherever they might be found. This idea utilizes the power of national criminal law against individual criminals, rather than the power of international law against governments. It builds on analogous developments in the law of piracy and treaties declaring the criminality of airplane hijacking, crimes of maritime navigation, theft of nuclear materials, and crimes against diplomats.

We are also concerned about the actions of governments. Over time, we hope the burden of proof in demonstrating compliance with international conventions will shift away from those alleging that others are not in compliance to those states or groups whose compliance is in doubt. International norms should adapt so that such states are obliged to reassure those governments who are concerned and to take reasonable measures to prove they are not secretly developing weapons of mass destruction. Their failure to supply such proof, or to prosecute terror-weapon criminals living within their borders, should justify defensive actions by concerned nations.

NATIONAL INFORMATION ASSURANCE INSTITUTE. Cyber-terrorism is a special problem in which private-sector cooperation is vital but elusive. The president's Commission on Critical Infrastructure Protection (often called the Marsh Commission) noted that industry was reluctant to deal with these problems on its own because the solutions cost money, the risk is unclear, and there was fear of heavy-handed government action. On the other hand, although the FBI has created a National Infrastructure Protection Center, which can help identify potentially vulnerable installations and functions, we do not think the FBI, with all its operational duties, is the place to build a bridge with the private sector. Nor is it the right place to harness the significant resources and expertise on the cyberattack problem that are found within the Department of Defense.

Instead, we propose the formation of what we would call the National Information Assurance Institute, based within the private, nonprofit sector, to serve as an industry laboratory with a central focus on assuring the integrity and security of information and computer systems against potential cyberterrorism. The institute would not itself own the infrastructure, nor would it be part of the government, but it could deal with both sides. It would implement the Marsh Commission recommendation, which advocates seeking a way for industry to organize itself better to deal with this problem as part of a public-private partnership, and it offers a way for industry to respond to President Clinton's PDD-63.

For industry, this institute could become a clearinghouse for sharing information assurance technology; a developer of new techniques and technology for information assurance; a repository for proprietary information that would not pose any competitive threat; a unified point of contact with law enforcement, national security, and other agencies of the federal government; and a resource for training and familiarization of industry personnel with technical best practices and government concerns, policies, and regulations.

For government, this institute could become a channel for sharing sensitive intelligence about threats to the information infrastructure with the private sector; a center for technical excellence for developing and improving technology for protecting critical infrastructure; and a unified government-industry forum for coordinating federal policy, regulation, and other actions affecting infrastructure providers.

The institute we propose would be established as a not-for-profit research organization by a group of private companies, universities, and existing not-for-profit laboratories. The institute would be governed by a board of directors drawn from the private sector and academia. The institute staff could be supplemented by staff detailed from both industry and government. Industry affiliates would include the manufacturers and maintainers of information systems, service vendors, their trade associations, and major companies and trade associations from the power, telecommunications, banking, transportation, oil and gas, water and sewer, and emergency service sectors (multinational companies would be included, with appropriate protection for circulation of U.S.-only classified information).

This new institute could perform information assurance assessments for industry on a confidential basis. Industry representatives would be educated and trained on threats, technical best practices, and government policies. The institute would receive research and support contracts from government. It could sponsor and conduct research on security assessment tools, intrusion detection, recovery, and restoration of data and services. It would identify and develop industry-standard best practices, and evaluate the vulnerability of commercial products; enforcement would be informal, in the private sector, using the marketplace (through insurance ratings, for example), rather than through formal government regulation. The institute could also perform incident evaluations, create a monitoring center for information assurance, provide on-call assistance, and help industry develop contingency plans for failure.

AN INTEGRATED STRATEGY.   Efforts to combat catastrophic terrorism require shrewd analysis of where more resources could make a difference. Not all worries merit equal concern. The allocation of resources by the government should be guided by risk analysis. In this form of analysis, well known to engineers, a dangerous system is analyzed to identify the key sequences of errors that could lead to catastrophic failure. Those are the sequences that then command the highest-priority engineering attention.

The role of risk analysis, or strategic analysis for risk control, is to analyze threats and define risks realistically (avoiding the temptation to define them in terms of existing agency boundaries or capabilities), to commission further data gathering and analysis to assess relative significance, and then to subdivide acute risks into components where additional resources can make a difference.[8] A systemic approach is needed that encompasses broad-area surveillance, specific threat identification, targeted surveillance and warning, prevention, protection, deterrence, interdiction, covert action, consequence management, forensic analysis of a site to determine responsibility, punitive action, and after-event analysis of lessons.

Government agencies can do many things reasonably well, but strategic risk analysis is not one of them. We recommend, therefore, that the FBI offer a substantial multiyear contract for terrorism risk analysis to a not-for-profit research center established to perform such analysis, to devise and evaluate exercises and tests, and to develop concepts of operation for countering catastrophic terrorism. The appropriate parallel is the role the RAND Corporation played, early in the nuclear era, in helping the government think about a new set of security concerns. The Department of Defense has made a start by establishing an advanced concepts office in the newly formed Defense Threat Reduction Agency, which is dedicated to counterproliferation but whose mandate extends to counterterrorism. Risk analysis will require a parallel effort on a national level, not just by DOD.

Crisis and Consequence Management

Crisis management for catastrophic terrorism should include a U.S. capacity to employ appropriate force in any part of the world, with minimal collateral damage, to thwart a possible attack using weapons of mass destruction and to undertake urgent protective efforts that employ every resource of federal, state, and local governments. The U.S. government should also acquire capacities and plans for forensic investigation of the site of an attack to collect evidence and identify those responsible in order to take further action against them.

Consequence management involves the capacity to deal with the aftermath of an attack. The United States, at all levels of government, must develop the ability to respond effectively and promptly to any use of a weapon of mass destruction—nuclear, biological, chemical, or cyber—against American targets, with appropriate and specific measures to mitigate casualties and damage. This is a large order. The needed capabilities include emergency medical care, distributions of protective gear or medications (including vaccines), and planning and implementation of evacuations and area quarantines. Extensive preparations are needed to ready these capabilities in central locations, to mobilize them on sudden notice, to transport them where needed, and to organize local authorities and caregivers so that they are ready to receive and use them. The United States must also prepare emergency plans, including redundant or alternative control systems, for sustaining the operation of the infrastructure that provides the necessities of life, if this infrastructure were to come under attack.

The present system for handling terrorist emergencies is based on the FBI, or—if overseas—on initiatives by State Department representatives or local military commanders. If an acute threat emerged in the United States, local authorities would be expected to alert the local FBI office. The FBI's special agent in charge would organize the intergovernmental response through activation of a strategic intelligence center in Washington and a joint operations center and joint public affairs efforts in the local area. If there were a threat of nuclear, chemical, or biological weapons, the FBI could call on its Weapons of Mass Destruction Operations Unit, which is subject to domestic guidelines about how it should coordinate with other agencies and with Defense Department assistance. There is ample legal authority for the FBI to seek military aid in dealing with such a crisis on U.S. soil. The FBI can call on a small interdepartmental Domestic Emergency Support Team (or, overseas, a Foreign Emergency Support Team), and the FBI has its own Hazardous Materials Response Unit. More military assistance would likely come, not from a joint interservice command, but from the Army's Chemical and Biological Defense Command. Consequence management would be organized by the Federal Emergency Management Agency (FEMA) under what is called the Federal Response Plan.

This structure is adequate for responding to ordinary terrorist threats or attacks, or perhaps even small scares related to weapons of mass destruction, as in February 1998 when the FBI learned that two people in Las Vegas, one of whom had earlier been convicted of fraudulently obtaining bubonic plague virus, might be in possession of some anthrax. It turned out that the suspects did not have live anthrax, only veterinary anthrax vaccine, but the event was a useful exercise: the crisis response went well, including coordination with limited Defense Department resources.

However, if some agency of the U.S. government learned that a large-scale attack with weapons of mass destruction might actually be imminent, threatening tens of thousands of lives, this structure for responding would probably be pushed aside almost instantly. The White House would immediately become involved and would seek to use every bit of power at America's disposal to avert or contain the attack. The operational command structure would need to be capable of directing everything from CIA covert actions to FBI raids to military strikes; setting up interdiction involving ground, sea, and air forces; and mobilizing and moving thousands of law enforcement and emergency management personnel and active duty military, ready reserve, and National Guard as well as thousands of tons of emergency supplies and matériel for deployed units.

None of these actions can happen quickly unless plans have already been drawn up and units designated to carry them out, with repeated training and exercises to create the necessary readiness to execute the plans. In such a situation, the Defense Department's capabilities would immediately become paramount. The

FBI does not command such resources and has no plans to command them.

What is needed, therefore, is a two-tier structure for response, one for "ordinary" terrorist incidents that can be managed by federal law enforcement with interagency help, and a second structure for the contingency of a catastrophic terrorism attack. The parallel is to U.S. unified combatant commands that prepare for remote but extremely serious contingencies of regional aggression, such as U.S. Central Command's response to Iraq's 1990 invasion of Kuwait. The United States must develop a similar structure to respond to this new, perhaps even more likely, contingency of the future.

Rather than create a new combatant command, however, we suggest two new offices, one set up within the Office of the Secretary of Defense and the other within the U.S. Atlantic Command, the combatant command that is already responsible for the security of the American homeland and has training and exercising responsibility for the majority of the U.S. armed forces. Our working title for these offices is Catastrophic Terrorism Response Offices, or CTROs. The new offices would build a capability that is centered in the federal government, but that also includes state and local authorities along with relevant parts of the private sector. This capability would be activated only when authorized by the president and the secretary of defense to respond to validated catastrophic terrorist threats that would cause massive loss of life (measured in the thousands, that is, significantly larger than the attack on the federal building in Oklahoma City) or that would otherwise jeopardize the operation of American government or the critical infrastructure necessary to public health or the functioning of the economy. The president and his advisers would not find it easy to determine when this threshold had been met, but such judgments are required in other areas of national security policy and can be made here.

The CTROs would plan and organize for a U.S. response to catastrophic terrorism by all elements of the U.S. government. They would:

— assess intelligence and warning information in order to alert the National Command Authority of catastrophic terrorist threats;

— establish requirements for the collection and analysis of intelligence carried out by the proposed National Terrorism Intelligence Center;

— define needed resources and assure that resources, procedures, and trained personnel are available at the federal, state, and local level to respond to validated catastrophic threats;

— sponsor training and exercises involving federal, state, and local authorities for responding to catastrophic terrorist attacks;

— direct operations by other organizations, such as covert actions by the CIA, military operations through the Joint Chiefs of Staff, or law enforcement actions by the FBI; and

— coordinate international preparedness to join in a multinational response against catastrophic terrorist threats.

The two CTROs should have the legal responsibility to establish an overall U.S. government readiness to respond to catastrophic terrorism threats. This would be activated at the request of the president, acting through the secretary of defense, who would be the executive agent for both offices and for their budget program. The CTROs would thus be able to program elements in the DOD program budgeting system and would submit a consolidated catastrophic terrorism response program to the White House for inclusion in the president's proposed budget. Congress pointed toward such a goal in the Defense against Weapons of Mass Destruction Act of 1996 (also known as the Nunn-Lugar-Domenici amendment, or Nunn-Lugar II), which mandated that the Defense Department train civilian emergency personnel at all levels of government and establish rapid terrorism response teams. Our idea broadens the scope of the initiative and suggests a way to give it a stronger and more operational institutional base.[9]

However, the Department of Defense would play a strong, supporting role, not the leading one, in such a capability. DOD resources and capabilities for dealing with biological and chemical weapons would be needed for crisis and for consequence management, but only as part of a larger national effort.

Why two offices, rather than one? The CTRO centered in the Office of the Secretary of Defense should concentrate on planning and preparedness for preemptive or retaliatory strikes, utilizing covert action or the uniformed armed forces. It should involve a relatively narrow set of agencies and their staff: the Joint Chiefs of Staff, the CIA, and the FBI. This is a highly secret, delicate activity now done only in an ad hoc manner between the CIA and the Joint Chiefs of Staff and has not previously included the FBI.

The second office must be prepared to handle a much broader range of activities that affect containment and management of the consequences of a catastrophic attack. The number of agencies involved must also be inclusive. This consequence management function must draw on the resources of the National Guard, FEMA, the Department of Health and Human Services, and other federal, state, and local agencies. This is a much larger orchestra to be activated in an emergency, and we think it can be better prepared and conducted by an integrated structure like U.S. Atlantic Command.

Neither of these new offices need be very large. Their jobs are planning and preparation, not day-to-day operations. Yet the work they do will be invaluable when the crisis comes.

Acquisition

A national policy must include a concept for buying what is needed. The government is already ordering everything from vaccines to new research, but nearly two dozen agencies have their own separate shopping lists and ways of doing business. When these budget requests arrive in Congress, the lack of overall acquisition planning creates difficult choices for the affected committees as well as budget competition on Capitol Hill. In November 1997 a conference report accompanying appropriations for the Department of Justice correctly warned that "additional emphasis is needed to coordinate efforts among the many participating departments and agencies that have personnel, resources, and expertise to contribute" to the counterterrorism mission.[10]

We urge the creation of a coordinated, broadly focused budget program that will plan, coordinate, and track all R&D and acquisition projects intended to improve counterterrorism capabilities—conventional and unconventional, defensive and offensive, domestic and foreign—and conduct field testing of new operational capabilities. This national counterterrorism acquisition program should be based on a government-wide five-year plan to develop and acquire the needed technology and operational skills, including improved detectors of special materials such as radioactive substances or biological agents; forensic investigation tools; automated tracking and analysis systems; and improved protective clothing or equipment. The Clinton administration has already started a significant effort to acquire stockpiles of vaccines, antidotes, and antibiotics, adding to such a program already under way for the U.S. armed forces. Resources are needed for storage, transportation, and shipment of such medications.

There is a further need for renewed research into defense against biological weapons, including genetically altered pathogens that defy available vaccines or antidotes. Improved detection devices need to be complemented by specialized laboratories that can rapidly analyze substances and validate field identifications.

Attorney General Janet Reno warned Congress of the extraordinary acquisition requirements involved in a serious policy to cope with the threat of catastrophic terrorism. In April 1998 she explained that "we may need to develop an approach which will permit the government to accelerate the normal procurement procedures to quickly identify and deploy new technologies and substances needed to thwart terrorist threats and respond to terrorist acts. These procedures would be used not only to purchase medications and other needed tools, but also, in some instances, to borrow medications or tools from, or to enter into effective partnerships with, both academia and industry."[11]

We believe that such a policy requires an interdepartmental acquisition program that draws on Defense Department expertise. Despite its limitations, the department still has the best track record in the government for successful sponsorship of technological development and rapid, large-scale procurement. This proposed acquisition program would be separate from other acquisition programs for cooperative threat reduction (such as the Nunn-Lugar programs for the former Soviet Union), efforts to counter narcotics trafficking or organized crime, and nonproliferation activities; its focus would be counterterrorism.

An effective interdepartmental committee system is needed for the success of this acquisition program. We suggest a National Counterterrorism Acquisition Council that would be chaired by the undersecretary of defense for acquisition and technology. Such an acquisition council should include representatives from other departments, including top subcabinet officials from Justice, Energy, Treasury, State, and Health and Human Services, as well as the FBI deputy director, the CIA deputy director for science and technology, and the FEMA director.

This acquisition council would oversee the field testing and evaluation of new capabilities, with the participation of concerned agencies. Some agencies might worry about Defense Department usurpation of their procurement decisions, but we argue that it is exactly these agencies that would benefit from a national program. The Defense Department will in any case be acquiring vast quantities of equipment for its own needs, and suppliers will naturally configure themselves around this demand. Civilian agencies need a way to be sure that their particular requirements are also taken into account, and the acquisition council we propose is the best way to ensure this.

We suggest that the Defense Department establish an initial program with at least $100 million to fund the development of promising counterterrorism technology. Where appropriate, the acquisition council would designate lead agency responsibilities. The acquisition council can also facilitate sharing of technology, tactics, and matériel between one agency and another and provide a point of contact for international programs and technology sharing with other nations. It can provide government-wide procedures controlling access to especially sensitive projects within the national counterterrorism program. Although the program would be executed by various departments, the acquisition council would be responsible for monitoring the progress of each program element and should be expected to report annually on progress to both the president and Congress.[12]

Conclusion

Extrapolating from the Atlanta scare, the Oklahoma City bombing, the Aum Shinrikyo subway gassing and the attempted anthrax attack in Tokyo, and the World Trade Center bombing, one must judge an incident of catastrophic terrorism more likely than not in coming years. Steps similar to those described above will surely be taken in the aftermath of such an event, if they are not taken before. But if we wait for such a terrorist strike before we plan in earnest for society's protection, the result will be a response forged in fear and anger. In a matter where it is not only our survival but the freedoms and values of a civil society that are at stake, a considered and farsighted program of Preventive Defense is far preferable.

CHAPTER 6

The Threat Within: Shaping a Force for the Future

It was a beautiful spring day in 1993 as I drove to Lancaster, Pennsylvania, to speak to the senior officials who specified and bought goods and services for the U.S. Department of Defense. They were holding their annual conference on acquisition issues and problems and had invited me to share with them my ideas on acquisition reform. While the climate outside was sunny, I feared that the climate inside would be stormy. I had been on the job three months as deputy secretary of defense—Les Aspin was secretary and would remain so until the following February—and I had already announced that my highest priority would be radical reform of the acquisition system. Now I was going to meet with the officials whose support and energy would be necessary to make that reform a reality. They had managed the defense acquisition system for many decades and had become expert in the intricate and convoluted process that I wanted to change. Moreover, one of the fruits of acquisition

Carter was not present for the events described in the first section of this chapter, so Perry tells this story himself.

reform would be a reduction of overhead, and these officials were part of that overhead.

As I arrived at the conference center, I sensed anticipation and some apprehension among the 500 or so officials who had gathered to hear what I would say. I chatted first with Colleen Preston, a capable and dedicated lawyer who for many years had been on the staff of the House Armed Services Committee. She had come to the Pentagon specifically to help me create a new and more efficient way for the Pentagon to buy goods and services and had already drafted the new legislation that would be necessary. She told me that although some of the acquisition officials at the conference were concerned primarily with how reform might adversely affect their jobs, most of them believed that the acquisition system was long overdue for reform. Preston thought that they could be won over as allies if they became convinced that we were on the right track and that we were prepared to stay the course.

I started my talk to the assembled officials by quoting Victor Hugo: "More powerful than the tread of mighty armies is an idea whose time has come." After decades of false starts, I said, acquisition reform was an idea whose time had come: we really were going to transform the way we specified and bought goods and services, and, I told them bluntly, they should either get on the team or get out of the way. This was highly risky for my first meeting with this group and might easily have backfired. But it turned out that this message was exactly what most of them wanted to hear. They were frustrated with administering a system that they knew was inefficient and that did not serve well either the taxpayers or the military personnel who depended on the goods and services they bought. So most of them did get on the team, and their dedicated support was essential to our ultimate success in truly transforming the system. Indeed, that experience confirmed a valuable lesson about human nature: most people really want to do the right thing and, given an opportunity and some support, will perform much better if they believe that their task is important and that they are a part of a winning team.

The "Last Supper": Defense Industry Consolidation

The support of Defense Department acquisition officials was a necessary but not a sufficient condition for success. Acquisition reform also depended on the cooperation of the defense industry. So, shortly after the Lancaster meeting, I asked Secretary Les Aspin to schedule a dinner at the Pentagon for about twenty leaders of the defense industry. Aspin had been a strong supporter of acquisition reform when he was chairman of the House Armed Services Committee and was enthusiastic about my efforts to bring about real change, so he was happy to schedule the dinner and participate in it. Also supporting my goal of acquisition reform was John Deutch, who had just been confirmed as the undersecretary of defense for acquisition and technology. In his new position, he was the "defense acquisition executive": the Defense Department official who would be responsible for implementing the reform program. Although he had just been formally confirmed, he was instrumental in helping me organize this meeting with defense leaders and was already applying his enormous talent and energy to formulating a defense-industrial strategy.

At the dinner, I spoke as frankly to the executives as I had to the Defense Department officials. I told them how large the post–cold war reductions in Pentagon weapons-buying budgets were going to be, and I warned them that they would be making a serious mistake if they expected the current downturn to be merely cyclical or temporary. I suggested that they should prepare for a long dry spell, and that this would certainly entail a consolidation of the defense industry, because the Defense Department would not support the excess overhead entailed by unused and unneeded facilities. I concluded by saying that they would be on their own in the upcoming consolidation: it would not be directed by the government but, except for ensuring compliance with antitrust laws, the government would not get in their way.

It was a sobering message, and the executives listened intently. Norman Augustine, who was head of Martin-Marietta at the time, told me some years later that when he heard this message, he looked at the executives on his left and right and said, "Next year at this time, one of us is not going to be here!" In a speech the following year, Augustine referred to that dinner meeting as "The Last Supper," but he also declared that this was the message that industry leaders had needed to hear in order to get moving on their consolidation. He himself, together with Dan Tellep, the head of Lockheed, led the industry with the dramatic merger that formed Lockheed-Martin, today the country's largest defense contractor. That merger and later industry mergers have been a subject of some controversy, but in my judgment they have been classic "win-win-win" moves: the Defense Department won by saving billions of dollars of unneeded overhead; defense companies won as the market rewarded their increased efficiencies with increased stock prices; and the taxpayers won, since the consolidation reduced unneeded overhead that otherwise would have resulted in higher costs of weapons purchased by the Defense Department.

Early Efforts at Defense Acquisition Reform: "Unblemished by Success"

Consolidation was largely in the hands of industry, but acquisition reform was our responsibility in the Pentagon. The Defense acquisition system has long been the subject of scorn and jokes. The media has had a field day writing stories about, say, fruitcakes ordered to unique military specifications, or "milspecs." These stories now have a legendary quality about them, but unfortunately, the truth is even worse than the legends. The use of milspecs for computers and microchips, which made good sense in the early days of the electronics industry when these products were often unreliable, had become counterproductive by the 1980s, and the continued use of milspecs was costing the Defense Department billions of dollars. Defense acquisition had been the subject of Defense Science Board panels, congressional committees, and blue ribbon commissions, all of which recommended reforming the system. Nearly all defense secretaries from 1960 on had recognized that defense acquisition was a problem, and many had vowed to fix the problem. But none had succeeded. Indeed, when we started this crusade, the conventional wisdom was that acquisition reform had been "unblemished by success."

During the late 1970s, when I was the Defense Department's acquisition executive responsible for the acquisition system, I recognized that major reform was needed and seriously considered taking it on, but at that time I decided not to try. I realized what a monumental problem it would be to bring about meaningful change and judged that I would not have the necessary support from either the executive or the legislative branch of government; it would have been a lonely and ultimately futile battle. Moreover, my first priority at that time was a different problem that was even more important. The world was then in one of the most dangerous periods of the cold war, and the United States confronted a Soviet Union whose army outnumbered American forces by more than three to one in ground divisions, tanks, and artillery pieces; the Soviets were also striving to overtake America's lead in strategic nuclear weapons. In short, I believed that the United States was in danger of losing the military edge that was the key to deterrence of the Soviet Union. Harold Brown, who was then secretary of defense, agreed with this assessment and provided unwavering support for my efforts.

The Offset Strategy: What We Buy as Well as How We Buy It

Thus in the late 1970s I devoted my tenure as acquisition head to two priorities. The first was to preserve America's nuclear deterrence capability by modernizing the strategic nuclear forces. I concentrated on the development of the Trident submarine, the Trident D-5 missile, the Peacekeeper (MX) missile, a new family of cruise missiles (including the Tomahawk, now famous from the Gulf War), the stealth bomber, and advanced reconnaissance and command and control systems for these new weapons.

My second goal was to offset the Soviet numerical advantage in conventional weapons by upgrading American tactical forces with modern technology, with special emphasis on information technology. Thus, I focused on the development of a new tactical weapon strategy based on three related priorities. The first was to develop greatly improved sensors that would allow American troops to detect and locate targets on the battlefield. The second was to develop precision-guided weapons that could destroy those targets with a single shot. The third priority was to develop stealth technology to protect American aircraft from Soviet air defense systems.

Harold Brown called this new strategy the "offset strategy," because these new weapons would give qualitative advantages to American forces to offset the quantitative advantage that the Soviet forces enjoyed. Although initially it had many skeptics, the offset strategy was an outstanding success. Even though, happily, it never had to be tested against the Red Army, it was tested against the Iraqi Army, a large force equipped with Soviet weapons. The result was a rapid, decisive victory for the allied forces, with remarkably few casualties.[1] The Defense Department still pursues this strategy of using information technology to achieve a decisive edge on the battlefield. Today it is not called the offset strategy; instead it has achieved the status of a "revolution in military affairs," and is the subject of study and of admiration (or fear) by military forces around the world. So when I left the Pentagon in 1981, I had a real sense of success for having seized the opportunity to introduce the revolution in military affairs; I also had a sense of failure, however, for having passed up the opportunity to tackle acquisition reform. But as it turned out, this was not to be my last chance.

A Second Chance at Reform

In the mid-1980s a blizzard of articles swept through the media that ridiculed the Pentagon for the outrageous prices it had paid for hammers and toilet seats. To deal with this intensely negative press, President Reagan took the time-honored approach of appointing a presidential commission to investigate the problem and make recommendations for corrective action. Often these commissions are set up simply to show the public that something is being done, and generally the commission reports are filed away and forgotten. But if that was what President Reagan wanted, he appointed the wrong chairman. David Packard, as deputy secretary of defense during the Nixon administration, had made a serious effort to improve the acquisition system, but he was only in office two years, not long enough to implement some of his best ideas. When President Reagan made him chairman of the commission, Dave Packard had a second chance and intended to take his charge seriously. And now the commission gave me a second chance too. I had returned to California and was working as an investment banker, but I maintained my involvement in national security affairs through the Center for International Security and Arms Control (CISAC) at Stanford University. Dave Packard asked me to join his commission and to prepare the recommendations for changes in the procurement system. With his wise guidance and support, I was able to put together a blueprint for transforming the acquisition system. My plan was based on dropping the requirement that defense equipment be built to military specifications and using instead commercial standards and commercial buying practices.

The commission's report, published in April 1986, contained a section on acquisition reform called "A Formula for Action." Its conclusion was stated in simple and unambiguous language:

> All of our analysis leads us unequivocally to the conclusion that the defense acquisition system has basic problems that must be corrected. These problems are deeply entrenched and have developed over several decades from an increasingly bureaucratic and overregulated process. As a result, all too many of our weapon systems cost too much, take too long to develop, and by the time they are fielded, incorporate obsolete technology.[2]

The commission recommended many changes in the organization of the Defense Department's acquisition system, some of which were accepted by DOD and implemented the next year. The heart of the recommendations, however, called for changes in process and procedures: to change from milspecs to commercial industrial standards, and from buying practices unique to defense procurement to those used in traditional commerce. "A Formula for Action" stated a case that I would make again years later: "Rather than relying on excessively rigid military specifications," I urged, "DOD should make greater use of components, systems, and services available 'off-the-shelf.' It should develop new or custom-made items only when it has been established that those readily available are clearly inadequate to meet military requirements." I went on to explain the reasoning:

> No matter how DOD improves its organization or procedures, the defense acquisition system is unlikely to manufacture products as cheaply as the commercial marketplace. DOD cannot duplicate the economies of scale possible in products serving a mass market, nor the power of the free market system to select and perpetuate the most innovative and efficient producers. Products developed uniquely for military use and to military specifications generally cost substantially more than their commercial counterparts. DOD program managers accordingly should make maximum use of commercial products and devices in their programs.

To illustrate the problems of excessive reliance on milspecs, I cited the case of the integrated circuit or microchip, an electronic device already widely used in military equipment and which would become even more ubiquitous as time went on. I pointed out that, in 1986,

> DOD will buy almost $2 billion worth of microchips, most of them manufactured to military specifications. The unit cost of a military microchip typically is three to ten times that of its commercial counterpart. This is a result of the extensive testing and documentation DOD requires and of smaller production runs. (DOD buys less than ten percent of the microchips made in the U.S.) Moreover the process of procuring chips made to military specifications involves substantial delay. As a consequence, military microchips typically lag a generation (three to five years) behind commercial microchips.

The use of milspecs had made sense when established, but over time the drawbacks had begun to outweigh the benefits:

> When military specifications for microchips were first established, they assured a high standard of quality and reliability that was worth a premium price. The need for quality and reliability

in military equipment is as great as ever. In the last few years, however, industrial consumers of microchips have come to demand equivalent standards, and manufacturing processes and statistical methods of quality control have been greatly improved. It is now possible for DOD program managers to buy the bulk of their microchips from commercial lines with adequate quality and reliability, and thus to get the latest technology at a substantially lower cost.

This same principle—the expanded use of commercial items—can apply to a great variety of products and services bought by the Defense Department. These range from personal computers, computer software and professional services, to a host of nontechnical products such as bath towels and steak sauce. We [the Packard Commission] recommend that the Defense Acquisition Executive take steps to assure a major increase in the use of commercial products, as opposed to those made to military specifications. He should direct that program managers get a waiver before using a product made to military specifications, if there is an available commercial counterpart. When a "make-or-buy" decision must be made, the presumption should be to buy. This would invert present procedures, biasing the system in favor of commercial products and services, but permitting the use of items made to military specifications whenever a program manager believes it necessary to do so.[3]

David Packard urged this plan on President Reagan, and the president approved it in principle, but his secretary of defense, Caspar Weinberger, did not approve it in practice. And so the blueprint, like many other recommendations of presidential commissions, was put on a shelf and forgotten.

An Idea Whose Time Had Come

Thus when I was appointed deputy secretary of defense in 1993, the position David Packard had held in the early 1970s, my first action after being confirmed was to pull this blueprint off the shelf and use it to lay out the department's plan of action for acquisition reform. In retrospect, the preceding history was probably the only sequence of events that could have allowed the department to succeed in acquisition reform. David Packard had only had two years to implement his ideas, which is not long enough to move the huge bureaucracy that implements the department's acquisition programs. In contrast, not only was I committed to staying the full four years, but I would be able to hit the ground running, having invested a year in preparing the action plan in 1986 and having benefited greatly from Packard's wisdom and experience.

By 1993, then, acquisition reform truly was "an idea whose time had come." Both President Clinton and Vice President Gore supported a strong reform program; in fact, Vice President Gore was making "re-inventing government" his personal objective, and defense acquisition reform was an integral part of that program. There was strong bipartisan support in Congress for acquisition reform; indeed, the necessary legislative changes were passed during the first year I was in office as secretary, which was nothing short of miraculous.

President Clinton and Secretary Aspin gave me the leeway to bring on an acquisition team that was both experienced in defense program management and totally dedicated to carrying out the blueprint for reform. I assembled the strongest acquisition team the Pentagon has ever seen. John Deutch was acquisition executive, and when he was appointed director of central intelligence, he was succeeded by Paul Kaminski; both were superb managers and outstanding technologists, and both had the respect of the military leadership and the defense industry leadership. The acquisition executive's senior staff and their counterparts in the services were also experienced and dedicated to reform. This team consisted of Noel Longuemare, Gil Decker, John Douglas, and Clark Fiester. Art Money would replace Clark Fiester after Fiester was killed in an airplane crash while traveling to an acquisition reform meeting in Texas. Three of these executives were Republicans, and I had to get special support from the president and vice president to get their appointments through the Political Office in the White House. Although at the time there was much skepticism and foot dragging, today everyone agrees that this was an acquisition "dream team." All of the stars were aligned; if ever in the history of the Pentagon the cumbersome acquisition system could be reformed, this was the time.

Turning "Milspecs" on Its Head

I laid out the entire program of reform in a major statement of acquisition policy entitled "Acquisition Reform: A Mandate for Change" in February 1994.[4] Congress, enthusiastic about reform, promptly passed two landmark pieces of legislation, the Federal Acquisition Streamlining Act and the Clinger-Cohen Bill. These laws gave the Department of Defense the legal authority to un-shackle the acquisition system.

It was therefore just a few months after becoming secretary that I issued a directive making the Packard Commission's "For-mula for Action" a reality. This directive guides acquisition reform today. Previously, a program manager had had to obtain a waiver to buy commercial components rather than ones made to special military specifications. The new directive stood this milspecs policy on its head. A far-reaching reform was stated in a single sentence, clear and direct; the idea thus expressed was, in Victor Hugo's words, "more powerful than the tread of mighty armies." It read: "the use of military specifications and standards is authorized as a last resort, with an appropriate waiver."[5] The time had come; acquisition reform was launched.

From Hollow Army to Fit Force

When I developed the weapon systems for the offset strategy in the late 1970s, many critics had questioned whether such high-tech weapons systems could be effective in the field. They feared that U.S. military personnel would not be able to operate or maintain them effectively. The best articulation of this point of view was a book by James Fallows in 1981.[6] I did not agree with these argu-ments and published a rejoinder to Fallows.[7] But the critics were right on one point: the quality of American military personnel was declining in the 1970s.

This problem was especially acute in the army, which was at a low point in morale and effectiveness. In fact, General Edward C. ("Shy") Meyer, then chief of staff of the army, described his force as a "hollow army." The country had just come out of the Vietnam War, and most midgrade officers and noncommissioned officers were badly demoralized. They had been through a war whose unpopularity rubbed off on them. The soldiers were poorly disciplined, and many of them were on drugs. The officers and NCOs felt that their country and their service had let them down, and they were deeply disillusioned; many of them were so frustrated that they left the service. But others decided to stay and rebuild their army, to restore its discipline, morale, and fighting effectiveness. They had a valuable new tool available to them: the all-volunteer force (AVF). The AVF changed the recruiting paradigm. Instead of being required to accept reluctant and often unhealthy or undereducated draftees, the army could demand quality and commitment from its recruits. This created an opportunity to build a truly professional military service, with enlisted personnel who would stay on for a full career, not just eighteen months. This started the rebuilding process.

There were many heroes in this long, hard, and ultimately successful struggle, but perhaps one stood out above all others. That hero was General Max Thurman, who approached this task with enormous dedication, determination, and intelligence. As a young major general, Thurman had taken over the U.S. Army Recruiting Command and transformed it. He reasoned that the first step in the rebuilding process was to recruit healthy, smart, motivated soldiers, so he organized a uniquely successful recruiting effort, which aimed for quality, not quantity. He knew that education was both a powerful training device for the new army, and a powerful incentive to attract bright young people. The army's recruiting motto became: "Be all you can be!" General Thurman set out to put substance behind the slogan. This effort was given an enormous boost with the passage of the new GI Bill in 1985. This legislation, sponsored by Congressman Sonny Montgomery, gave the services the means to attract some of the best high school graduates. These bright young recruits had to be trained, so the services also instituted a training program that today is the best in the world, in or out of government.

MAKING THE SCRIMMAGE TOUGHER THAN THE GAME.   A decade later, as secretary of defense, I had the privilege of seeing the results in action. I was astonished when I saw the thoroughness of the training for the mission of enforcing the Dayton peace accords in Bosnia. In November 1995, a few weeks before our troops were to go into Bosnia, I went to Germany to assess the readiness of the First Armored Division, which was to be the core of the American ground forces sent there. After I met and talked with the troops at their base camp, General Bill Nash, commander of the division, took me to the training grounds at Grafenwoehr and Hohenfels. These were two of a number of the major training facilities created since the 1970s (the rest were in the United States) to improve the quality of the training given to U.S. military personnel. I was accompanied by the German defense minister, Volker Rühe, with whom I had formed a close friendship when we worked together to get NATO to take decisive action in Bosnia.

Rühe and I arrived at Hohenfels in a biting wind, with snow flurries chilling our bones. There we were met by Colonel Dean Cash, who was in charge of the training at Hohenfels. He took us on a tour of the miniature Bosnia he had created, complete with towns, villages, and farms. He had simulated all of the hazards our troops would face in Bosnia: opposing paramilitary forces, land mines, smugglers, provocateurs, even CNN reporters. Each battalion, before it was cleared to go to Bosnia, had to pass a number of tests dealing with crisis scenarios. If it failed any of the tests, they had to be repeated. He explained that history showed that a disproportionate number of casualties occurred in a unit's first battle because green troops make mistakes. He wanted these troops to make all of their mistakes at his test range, rather than in a real, and deadly, combat situation. When Minister Rühe asked Colonel Cash whether he was satisfied with the adequacy of the training, he said, "Yes, except that I wish we had more snow and ice. I would like the weather to be even worse than our soldiers will experience in Bosnia!"

A few weeks later, I crossed the Sava River bridge into Bosnia with Joint Chiefs Chairman General John Shalikashvili and General George Joulwan, supreme commander of allied forces in Europe (SACEUR) and in overall command of the Bosnia operation. I told General Joulwan of that conversation, and he smiled proudly and said, "Of course. I teach them that they should always make the scrimmage tougher than the game!"

On that river crossing, we met a construction engineer whose army enlistment was up that week, and he asked us if we would reenlist him. So the three of us—the secretary of defense, the chairman of the joint chiefs of staff, and the SACEUR—gave Sergeant First Class Charles Kidwell his oath of office, there in the mud and ice, as the First Armored Division rolled into Bosnia. When I reflect now on the remarkable success of American forces in that dangerous and difficult mission in Bosnia, my thoughts go back to the training range at Hohenfels and the swearing-in ceremony on the Sava River bridge to bring home the key lessons: Training counts! Quality counts!

THE BEST DAMN NAVY IN THE WORLD.   Step by step, year after year, the rebuilding took place over a decade. All of the army leaders of this period participated in the rebuilding process, including Colin Powell, John Shalikashvili, Hugh Shelton, John Wickham, Carl Vuono, Gordon Sullivan, Denny Reimer, Norman Schwarzkopf, George Joulwan, Gary Luck, Barry McCaffrey, Binny Peay, Wes Clark, John Tilelli, Dan Christman, Paul Kern, and Randy House. As a consequence, when the U.S. Army was tested in Desert Storm and later in Bosnia, the forces were ready, and the world was awed by their prowess. They were equipped with the extraordinarily effective weapons that had been developed as part of the offset strategy, but these weapons depended on well-trained, well-disciplined troops to operate and maintain them. One American general said that even if he had had to swap weapons with the Iraqi army, he would still have won because of the superior quality and training of the U.S. forces. In about a decade, the army had come out of the pits to become the most effective in the world.

The same is true of all of the U.S. military services, although it was the army that had the greatest distance to go. A few days after I announced the deployment of two carrier battle groups to the waters around Taiwan at the height of the Chinese missile-firing episode (related in chapter 3), I was speaking to a congressional audience about that deployment and I said to them—and the world—that "America has the best damn navy in the world." I made that point because I thought it was especially important to do so during that crisis, but it was not just hyperbole: I was simply stating a fact. Nor is that just my opinion. I have met with the defense ministers and chiefs of staff of sixty-seven nations, both in their countries and in the United States, and I have come to know some of them very well. They also believe that America has the most effective military forces in the world today. One chief of staff in particular, after a visit to Fort Bragg, was incredulous at the quality, education, and training levels of the NCOs he met. They were all performing tasks that he would have assigned to midgrade officers, and they were performing them exceptionally well.

TAKE CARE OF THE TROOPS AND THEY WILL TAKE CARE OF YOU.   With this good news about the quality of America's military services today, there is also bad news: it will be difficult—and expensive—to maintain that quality. Early in my tenure as secretary of defense I established a close working relationship with the senior NCO of each service. We went to bases together once a quarter and talked with enlisted personnel about what was good and what was not so good about military service. We asked whether they planned to reenlist, and if so, why, and if not, why not. We learned that the one big issue across all services and across all enlisted grades was quality of life.

I had made readiness my top budget priority, and I concluded that readiness was inextricably linked with the quality of life of our military personnel and their families. So I appointed a quality of life task force under the former secretary of the army in the Reagan administration, Jack Marsh, a devoted public servant who had developed a real bond with the military. His commission made a number of thoughtful recommendations; among the most important were those calling for steps to increase compensation and to provide better family housing. But these actions were expensive, and funds for them were not in the planned defense budget. So I made a special appeal to President Clinton to allow me to propose to Congress a one-time allocation to make a significant improvement in quality of life. The president authorized me to request a $15 billion addition to the budget for that purpose, and the Congress quickly approved that request.

On subsequent visits to military bases, I saw the improvements these additional funds brought about in the lives of our personnel and their families and the resulting improvements in morale. Some of the morale improvements came from the tangible benefits these new programs provided, and some of them came simply because the soldiers saw that their leaders cared. This phenomenon was explained to me simply but eloquently by Sergeant Major Richard Kidd, who distilled his wisdom on personnel management in one pithy phrase, "Take care of the troops, and they will take care of you." This slogan applies not only to quality of life programs, but to all the innovations that are necessary to preserve the effectiveness of the Department of Defense and thus the safety of our uniformed personnel and of all Americans.

The Threat Within

Throughout the postwar period, U.S. military forces have maintained an admirable standard. Their strength and their ability to deter helped bring us safely through the cold war. Now, however, the A-list threats of the cold war have dissolved, and the resulting tendency to focus strategy on lesser contingencies and on the many worthy opportunities to use the U.S. military for peacekeeping or humanitarian operations risks squandering the opportunities for lasting security afforded by the post–cold war period.

Post–cold war complacency might also lull us into mismanagement of our defense resources. During the cold war, an imminent threat focused the executive and legislative branches on the hard duty of providing strong and ready military forces. But in an era when U.S. military supremacy is unquestioned and major threats seem remote, it is easy to lapse into undisciplined patterns of spending defense dollars in ways that are comfortable to defense managers and to the political process, but wasteful and ultimately dangerous.

Such complacency is what we call "the threat within." It threatens a steady erosion of the military superiority the United States inherited from the cold war. It is vitally important not to repeat, at the end of the cold war, the mistake made at the end of World War II and the Vietnam War, when the Defense Department let the readiness and capability of our military forces decline to where the nation had a "hollow army" and was not prepared to deal with military contingencies. Thus a primary challenge of the Pentagon is to manage the present decreased budget levels without hollowing out our forces.

The previous chapters have described the dangers to U.S. security that could transform themselves into A-list threats if they are not forestalled through imaginative Preventive Defense strategies. We have argued that a traditional approach to national defense based on shaping military forces to defeat or deter already extant threats is not enough, because it would result in lost opportunities to prevent new and larger threats to America's vital interests from emerging. However, Preventive Defense strategies, for all their promise, are not guaranteed to succeed. If they fail and new A-list threats emerge, the United States will need a well-equipped, well-trained, and well-motivated military. Sound shepherding of the quarter-trillion dollar defense budget is therefore a necessary complement to a strategy of Preventive Defense. It is to the struggle against "the threat within" that the rest of this chapter is devoted.

Managing a Very Large Company

With the end of the cold war, the Department of Defense faced an imperative to change, and in managing this change it faced the problems of a very large company. Indeed, the Department of

Defense may be thought of as the largest company in the world, with more than 3 million employees and more than 200 million shareholders—the American people. This "company" has an annual budget of a quarter of a trillion dollars and a board of directors—the Congress—with 535 members. But while there are similarities to managing a company, there are also important differences quite apart from the enormous scale of the operation. In particular, the secretary of defense faces unique problems because of the political environment in which decisions are made and questioned and because of the life-and-death importance of getting the decisions right the first time. A judgment error in a tactical deployment decision can put thousands of lives at risk, and a failure to execute the "company's management plan" can jeopardize the security and freedom of 270 million Americans.

Creating a Management Plan

The chief executive officer of a corporation must determine the business goals or mission of the corporation and create a management plan for achieving them. The mission of General Motors, for example, may be described as serving the transportation needs of the world market by building the most competitive automobiles and trucks. Each year the company's managers prepare a plan that defines its business goals and describes the operations and resources needed to achieve them. Similarly, the business of the Defense Department may be described as providing for the security of the United States by maintaining well-trained, well-led, and well-equipped military forces.

Each year the Defense Department prepares a "management plan" called the Future Years Defense Plan (FYDP), which defines defense goals and describes the operations and resources needed to achieve these goals. Preparing a FYDP involves determining specific defense missions, which in turn establish the appropriate size of the defense budget and the relative priority of the different accounts within the budget. The defense budget includes accounts that cover the activities of the current force structure and its readiness to fight, such as the salaries and benefits that affect the quality of life of military personnel, training and exercising, and the actual conduct of operations. It also includes accounts that constitute investment in modernization of the forces for the future: acquisition of new weapons, as well as research and development. Each year the budget must be approved by the president, who must reconcile the defense budget with the budgets of all other government agencies, and then by the Congress, just as a company's management must get approval for capital expenditures from its board of directors.

How Much Is Enough?

When the secretary of defense prepares a management plan—the FYDP—the first question he considers, and the first question asked by the president and the Congress is, "How much is enough?" But an informed answer to this question requires first answering another question: "Enough to do *what*?" That is, the secretary, together with the president and the Congress, must determine the missions that the Defense Department must perform to protect the nation's security interests. During the cold war there was broad consensus that DOD needed to field conventional military forces that, in conjunction with allies, would be capable of containing the Warsaw Pact military forces, while at the same time fielding strategic nuclear forces capable of deterring a nuclear war. Therefore, defining defense needs was largely a matter of defining in some detail the potential Soviet threat, and thus threat assessment became a major part of defense planning.

We have argued that the dangers to U.S. security now and in the future will, in contrast, not always take the form of imminent threats defined in traditional cold war terms. Today the United States faces no threats comparable to those it faced during World War II and the cold war. It does face serious threats of major regional conflict in the Persian Gulf and on the Korean Peninsula, and must be prepared to deter and defeat them, but these regional threats do not fully characterize all of the challenges to American defense, and so a different calculus of budget sufficiency is needed. The budget plans put together by the secretary of defense must, of course, include the military forces capable of dealing with regional conflicts (what Les Aspin, when he was secretary of defense, called the "two major regional contingency" or "2MRC" strategy). But in addition to these, and to the programs designed to keep threats to U.S. survival from reemerging—the Preventive Defense programs detailed in the previous chapters of this book—it must also include a general plan to maintain military excellence as a hedge against the failure of Preventive Defense. In this chapter, we discuss some of the management actions necessary for successful execution of this complex defense program.

The Bush administration was the first administration that had to prepare a defense plan after the cold war ended. Secretary of Defense Dick Cheney and JCS Chairman Colin Powell responded to this challenge by establishing the "base force." This entailed a reduction in force of 25 percent, including a major reduction in American forces deployed in Germany and the initiation of the reduction in nuclear forces required by START. But the question of the proper size and shape for American military forces continued to be debated with widely diverse views. The Clinton administration initially addressed this question through the bottom-up review (BUR), which postulated that America's security needs could be met with military forces capable of conducting two major regional conflicts nearly simultaneously. The BUR, approved by President Clinton in late 1993, concluded that these missions were compatible with force reductions of 33 percent and budget reductions of 40 percent in real terms, both measured from cold war highs in the mid-1980s.

Linking Ends with Means

The conclusions of the bottom-up review were questioned by many, but the administration was able to frame the debate by referring critics to the analysis in the review process. The great merit of the BUR was that it linked the ends or missions of the defense plan with its means, that is, the required budget and force levels. Thus, any debate on decreasing the budget logically led to a discussion of how much of a reduction in mission requirements it would impose; any debate on adding missions necessitated grappling with the concomitant budget increase.

Nevertheless, questions persisted as to the adequacy of the defense budget. Some argued that the operational funds budgeted were not sufficient in light of the heavy deployments required by peacekeeping operations that had not been envisioned in the 2MRC strategy, and others argued that the modernization budget was too low and would soon result in weapons obsolescence. As a consequence of these concerns, the Congress mandated that a second review be submitted with the fiscal 1998 budget and every four years thereafter.

The first such Quadrennial Defense Review (QDR) was begun in the last half of 1996, when we were still in office, and finished in the first half of 1997, when William Cohen had become secretary of defense. Major direction was supplied by Deputy Secretary John White for both secretaries. One major focus of the Quadrennial Defense Review was strategy. As with the bottom-up review, the emphasis was on regional conflicts of the kind America might face in the Persian Gulf and the Korean Peninsula. We have no reason to expect that such regional threats will magically disappear, so America needs military forces that can deter regional aggressors or, if deterrence fails, can win quickly, decisively, and with minimal casualties. Therefore, prudent planning requires maintaining an adequate forward presence, sufficient strategic lift, and a level of ready forces that are sufficient to give America the ability to move forces rapidly to a crisis area and to gain dominance quickly over any potential regional aggressor. The primary challenge was to formulate a long-term defense budget capable of maintaining such a force structure and readiness posture, while at the same time giving high priority to the less costly but vitally important programs for Preventive Defense (which the QDR referred to as "shaping the environment"), as well as hedging for the long term against the failure of Preventive Defense (which the QDR called the task of "preparing").

The QDR concluded, and we agree, that these three missions can be sustained for the foreseeable future and within the current budget levels of about $250 billion a year. But this conclusion depends on certain assumptions, some made explicit in the Quadrennial Defense Review report, and others implicit. Explicit in the QDR report was the requirement that the Defense Department must achieve significant management economies, reform its acquisition procedures, increase efficiencies in operating the support structure, and reduce unneeded defense infrastructure. Implicit was the requirement to sustain into the future the present superb quality of American service personnel and the technological superiority of their equipment. The QDR thus pointed beyond the defense management tasks of budgeting and force planning to the major task of execution, so that the planned force is actually achieved. The challenge posed by the QDR (and the BUR before it) is to reduce the budget 40 percent and the force 33 percent from cold war highs without "breaking the force," that is, without causing the force to lose its military effectiveness.

The key to successful execution is to transform the way the Pentagon does business so as to improve efficiency dramatically, thereby reducing overhead costs. If this can be done, then a higher percentage of the defense budget can be spent sustaining the quality of our service personnel and modernizing to sustain our technological lead. It is clear that the successful implementation of the Pentagon's "management plan," the Quadrennial Defense Review, will put a particularly heavy burden on Pentagon management for years to come.

What is needed is not a simple extension of Pentagon business-as-usual, but a revolution in defense management, or rather three related revolutions: a revolution in military affairs, to maintain the exceptional technological edge of our military equipment; a revolution in business affairs, to bring sound business management to the department, reducing unneeded overhead through management reform and reducing the unit cost of equipment through acquisition reform; and a revolution in personnel management, to sustain the exceptionally high quality of American service personnel achieved painstakingly since the post-Vietnam period. In the balance of this chapter, we describe our specific recommendations for each of these revolutions.

A Revolution in Military Affairs

America's military strategy depends on the full use of its technological leadership, especially its leadership in information and aerospace technology. The cold war strategy of maintaining technological superiority was a way to offset the numerical superiority of Soviet ground forces. In Desert Storm, American forces were equipped with the new weapon systems that had been developed during the 1970s and procured during the 1980s; these weapon systems used information technology to locate enemy targets on the battlefield, embedded computers to guide weapons precisely to those targets, and stealth technology to evade enemy weapons. As a consequence, the allied forces won quickly, decisively, and with remarkably few casualties. America's military leaders, having seen the results of battlefield dominance in Desert Storm, decided that they liked it and wanted to keep it. And so today, America's military strategy calls for maintaining battlefield dominance over any regional power with whom we might be engaged in conflict in the near term, for sustaining that lead against the new threats that might emerge through failures of Preventive Defense, and to do so through leadership in technology, especially information technology.

This is the same strategy of technological superiority the United States had during the cold war, but now not only has the reason changed, but so also has the way of applying this technological superiority. During the 1950s, 1960s, and 1970s, the Defense Department was the principal supporter of R&D for the computer, communications, and semiconductor industries. Some of the most significant technical advances in these fields were developed first for military systems: supercomputers, geosynchronous satellites, computer networks, and integrated circuits were all developed first for military programs. In effect, a large part of our nation's commercial industry was riding on the shoulders of the Defense Department.

Today that has all changed: the technological explosion in computers, communications, and semiconductors has led to an amazing new set of commercial products for industry, businesses, schools, and the home, and all of these different users are being tied together by the World Wide Web in a way few could have predicted even a decade ago. Commercial applications of computers are ahead of military applications in all of these fields, and the commercial revenues and technology investments dwarf defense expenditures and R&D budgets. Today defense is obliged to ride on the shoulders of America's commercial industry.

This has required a profound change in the way the Defense Department does business with industry, and the way it supports R&D. First and most important, the department can no longer support a unique defense industry isolated from commercial industry. During the 1980s, for example, the Defense Department spent years and more than a billion dollars developing a family of defense-unique desktop computers, but by the time the military development cycle was completed, these computers were obsolete and were incompatible with the standards evolving in the commercial computer industry. This example was just one of many that made it clear that America should have a single computer industry that supplies defense and commercial needs alike. This requires DOD to give up its unique specifications and conform to industry standards and to give up its unique buying practices and employ best commercial practices. The introduction of commercial practices and components in defense acquisition will save money, and it is also essential to getting modern technology into weapon systems by drawing on the American commercial lead in information technology.

The potential show-stopper in this strategy is getting the best technology into the hands of our troops in a timely way. Major weapon systems generally take ten to fifteen years to develop and then are in the inventory twenty to forty years. But the computer technology that most influences their competitive advantage changes every two or three years. So DOD needs more than a new procurement strategy; it needs an evolutionary systems strategy that keeps major weapon systems in the field for several decades, but updates them every few years with new information technology.

The army has established a large-scale experimental program to do just that. The army chose Fort Hood, Texas, and the Fourth

Infantry Division to experiment with ways to develop "Force 21," the digitized battlefield of the twenty-first century. The concept behind the experiment is simple: to insert digital subsystems into our current weapon systems—tanks, artillery, attack helicopters—thereby giving them a quantum leap in capability. In aggregate, these applications meld the various force elements into a "system of systems" through an integrated network of powerful computers and high-speed communications. This will transform the way commanders and troops see and communicate on the battlefield. In the past, information was passed around the battlefield via radio conversations or typewritten messages. Commanders got only a fraction of the information they could really use in combat. With the system of systems envisioned in Force 21, commanders will have the ability to send and receive, in digital bursts, critical information about the location of enemy and friendly forces; the rate of use of food, fuel, and ammunition; the progress of current operations; and plans for future operations.

The effect on combat operations will be revolutionary. Every commander will have "battlefield awareness": a constant, complete three-dimensional picture of the battlefield. Every field unit will be better able to carry out its commander's orders because it will be able to see more clearly through the "fog of battle." An entire division will be able to fight as a single integrated combat system.

In battle, when a tank commander spots enemy forces, he will have a choice. He could engage the enemy with the weapons on his tanks, or he could call in attack helicopters, artillery, strike aircraft, or naval gunfire. Because of digital technology and the constant flow of battlefield information to all combatants, these other units will see exactly what the tank commander sees, and any one of them—or any combination of them—will be able to respond with equal precision in attacking the targets. As combat is under way, the supporting logistics unit will monitor the ammunition usage, so it will be able to resupply at the time and amount needed, thereby reducing the huge logistics tail otherwise needed to support combat operations. This system of systems is a brilliant application of information technology to achieve battlefield dominance without designing all-new weapons platforms. This is the army of the future: the experiment is bringing a capability like the Internet to the battlefield and doing so with commercial technology and commercially available components.

These examples show that computers are adding major new capabilities to America's weapon systems. But the information revolution is also playing a key role in the design of those weapons and in the training of troops and commanders. Powerful new simulation technology is revolutionizing the way that engineers design and test new weapons. Today in commercial companies, new integrated circuits, new computers, and new telecommunication products—even new automobiles and aircraft—are designed and tested on simulators before the first prototype is built. This same simulation technology can and should be used to a greater and greater extent in military systems. Such simulation lowers development cost and time and ensures that the first model built will be much closer to the final design. "Cut and try" as a design technique is becoming a relic of the past.

The impact of computer simulation on military training promises to be even more dramatic. Military history is replete with surprises because, unlike industrial operations, which are generally repetitive, military operations are generally first-ever experiences for most concerned. Unlike a company such as, say, Federal Express or General Motors, which can hone its operations through everyday experience, military organizations have to strive to simulate "the real thing" through field exercises and training. They spend most of their time planning for operations rather than conducting operations. A key determinant of their success in combat is the realism with which they can practice in peacetime.

Computer simulation can never replace field training or dispel the "fog of war" entirely, but the same computer-enabled techniques that are revolutionizing the entertainment industry's special effects have an enormous potential to allow military organizations to gain realistic wartime experience in peacetime training. Today, every commercial airline uses flight simulators as a low-cost way to maintain and test the proficiency of their aircrews. Military aviation also makes extensive use of such flight simulators, and in the

army today, soldiers train on tank simulators. For the military services, simulators not only reduce training costs, but also allow
training in combat situations that would be too dangerous for field
training. Information technology is permitting simulations that
involve more than one aircraft or tank and show entire engage-
ments in an integrated fashion. Once again, as in the "offset strategy," America can leverage its strength in information technology
to perfect military operations before they have to be conducted.

A Revolution in Business Affairs

During the Bush administration and Clinton's first term, the
Defense Department discontinued or drastically reduced programs
that were no longer needed at the end of the cold war. More difficult were the steps such as those a company president would take
if his business had decreased 40 percent, namely, cutting overhead.
Deputy Secretary of Defense John White, confronted with this
problem, decided that the Pentagon needed a revolution in management as a companion to the ongoing revolution in technology,
and he coined the term "revolution in business affairs" to describe
the effort to improve the overall effectiveness of the DOD by
increasing the efficiency of its support operations. This revolution
is inspired and in part enabled by the marked increase in manage-
rial efficiency of U.S. industry over the last two decades. The private sector has achieved its improvements by focusing on core
competencies while outsourcing other functions, by flattening
organizations, by stressing innovation, and by emphasizing measured performance. These same practices can also apply to the
Defense Department and are necessary for the accomplishment of
the Quadrennial Defense Review's management plan, particularly
modernization. Just as a revolution in military affairs represents
the Defense Department's adoption of industry's technological
advances, the revolution in business affairs is the department's
adoption of industry's management advances.

Since 1987, the overall DOD budget has decreased by almost
40 percent, but the modernization budget has decreased even

more, dropping by almost 60 percent during the same period. This dramatic decline in modernization spending has not yet resulted in a significant extension of the average age of equipment with deployed forces because of the concomitant decrease in force size. But the force size has now stabilized, and modernization spending must increase or the equipment with deployed forces will get a year older with each passing year instead of remaining up to date. Some have argued that therefore America needs a higher defense budget. To the extent that needed modernization programs are not funded by increases in the defense budget, then DOD must move resources from the accounts that support current activities to those that support investments in the future.

The Defense Department has three options for shifting resources from current to future accounts. It could reduce expenditures on operations and maintenance and personnel (readiness), reduce the number of active military units (force structure), or reduce the cost of support services and infrastructure. The last alternative is clearly the preferred choice. But it is also the most difficult because it requires fundamental changes in the way the department does business; that is, it truly does require a revolution in business affairs.

The Example of Military Housing

One view of the revolution in business affairs limits it to reforming the "yellow pages" activities of the Department of Defense: food, clothing, business travel, and other functions that are not unique to a defense organization should be outsourced to the most efficient commercial provider rather than accomplished internally by department personnel. But we believe that a broader view is necessary. The revolution in business affairs must encompass a fundamental reexamination of a larger array of military support functions that do not have common civilian counterparts such as logistics, medical support, management information systems, housing, and training. DOD's goal should be to improve the efficiency of all functions that support military operations.

A prime target for the revolution in business affairs is military housing. Now that the United States has an all-volunteer force, a large number of our active duty military are married, and most of them have dependent children. Providing World War II–type barracks for this force is not compatible with long-term retention of the best qualified of our professional force. But base housing for families is available for only a fraction of the force, and some of that dates back to the nineteenth century, when many of the army forts in the West and Midwest were built during the days of the Indian Wars. However, launching a serious program to build family housing on military bases would overwhelm the defense budget at the expense of training and modernization. Therefore, at the recommendation of the quality of life task force headed by Jack Marsh, the Defense Department initiated a pilot program in 1995 to outsource military housing. The idea was simple: DOD would supply what amounted to a guaranteed market for housing developers. This would give them the financial incentive to build houses on or near military bases, meeting general quality standards rather than detailed specifications established by the department. The developer would then lease the houses to individual soldiers, at monthly rates compatible with the housing allowance provided them by their parent service.

The pilot program demonstrated that there is real potential for attracting very large amounts of private capital to investment in housing that meets military needs. In that sense, the pilot program has been a success. But it was only a pilot program, dealing with a small percentage of the military's housing needs. What is needed at this time is a strong push in both the Defense Department and the Congress to scale up this pilot program to deal with still largely unmet needs.

The Base Closing Imperative

To accomplish the revolution in business affairs, the Pentagon management set out to cut overhead that was no longer needed by the reduced force. But defense management has a much more complicated task than private-sector management because all of the required actions are political dynamite. Every member of Congress wants to reduce unnecessary defense spending, but no member wants to close a base or a government depot in his or her district. Indeed, every defense secretary soon learns that hell hath no fury like a member whose base is about to be closed.

Even though this issue is so politically charged, the Bush and Clinton administrations did make major reductions: DOD civilian manpower has been reduced by 25 percent, on the way to 33 percent, and more than 100 bases have been closed or realigned. This progress has been made possible by legislation passed by Congress in 1988. For years before that, no secretary had been able to close bases that were thought unneeded because their proposed closures would inevitably be blocked in Congress.

A few farsighted congressional representatives conceived of an approach to unblock this bottleneck. They proposed, and Congress passed in 1988, legislation that created a Base Realignment and Closing Commission. Under the legislation, the commission's task would begin with a review of all base realignments and closings that were proposed by the secretary of defense. The commission would then conduct extensive hearings and determine which of these proposals should be accepted. The commission's recommendations then went to the president. He could reject the plan as modified by the commission, but he could not change it. If he approved the plan, then it went to the full Congress, which again could reject it, but not change it. The wisdom of this legislation was soon evident. As noted above, more than 100 bases have been closed or realigned since the enactment of the law, whereas almost none had been closed before.

But base closing does not lead to immediate savings; in fact, it requires an expensive and sometimes time-consuming front-end process because of the environmental problems at many bases and because of the need to protect the interests of the communities affected by the closing. During the early 1990s, when base closing was in its early stages, the process was costing $4 billion a year; by the end of the 1990s, the process will be saving more than $6 billion a year. The net change from an annual cost of $4 billion to an annual savings of $6 billion has allowed the Defense Department to begin to swing about $10 billion annually from unneeded bases to badly needed equipment modernization.

But even with a $10 billion increase in the modernization budget, and even if the overall defense budget holds firm at present levels, there will still not be enough to meet the services' equipment modernization goals. That is, military equipment will be aging faster than the services can afford to modernize, so each year the average age of weapons will increase. If that is allowed to happen, then the readiness levels that are so critical for force effectiveness will suffer beginning early in the next decade. Even if military forces continue to be high quality and well trained, their effectiveness will decline if they are using obsolescent equipment.

Thus further rounds of base closings, as recommended by the Quadrennial Defense Review, are imperative. But this requires Congress to extend the Base Realignment and Closing Commission legislation, which to this point it has not been willing to do. Therefore other strategies for increasing modernization must also be pursued as part of the revolution in business affairs.

Continuing the Reform of the Acquisition System

One of the key strategies in dealing with the modernization problem is to get more bang for the available modernization buck by continuing the reform of the acquisition system. Defense acquisition is the largest and most complex purchasing operation in the world, and its processes and procedures have evolved over many decades and are administered by more than 150,000 people in whom these procedures are deeply ingrained. This makes any changes in the system difficult to execute and really fundamental changes almost impossible. However, on June 24, 1994, the landmark directive reforming military specifications policy was issued: it stated that military specifications could be used only if a waiver were approved by the acquisition executive. This directive empowered program managers to buy commercial components unless there were a compelling reason to insist on military specifications. DOD thus turned the previous acquisition system on its head by moving from a preference for military specifications and standards to a preference for commercial standards. Most program managers welcomed this empowerment and acted on it with great effectiveness.

Some skeptics have questioned whether the financial savings that could be achieved by the reform initiative were sufficient to justify the daunting task of changing over to commercial components and standards. The annual modernization budget, covering spending on weapons systems, is currently about $50 billion. But additional expenditures on large numbers of relatively small quantities of nonweapons items, from jet fuel to stationery, total tens of billions of dollars, and are contained in the operations and maintenance budget rather than the modernization budget. Efficiencies of as little as 10 percent in total procurements would amount to annual savings of about $10 billion, and we believe that even greater savings are possible. This was a primary impetus for establishing the acquisition reform initiative and a primary basis for the support given to it by the services and the Congress. As a result, it is fair to say that the Defense Department has built a foundation for long-lasting reform of its acquisition system.

The early results have been reflected in savings on a variety of procurements, from very small and mundane purchases to major weapons procurements. The Defense Logistics Agency is now buying better quality T-shirts at a 10 percent lower price than the previous milspec T-shirts. The U.S. Air Force, by allowing the program manager to buy commercial components, is now buying Joint Direct Attack Munition (JDAM) precision-guided bombs at about half the previous price, with an overall program savings of more than $2 billion. The C-17 airlifter, a program on the verge of cancellation in 1993, became under the new system a model program delivering ahead of schedule and savings on the order of $5 billion. The C-17 savings were a result of multiyear procurement, use of commercial components, and empowering the contractor to use "continuous process improvement" techniques in the factory.

There has been a very solid beginning, with major program achievements and the establishment of new procedures, but much hard work lies ahead to institutionalize these new procedures fully. To understand just how much has been done in addition to the reform of military specifications, and how much still lies ahead, it is instructive to summarize the most important of these new procedures.

ADOPTING COMMERCIAL BUYING PRACTICES.   The use of commercial items allows the program manager to take advantage of the innovation and economies of scale offered by the commercial marketplace and ensures that the Defense Department will have access to state-of-the-art technology. Equally important is the use of commercial buying practices, giving the department program manager access to vendors who are not willing to take on the added cost and trouble involved in incorporating the unique defense accounting system in their business practices.

REWRITING OF DEFENSE DEPARTMENT DIRECTIVES.   The department has revised and streamlined the phonebook-thick directives that once provided detailed guidance for the acquisition of major systems. The new directives manage to fit all of the new laws, policies, and procedures into a single document. On the one hand, they make explicit the guidance that was mandatory, and on the other hand, they encourage and facilitate the use of professional judgment by program managers.

SINGLE PROCESS INITIATIVE.   If the new acquisition procedures were only applied to new contracts being negotiated with industry, much of the benefit of reform would be missed. It was therefore important that program managers and industry managers be able to apply the reforms retroactively to existing programs already under contract. Rather than rewrite these many existing contracts, the single process initiative provided a mechanism for specified process reforms to be applied to all of a contractor's contracts simultaneously.

INTEGRATED PRODUCT AND PROCESS DEVELOPMENT TEAMS. "Integrated product and process development" teams have been used by industry for about a decade with great effectiveness. They bring together the various members of the design and production team at an early stage of the design process to consider simultaneously what is to be made and how it is to be made, allowing for cost-effective tradeoffs in design specifications and production techniques. Such teams are now used throughout the department.

ELECTRONIC COMMERCE.   The Defense Department led the federal government in the implementation of electronic commerce and electronic data interchange. DOD has automated more than 200 contracting offices doing over 60 percent of the department's contracting actions. Electronic buying has long been standard in industry and saves both time and money.

STREAMLINED TESTING.   Testing has always been an indispensable part of the defense acquisition system, but it takes on a special significance with the reformed acquisition processes. Accordingly, DOD has reformed the test and evaluation system along with other acquisition reforms. Changes include the earlier involvement of operational testers, combining development and operational testing when feasible, and greatly expanding the use of modeling and simulation.

PILOT PROGRAMS.   At the request of the secretary of defense, in 1995 Congress authorized five pilot programs and gave the managers of those five programs sweeping authority to use commercial components and practices. These five programs were important not only for the savings they could generate, but because they could serve as pathfinders for all other defense procurements by demonstrating that extensive use of commercial components could not only save money but also lead to a better product. The five programs selected were the JDAM precision-guided bomb; Fire Support Combined Arms Tactical Trainer; Joint Primary Aircraft Training System; Commercial Derivative Engine; and Commercial Derivative Aircraft. The pilot programs were given statutory relief by the Federal Acquisition Streamlining Act from the onerous requirements of long-standing procurement law and regulatory relief under the authority of the Defense Department's acquisition executive. The pilot programs are making substantial progress and demonstrating that, through the use of commercial products and commercial practices, military items can be acquired with improved development and delivery schedules, at reduced cost, and with substantial gains in in-house efficiencies.

These initiatives highlight the extensive changes in the defense acquisition system. Other changes include the preparation of automated reference tools for all service and department agencies; important new initiatives in the education, training, and career development of acquisition officials; reform of the contract administration and pre-award contract process; and the introduction of predetermined cost targets for defense procurements. All of these landmark changes were initiated by John Deutch and Paul Kaminski in their combined four years as head of defense acquisition. These were heroic achievements that will serve the department and the nation for decades to come. However, much work still lies ahead.

The initiatives described above have already shown acquisition reform to be a "win-win-win" situation. The defense industry has won through greater profits and higher stock prices; the Defense Department has won through systems that embody modern technology; and the taxpayer has won through lower costs of equipment purchased by the Defense Department. But this has been only a beginning. The course has been set; the pilot programs have shown the way; now the Defense Department, the defense industry, and Congress must stay the course. They must be prepared, for example, to scale up the pilot programs in acquisition, in outsourcing, and in privatization of military housing so that the taxpayers and military personnel can get the full benefit of these initiatives.

A Revolution in Personnel Management

Even with the best technology, weapons, and management in the world, the future effectiveness of the U.S. military will turn on the quality and readiness of the soldiers, sailors, aircrews, and marines who are "at the point of the spear." People matter most. The looming challenge posed to modernization by lower budgets and accelerating technology requires a "revolution in military affairs," and the chronic wastefulness of defense management practices requires a "revolution in business affairs," so it is logical to call also for a "revolution in personnel management." But the people who make up today's U.S. armed forces are the best of any military force in the world, and we are far from the "hollow army" of the post-Vietnam era. Why, then, do we call for a revolution in personnel management?

The reason is that the hard-won professionalism of the U.S. armed forces is a fragile asset. It must be constantly renewed. It cannot be bought once and for all. As society and the economy change, the Defense Department must change its practices to ensure that the excellence displayed by the U.S. military in Iraq, Haiti, and Bosnia is preserved. Doing so will require a continuing revolution in personnel management, including recruiting, education and training, and retention policies.

Recruiting

When the all-volunteer force was established in 1973, the military services lost their guaranteed supply of personnel. From that time on, they would have to attract volunteers from all over the nation. The recruiting arms of each of the services were on the front lines of this mission, which seemed to some "Mission Impossible."

The first step in the rebuilding process was to set quality standards. Each of the services established standards based on a recruit's education level and scores on the general aptitude test. The army, for example, set goals that a certain percentage of its force should be in the top two categories in the aptitude test and that a certain percentage should be high school graduates. These goals have been generally met by all four services for almost two decades now. The results make it clear that these goals should be maintained. America's military personnel have to operate increasingly complex equipment and conduct military operations for which independence and initiative are increasingly important.

Setting standards was a necessary first step, but how could bright young high school graduates be persuaded to enlist? The recruiting arms received their greatest tool when Congress passed a bill supported by Representative Sonny Montgomery. This "new GI Bill" promised to pay most of the costs of a college education for recruits after they served their term of enlistment. This attracted high school graduates who wanted to go to college but could not afford the cost of a college education. The Montgomery bill not only increased the incentive to enlist; it also targeted the incentive directly to those bright and motivated young graduates who wanted to go on to college.

Military recruiters have always had an important arrow in their quiver—an exciting, interesting job, best represented by the navy's recruiting motto: "Join the Navy and see the world!" Now the Montgomery bill and the military's outstanding training programs gave them a second arrow, best represented by the army's recruiting motto: "Be all you can be!" These were powerful messages, but the services needed an equally powerful way of communicating these messages, so the recruiters got increased budgets for advertising. In the modern age, advertising had to do more than display Uncle Sam proclaiming "I need you" on billboards in front of post offices around the land. The services used their increased budgets for television advertising, especially on nationally broadcast sports events. This turned out to be a good strategy, and for almost two decades, the military services have generally met their recruiting goals without lowering their standards. As a consequence, the services have today a steady input of bright young recruits who are motivated to learn a new profession and have the ability to master the difficult training program provided by the services.

Education and Training

The U.S. military services have today the best large-scale education and training program of any military or any company in the world. It begins with access to college education for active duty personnel. Each of the services encourages its personnel to take part-time college courses, providing financial assistance and sometimes schedule adjustments to make this possible. This is easier to arrange for military personnel based in the states, but the services have also established a college program for overseas personnel. The program is run for the services by the University of Maryland, which has established campuses in Germany, Japan, and Korea, where most overseas American personnel are based. The services have established correspondence courses for personnel who cannot get to a campus. The navy, for example, has set up computer workstations on each of its combat ships to help navy and marine personnel continue their college educations while they are at sea.

Additionally, the services have an extensive program of graduate education in technical fields of relevance to the military, including two postgraduate schools: the Naval Post-Graduate School in Monterey, California, and the Air Force Institute of Technology in Dayton, Ohio. Each year, thousands of military and civilian personnel attend these two military schools, and thousands more attend top graduate schools located all over the nation.

The U.S. military also conducts a unique program of leadership training. Every noncommissioned officer (NCO), before he or she is promoted to the next level, must take a leadership course specifically preparing for the challenges of the higher-level position, and some of these courses are quite extensive. Less than 1 percent of army NCOs are tapped for promotion to sergeant major, but before they get their stripes, each must pass a very intensive nine-month program in NCO leadership.

The ultimate in military training is the combat training conducted extensively by all of the services. We have already described the superbly realistic training at Grafenwoehr and Hohenfels for troops going into Bosnia. At Fort Irwin, California, and later at Fort Polk, Louisiana, and at Hohenfels in Germany, the army established fully instrumented training facilities that have made it possible to achieve an unprecedented level of combat realism. Every active-duty army brigade is scheduled to undergo this intensive combat training about once every eighteen months. At Fort Irwin they face the resident "Red Force" brigade, and this is typically an exercise in humility for the visiting brigade commanders. The navy and marines also have an extensive training program for their active duty crews. Every carrier battle group, for example, spends months at sea before deployment, in a "work-up" that culminates in a mock combat engagement.

The most advanced air force training facility is at Nellis Air Force Base in Nevada. There the air force maintains the "Red

Force," a resident squadron that takes on all other air force fighter squadrons in combat exercises. These exercises are as realistic as it is possible to make them without endangering the flight crews, and they are followed by a brutally candid evaluation of the mistakes made by the visiting squadrons. These visiting squadrons then return to their home bases, sadder but wiser, and far less likely to repeat in real combat the mistakes they made against the "Red Force." These training programs are the best possible preparation for real combat, and they also serve as a deterrent, since other military forces around the world are aware of the peak readiness of American forces as a result of this training.

Retention and Quality of Life

The extensive training program is certainly the key to the current and continuing readiness of America's military forces. It also constitutes a large investment, which is the reason that it always comes under attack at budget time. But even if the budget battle is won, some of that investment is lost each time one of our trained personnel decides against reenlisting. So the high readiness of America's military forces depends on a high rate of retention of military personnel, and retention depends to a large extent on the satisfaction of military personnel and their families with their quality of life. There is a saying among army recruiting personnel: "The soldier decides whether to enlist; his family decides whether he should reenlist." Thus an iron logic connects readiness with quality of life: cutting budgets that affect quality-of-life measures is, over the long term, a very poor economy measure that squanders the costs of recruiting quality personnel and the costs of training them.

Many factors influence the quality of life for military personnel and their families; high on the list are compensation roughly comparable to civilian counterparts, adequate housing, and adequate facilities such as day care, schools, and recreation at bases, particularly remote bases. Separation of families is also an issue: in Korea, for example, nearly all U.S. troops are on unattached tours of one year, separated from their families. While such family hardships may be acceptable in wartime, they are not conducive to building the kind of morale that leads the military's best NCOs and officers, in whom so much has been invested, to reenlist. Recently the increased operational tempo ("op-tempo") of the U.S. military, as it responds to the many crises and peacekeeping missions of the post–cold war world, has taken personnel away from their families more frequently and for longer periods than they had reason to expect when they chose military service. There are many signs that the trends in retention have become adverse. In spite of the promising beginning of the program inspired by Jack Marsh's quality of life task force and incorporated into recent Defense Department management reforms, the program seems to be stalled. The operational tempo—and the time away from home base and families—is reaching 50 percent for some units, and the discrepancy between military pay and civilian pay has reached 13 percent.

The interlocking problems of recruitment, training, and retention must be given the priority of an ongoing revolution. That will entail devoting a greater portion of the defense budget to improving the quality of life of U.S. military forces and their families. One potential source of the needed funds is reduction in the force structure. Although we firmly believe that a small, highly ready force with high morale is always to be preferred to a larger but "hollow" force, this option to free up funds might actually exacerbate the quality of life problem, since fewer active duty units would imply even higher op-tempo for each. In addition, we believe that a significant cut in force structure would have to be accompanied by a reduction in America's global commitments, with attendant long-term adverse geopolitical consequences. A second option is to slow down the pace of modernization. A third option is to increase the defense budget. A fourth option would be to realize further savings from the acquisition reform, base closing, and privatization initiatives that make up the revolution in business affairs we have described.

The first two choices are very undesirable, but even these are preferable to a decline in the quality of American military personnel: such a decline must not be allowed to occur.

Meeting the Threat Within

This book is about the future that lies beyond the "post–cold war era." That future, we have argued, contains dangers that will rekindle A-list security threats to U.S. survival if they are not forestalled by an active and thoughtful strategy of Preventive Defense. But just as preventive medicine does not ensure good health, Preventive Defense is not a guarantee of American security. The future is not only potentially perilous, but it is above all uncertain. We believe, therefore, that a vigorous program of Preventive Defense must be complemented by a wise shepherding of U.S. military prowess.

Complacency born of post–cold war euphoria is the greatest challenge to Preventive Defense. Absence of imminent A-list threats falsely suggests that security strategy can concern itself wholly with the important but much less vital B-list and C-list threats. The first five chapters of this book describe the dangers that might fill America's A list once again in the future. These chapters also describe the Preventive Defense measures that can reduce the probability that these dangers develop into full-scale threats. The same post–cold war complacency threatens the stewardship of our military. In this chapter we have called such complacency "the threat within." We have prescribed ambitious measures to overcome the threat within, and implementing them will not be easy. We have termed the needed measures "revolutions." Because the Pentagon does its business amidst revolutions in the world around it, the Pentagon must also undertake a series of revolutions: revolutions in technology, in business practices, and in human organization. Without revolutionary change of its own, the U.S. military will end up like a rust belt industry overcome by change and foreign competition. Unlike the external dangers described in the first five chapters, however, the threat within is entirely of U.S. making, and it is within our power to overcome it if we choose to do so.

Epilogue

On November 23, 1998, while putting the finishing touches on this book, we found ourselves in Washington again. As we stood in a conference room on the seventh floor of the State Department, Wendy Sherman, counselor to Secretary of State Madeleine Albright, held up a little flag to add a touch of gravity to the brief ceremony, and we repeated the oath of office for public servants: "I, William J. Perry, do solemnly swear . . . to uphold and defend the Constitution against all enemies, foreign and domestic. . . . I, Ashton B. Carter, do solemnly swear. . . ." We had last taken this oath in the Pentagon in 1993, as the events related in this book began.

President Clinton and Secretary Albright had asked Perry in October to come back to Washington to serve as their special adviser and policy coordinator for North Korea. Perry, in turn, had asked Carter to join him as his special adviser. ("Special adviser to the special adviser: it makes me feel very special," Carter quipped.) We were to conduct a fundamental, no-holds-barred review of U.S. policy toward North Korea. We expected the effort to take an intense four months. Secretary of State Albright promised to contribute the considerable talents of Wendy Sherman to the effort. The State Department provided an office and a small staff, augmented by personnel from the Joint Chiefs of Staff and the Office of the Secretary of the Defense. We liked the team; the mission, however, was daunting.

We were soon reminded just how daunting: two weeks later, we traveled to South Korea, where we met first at the headquarters of General John Tilelli, commander of U.S. Forces in Korea and of the U.S.–South Korean Combined Forces Command. Tilelli briefed us on OPLAN 5027, the plan for the defense of South Korea against a North Korean invasion, just as his predecessor, General Gary Luck, had done in the summer of 1994. That summer, as we related in chapter 4, the Korean peninsula had come close to war over the North Korean nuclear weapons program. Crisis was averted by the negotiation of a so-called Agreed Framework with North Korea. The main provisions of the Agreed Framework called for North Korea to "freeze" and eventually dismantle its plutonium production capability, and in return two power reactors would be built in North Korea with financing from the United States, South Korea, and Japan. While the new reactors were being built, the United States would provide fuel oil to North Korea to substitute for whatever power the "frozen" bomb program's reactors might have generated. In the intervening four years, despite some difficulties, both sides had been implementing these provisions.

OPLAN 5027, like all military contingency plans, is updated periodically. Tilelli highlighted the changes made since 1994. Both U.S. and South Korean forces had improved their capabilities in several ways. The North Koreans had maintained their million-man army just north of the demilitarized zone (DMZ) and continued to deploy thousands of artillery pieces and missile launchers close to the DMZ. One important change in OPLAN 5027 reflected the U.S. emphasis on counterproliferation that had begun in 1994. Tilelli was ahead of most U.S. commanders in his preparations to deal with North Korean missiles, chemical weapons, and biological weapons, not only at the battlefront but also at the airfields and seaports through which crucial reinforcements would flow into South Korea from the United States. Tilelli's impressive briefing made it clear that a North Korean invasion would be repelled and defeated within a matter of weeks.

But one reality had not changed since 1994. War on the Korean peninsula would be horribly destructive. Seoul is no farther from the DMZ than Dulles Airport is from Washington, D.C. North Korean artillery shells would rain down on this teeming modern city. Hundreds of thousands of civilians could be killed and millions of refugees created in both South and North Korea. The 37,000 U.S. troops stationed in South Korea, many other U.S. government personnel, and more than 100,000 other American citizens living and working in South Korea would also be in harm's way. Though there were plans to evacuate the noncombatants, one had only to imagine this occurring in the midst of an artillery barrage to realize that many Americans would share the fate of the Korean citizens of Seoul. War on the peninsula would be no Desert Storm; it would be a human catastrophe. Koreans and Americans have faced the possibility of such a catastrophe for decades. In fact, we are still formally at war with North Korea: the fighting was stopped by the armistice of 1953, but no peace treaty has ever been concluded. Nothing in this grim picture has changed since 1994.

In other respects, however, the situation on the peninsula had changed fundamentally from 1994, when the Agreed Framework was signed and conflict averted. It was these changes that had moved President Clinton and his senior advisors to seek a review of U.S. policy.

For one thing, the government of North Korea had changed. Negotiation of the Agreed Framework had begun when Kim Il Sung, the founding president of communist North Korea, hand picked for the job by Stalin himself, was still alive. Shortly after the 1994 crisis passed, Kim Il Sung died. In a mysterious and protracted process of succession, leadership of North Korea passed to his enigmatic son Kim Jong Il. The younger Kim seemed to take literally Korea's ancient sobriquet as the "hermit kingdom." He rarely speaks in public and has not yet met with foreign leaders since his father died. No one could vouch for his personal commitment to the Agreed Framework or its broad road map for improving the relations of his government with South Korea and the United States.

Meanwhile, North Korea's economy had descended from stalled communist throwback into all-out, free-fall collapse. North Korea's industrial and agricultural output had plummeted. Never self-sufficient in food, the country now needed more imported food but had little to export in return. Malnutrition and starvation ensued to an extent still unknown to the outside world, but clearly massive and tragic. North Korea's response to these failures could take one of several courses: Kim Jong Il might open up North Korea to the world like China's Deng and the Soviet Union's Gorbachev; or a coup or revolt might take place despite the controls of what still appears from the outside to be a monolithic police state, dealing Kim a fate like that of his father's friend Nicolae Ceausescu of Romania; or Kim might hang on stubbornly to his ideology for years, eking out an existence for his people on foreign handouts and controlling them through fanatical propaganda. No one can predict the fate of North Korea or its leadership.

From Tilelli's headquarters in Seoul, we continued by U.S. military aircraft and helicopters to meet the leaders of the three states neighboring North Korea: South Korea, Japan, and China. Their views would have to be factored into any American policy toward North Korea. First, we went to South Korea's Blue House to meet with President Kim Dae Jung. South Korea's leadership had also changed since 1994, and in a sharp departure from his predecessors, Kim Dae Jung had championed a bold policy of engagement with North Korea. He believed North Korea could be persuaded that its only choice was to open up and reform its economy. This would take years, but in the meantime, he counseled, we should be patient with the enigmatic leaders up north.

From Seoul we traveled to Beijing. China is perhaps the closest thing to a friend North Korea has, but China, like Russia before it, has ceased to pour money into Pyongyang to support the regime. In our meetings, China's leaders professed to be as mystified by North Korea's actions as we were, and they were clearly concerned with the deterioration of the North's economy. As we met, both sides were aware of yet another new feature of the present situation: China's relationship with the United States has improved greatly since 1994. This new relationship, while still fragile, opens up new prospects for a measure of cooperation in dealing with the "hermit kingdom." Finally, we went to Tokyo to consult with America's closest ally in the region and to report to the Japanese government on our discussions in Seoul and Beijing. Japan, too, was concerned about North Korea. The relationship between Japan and the Korean peninsula is colored by the memory of Japan's brutal occupation there before and during World War II. But late in 1998, Japan formally apologized to South Korea for its mistreatment of the Korean people, a move that thawed relations with the South. Japanese attitudes toward North Korea, however, had hardened. In August 1998, North Korea had launched a three-stage ballistic missile over Japan without warning. Though apparently intended to put a small satellite into orbit, the North Korean missile was clearly capable of delivering a warhead to Japan. Japanese public opinion was aroused; Japan suspended its food donations to North Korea and even considered suspending its funding for the reactors for North Korea that were called for in the Agreed Framework.

Our journey through the region was sobering. Unlike in Europe, the cold war is not yet fully over in East Asia. There is no overarching security structure such as Europe's NATO and no new Partnership for Peace to encourage the region's militaries to put their difficult past behind them. Indeed, the wounds of World War II are still not completely healed. Square in the middle of this complex mix is the dilemma of North Korea.

Kim Dae Jung's approach to this dilemma turns on patience and "peaceful coexistence" with the Stalinist state. Just like the cold war with the Soviet Union, he argues, the logic of history will eventually catch up with the Pyongyang regime. Kim's policy of engagement, he says, will ease the regime's inevitable passage to reform. Pressure and confrontation might provoke the unpredictable North Koreans to lash out, with catastrophic consequences. In different ways, Japan's and China's leaders gave us the same advice.

This counsel of patience runs headlong, however, into another major development since 1994: evidence that North Korea might not in fact have given up its aspirations to have a nuclear arsenal despite signing the Agreed Framework. One indication is the construction of a huge underground facility that U.S. intelligence believes might be designed to house a reactor and reprocessing facility like those of the "frozen" program at Yongbyon. The possibility of a covert underground nuclear program operating in place of the one "frozen" by the Agreed Framework raises all over again the dangers that led to crisis in 1994. Nuclear weapons in North Korea would be a triple threat: they would further increase the carnage of war on the peninsula; they might provoke an arms race in the region, causing Japan and South Korea to reconsider their own decisions to forgo nuclear weapons; and they would undermine nonproliferation worldwide if others witnessed North Korea "succeeding" in thwarting the Nonproliferation Treaty or even selling nuclear weapons to other aspiring proliferators.

This last possibility is no academic concern. North Korea already markets a growing family of ballistic missiles it has managed to produce despite its desperately backward economy. The North's ballistic missile program was the second reason why it might not be safe to follow Kim Dae Jung's advice and wait for change to come to North Korea. The North's missiles are increasing in range. The so-called No Dong missile could reach Japan, and the so-called Taepo Dong could probably reach parts of the United States. With only high explosive warheads, such missiles pose a negligible military risk, but in tandem with a nuclear weapons program, they become a deadly threat. North Korea's willingness to sell missiles for desperately needed hard currency suggests that they might also sell nuclear weapons if they are allowed to get them.

We agreed with President Clinton and his advisers, and with many members of Congress, that a continuing weapons of mass destruction program in North Korea would rob us of the time needed for Kim Dae Jung's engagement policy to work. Unless a solution to the problem can be found, the situation could easily end up in a confrontation like that of the summer of 1994. Can a Preventive Defense approach be found that will avert a return to the summer of 1994? If so, can it be practiced in this complex region with its many players? And can the regime in Pyongyang be persuaded to give up its weapons of mass destruction ambitions without a destructive war? The answers to these questions are far from clear. They are the next challenge for Preventive Defense.

Notes

Introduction

1. The concept of Preventive Defense was introduced by William J. Perry when he was secretary of defense in "Defense in an Age of Hope," *Foreign Affairs*, vol. 75, no. 6 (1996).

2. Dean Acheson, *Present at the Creation: My Years in the State Department* (Norton, 1987).

3. Although we wrote all of the chapters together, some passages record events at which Perry was present but not Carter, so in these passages the first person refers to Perry.

Chapter 1: Pursuing Marshall's Vision

1. Before using NAOC, Perry had ordered Carter to analyze all possible scenarios for NAOC's other duties, including the remote but never negligible possibility of nuclear war and the possibility of a terrorist attack that would devastate Washington. Carter reported that there would always be at least one NAOC aircraft available for the president or his successors, even if the secretary of defense traveled on one of the planes.

2. The idea of the Partnership for Peace and its implementation had been brilliantly articulated in 1993 by Deputy Assistant Secretary of Defense Joseph Kruzel, who was killed in 1995 in a tragic accident in Bosnia.

3. Remarks by Secretary of Defense William J. Perry to the George Washington University International Affairs Forum, March 14, 1994.

4. Not all paranoia is Russian: when Russian troops arrived in the United States for the reciprocal exercise in Kansas, American "militias" broadcast on their web pages that the exercise heralded the takeover of the U.S. military by the United Nations.

5. Up the road from Hyde Park is the Culinary Institute of America, "the other CIA," which trains chefs in haute cuisine. This CIA had offered to cater the summit, and when Clinton and Yeltsin and their entourages sat down to lunch, the fare consisted of fancy and exotic tidbits gorgeously presented. However, they were tiny little portions dotted around the large formal plates, and Yeltsin complained that this was not enough to keep a man alive. Was there any bread, he asked, just good dark bread, like Russian bread? The CIA staff said they had none but would quickly put together a substitute. Minutes went by while Yeltsin looked around hungrily. Finally a plate was set down in front of him, and resting on it were three dainty little freshly baked biscuits. Yeltsin rolled his eyes and pushed them aside. (A few days later he had a heart attack, one of several that year.)

6. Shevtsov has written his own account of these events, "Russia-NATO Military Cooperation in Bosnia: A Basis for the Future?" *NATO Review*, March 1997, pp. 17–21.

7. *New York Times*, November 12, 1996, p. 1.

8. We called it the NATO-Russia Consultative Mechanism or "Nerk'm." It later became the "Permanent Joint Council."

9. Much of our discussion of the future of NATO draws on Coit D. Blacker, Ashton B. Carter, Warren Christopher, David A. Hamburg, and William J. Perry, *NATO after Madrid*, Stanford-Harvard Preventive Defense Project Report, vol. 1, no. 1, 1998.

10. A similar set of proposals is found in John M. Shalikashvili and Elizabeth Sherwood-Randall, *The NATO-Russia Relationship*, Stanford-Harvard Preventive Defense Project Report, vol. 1, no. 5, forthcoming.

11. See Ashton B. Carter, Steven E. Miller, and Elizabeth Sherwood-Randall, *Fulfilling the Promise: Building an Enduring Security Partnership between Ukraine and NATO*, Stanford-Harvard Preventive Defense Project Report, vol. 1, no. 3, forthcoming.

12. Gordon A. Craig, *Europe since 1815*, 3d ed. (Holt, Rinehart, and Winston, 1971), p. 554.

Chapter 2: Nunn-Lugar and Arms Control

1. We are grateful to Jeffrey Starr, Laura Holgate, and Susan Koch, who managed this project for the Office of the Secretary of Defense, and to others who must still remain nameless, for sharing with us their recollections of this operation.

2. The uranium is now being put to peaceful use: it is being processed and sold to entities that operate nuclear reactors to generate electricity.

3. See Kurt M. Campbell, Ashton B. Carter, Steven E. Miller, and Charles A. Zraket, *Soviet Nuclear Fission: Control of the Nuclear Arsenal in a Disintegrating Soviet Union*, Center for Science and International Affairs (CSIA), John F. Kennedy School of Government, Harvard University, CSIA Studies in International Security No. 1, November 1991; Graham T. Allison, Ashton B. Carter, Steven E. Miller, and Philip Zelikow, *Cooperative Denuclearization: From Pledges to Deeds*, CSIA Studies in International Security No. 2, January 1993; Graham Allison, Owen Coté Jr., Richard Falkenrath, and Steven E. Miller, *Avoiding Nuclear Anarchy: Containing the Threat of Loose Russian Nuclear Weapons and Fissile Material*, CSIA Studies in International Security No. 12 (MIT Press 1996).

4. This history is detailed in the senators' own words in Sam Nunn and Richard Lugar, "The Nunn-Lugar Initiative: Cooperative Demilitarization in the Former Soviet Union," in Allan E. Goodman, ed., *The Diplomatic Record 1992–1993* (Boulder, Colo.: Westview Press, 1995), chap. 7.

5. Campbell, Carter, Miller, and Zraket, *Soviet Nuclear Fission.*

6. The fissile material repository was proposed in Allison, Carter, Miller, and Zelikow, *Cooperative Denuclearization.*

7. "Mutual Assured Safety," remarks by Secretary of Defense William J. Perry to the Henry L. Stimson Center, September 20, 1994.

8. For this argument, see Ashton B. Carter and John M. Deutch, "No Nukes? Not Yet," *Wall Street Journal*, March 4, 1997, p. A18.

9. A possibility we do not discuss here is that the United States decides in coming years to deploy a national missile defense (NMD) to defend its territory against ICBMs in the hands of potential aggressor states such as North Korea or Iran. The NMD deployment concepts under consideration for this contingency are limited defenses capable of intercepting small numbers of incoming warheads—far fewer than Russia is expected to maintain in this scenario. Thus, provided Russia understands the limited nature of this U.S. defense, it should have little effect on the structure of Russian missile forces or on the intent of the ABM treaty. Of course, this matter might become a topic of negotiation between the

United States and Russia, in which case these negotiations could figure into the next round of arms control. For the purposes of this discussion, however, we set aside the NMD scenario.

Chapter 3: Dealing with a Rising China

1. The missile tests were conducted before dawn on March 8, local time, which was early in the afternoon of March 7, Washington time.

2. North Korea's nuclear program is discussed in chapter 4.

3. The Zangger Committee, established in the early 1970s, develops guidelines for implementing the export control provisions of the Nuclear Nonproliferation Treaty.

4. The Nuclear Suppliers Group comprises countries that supply nuclear materials and technology for peaceful uses; it established a comprehensive set of guidelines to ensure that their nuclear cooperation does not aid proliferation. The Wassenaar Arrangement on Export Controls for Conventional Arms and Dual-Use Goods and Technologies was created by the original western members of the Coordinating Committee on Export Controls (CoCom) in 1996 to improve coordination of export control policies and increase transparency on transfer of conventional arms and dual-use technologies.

5. Shirley A. Kan, "Chinese Proliferation of Weapons of Mass Destruction: Current Policy Issues," Congressional Research Service (CRS) Issue Brief 92056, March 1998.

Chapter 4: Counterproliferation

1. Team Spirit was the Korean equivalent of Reforger ("reinforcement of Germany"), which we conducted during the cold war to demonstrate to the Soviet Union the capability to reinforce our troops in Germany.

2. President Carter's visit to Pyongyang, the U.S. government's response to Kim Il Sung's offer, and the subsequent negotiations conducted by Ambassador Gallucci are described in detail in Don Oberdorfer, *The Two Koreas: A Contemporary History* (Reading, Mass.: Addison-Wesley, 1997).

3. Remarks prepared for Secretary of Defense Les Aspin, speech to the National Academy of Sciences, December 7, 1993.

4. The RMA is discussed further in chapter 6. See also William J. Perry, "Desert Storm and Deterrence," *Foreign Affairs*, vol. 70, no. 4 (Fall 1991).

Chapter 5: Catastrophic Terrorism

1. Although the Posse Comitatus Act was passed in the Reconstruction period after the Civil War, it still has relevance. Indeed, it is one of the protectors of the civil rights of citizens during a period when public hysteria after a heinous terrorist act could stimulate the government to take actions unnecessarily impinging on civil rights, including an inappropriate use of the military.

2. Parts of the following are adapted from Ashton B. Carter, John M. Deutch, and Philip Zelikow, *Catastrophic Terrorism: Elements of a National Policy*, Stanford-Harvard Preventive Defense Project Report, vol. 1, no. 6, October 1998. A version of this report was published as Ashton B. Carter, John M. Deutch, and Philip Zelikow, "Catastrophic Terrorism: Tackling the New Danger," *Foreign Affairs*, vol. 77, no. 6 (November/ December, 1998), pp. 80–94. Much of the thinking on which these publications were based arose from the Universities Study Group on Catastrophic Terrorism, established in November 1997 by the Stanford-Harvard Preventive Defense Project (Ashton B. Carter and William J. Perry, codirectors) and the John F. Kennedy School of Government's Visions of Governance in the Twenty-First Century Project (Joseph S. Nye Jr., director). The members of the Universities Study Group on Catastrophic Terrorism who materially contributed to its work were Graham Allison, Zoë Baird, Victor DeMarines, Robert Gates, Jamie Gorelick, Robert Hermann, Philip Heymann, Fred Iklé, Elaine Kamarck, Ernest May, Matthew Meselson, Joseph S. Nye Jr., William J. Perry, Larry Potts, Fred Schauer, J. Terry Scott, General Jack Sheehan, Malcolm Sparrow, Herbert Winokur, and Robert Zoellick. We are grateful for their contributions, but none is responsible for errors of fact or judgment contained here. We also thank Herbert Winokur and the Visions of Governance in the Twenty-First Century Project for their support of the group's work.

3. Recent comprehensive analyses of the weapons of mass destruction and cyberterrorism dimensions of catastrophic terrorism are Richard A. Falkenrath, Robert D. Newman, and Bradley A. Thayer, *America's Achilles' Heel: Nuclear, Biological, and Chemical Terrorism and Covert Attack* (MIT Press, 1998); and the report of the President's Commission on Critical Infrastructure Protection (Marsh Commission), *Critical Foundations: Protecting America's Infrastructures* (Washington, October 1997).

4. Address by President Clinton at the U.S. Naval Academy, May 22, 1998; and White House Fact Sheet on PDD-62, both distributed by the White House Press Office.

5. Philip Heymann has been especially helpful to us in our understanding of the legal capabilities and limits affecting counterterrorist investigations. His comprehensive analysis, Philip B. Heymann, *Terrorism and*

America: A Commonsense Strategy for a Democratic Society (MIT Press, 1998), is the best guide to this complex subject.

6. Discovery motions by the defense seek to find whether the police or prosecutors have any relevant information not already disclosed, including information that might tend to show the innocence of the defendant. Under our proposal, the arresting agency and prosecutor's office would remain subject to discovery, which the Supreme Court has deemed an aspect of constitutionally guaranteed due process of law. However, since the center would not itself carry out law enforcement operations or make prosecutorial decisions, it can be exempted from such discovery; any information it provided to police or prosecutors would then be discoverable under the procedures specified in the current Classified Information Protection Act.

7. For a summary, see Philip Heymann, Matthew Meselson, and Richard Zeckhauser, "Criminalize the Traffic in Terror Weapons," *Washington Post*, April 15, 1998, p. A19. A detailed copy of the proposal is available from Meselson at Harvard University.

8. We are especially indebted to Malcolm Sparrow of Harvard's Kennedy School of Government for sharing his thinking on this subject; we present his ideas here in abridged form.

9. The FBI has also been given funds for training local first responders to an emergency. The FBI should be involved in the effort, based on training plans that fully integrate what Defense and other federal agencies can and are doing. These useful but fragmentary efforts indicate the case for an office like the one we suggest.

10. Conference Report 105-405 for FY 1998 Appropriations to the Departments of Commerce, Justice, State, the Judiciary, and Related Agencies, November 13, 1997.

11. Statement of Attorney General Janet Reno, Hearings of the Senate Judiciary Subcommittee on Technology, Terrorism and Government Information and the Select Committee on Intelligence, *The Threat of Chemical and Biological Weapons*, April 22, 1998.

12. A useful analogy for such an acquisition program, on a smaller scale, is the Technical Support Working Group (TSWG), which develops counterterrorism equipment for use by all agencies of the federal government and for state and local law enforcement, principally with DOD funding. This program concentrates on acquisitions for dealing with "ordinary" terrorism, such as robots for municipal bomb disposal squads. The TSWG is unique in many respects: it is truly interagency and cooperative, and it emphasizes fielding equipment quickly rather than endless "hobby shop" development of prototypes that are never fielded.

Chapter 6: Shaping a Force for the Future

1. The manner in which the offset strategy's innovations were turned to victory in the Gulf War is detailed in William J. Perry, "Desert Storm and Deterrence," *Foreign Affairs*, vol. 70, no. 4 (Fall 1991).

2. Packard Commission, *A Quest for Excellence*, Final Report by the President's Blue Ribbon Commission on Defense Management, The White House, June 1986. The program of acquisition reform was further developed a few years later by the Carnegie Commission on Science, Technology, and Government, in which David Packard and Norman Augustine participated; see Ashton B. Carter and William J. Perry, *New Thinking and American Defense Technology*, Report of the Carnegie Commission on Science, Technology, and Government, Ad-Hoc Task Force on National Security, August 1990.

3. Packard Commission, *A Quest for Excellence*.

4. Office of the Secretary of Defense, February 9, 1994.

5. "Specifications and Standards—A New Way of Doing Business," Directive of the Secretary of Defense, June 29, 1994.

6. James Fallows, *National Defense* (Random House, 1981).

7. William J. Perry, "Fallows' Fallacies: A Review Essay," *International Security*, vol. 6, no. 4 (Spring 1982), pp. 174–82.

Index